AFTER THE PROGRAM ERA

THE NEW AMERICAN CANON:

The Iowa Series in Contemporary Literature and Culture

Samuel Cohen, Series Editor

AFTER THE PROGRAM ERA

The Past, Present, and Future of Creative Writing in the University

EDITED BY LOREN GLASS

THE UNIVERSITY OF IOWA PRESS | IOWA CITY

University of Iowa Press, Iowa City 52242

www.uiowapress.org
Printed in the United States of America

Design by April Leidig

The University of Iowa Press is a member of Green Press Initiative and is committed to preserving natural resources.

Printed on acid-free paper

Library of Congress Cataloging-in-Publication Data
Names: Glass, Loren, editor.
Title: After the program era : the past, present, and future of creative writing in the university / edited by Loren Glass.
Description: Iowa City : University of Iowa Press, [2017] |
Series: New American Canon | Includes index.
Identifiers: LCCN 2016007769 | ISBN 978-1-60938-439-5 (pbk) |
ISBN 978-1-60938-440-1 (ebk)
Subjects: LCSH: Creative writing (Higher education) | American fiction—Study and teaching. | Literature—Study and teaching (Higher) |
BISAC: LANGUAGE ARTS & DISCIPLINES / General.
Classification: LCC PN181 .A38 2017 | DDC 808/.00711—dc23
LC record available at https://lccn.loc.gov/2016007769

CONTENTS

ACKNOWLEDGMENTS

First and foremost, I thank the graduate students in my 2014 seminar on the Program Era, four of whom appear in this volume. It was in this class that we realized not only how groundbreaking Mark McGurl's book is but also how much more there is to be said about the rise of creative writing as an academic discipline. Thus, I also thank Mark for providing us with the premise on which this collection is based and for his gracious agreement to contribute an afterword. Finally, I thank Elisabeth Chretien at the University of Iowa Press and Sam Cohen, editor of the New American Canon Series, as well as the two anonymous readers they solicited for this manuscript.

INTRODUCTION

From the Pound Era to the Program Era, and Beyond

LOREN GLASS

The publication in 2009 of Mark McGurl's *The Program Era: Postwar Fiction and the Rise of Creative Writing* provoked a sea change in the study of postwar literature. Even though almost every English department in the United States housed some version of a creative writing program by the time of its publication, it had somehow not occurred to anyone that this institutional phenomenon was historically significant. McGurl's groundbreaking book effectively established that "the rise of the creative writing program stands as the most important event in postwar American literary history," forcing us to revise our understanding not only of the relationship between higher education and literary production but also of the periodizing terminology we had previously used to structure our understanding of twentieth-century literature.[1]

This anthology explores the consequences and implications, as well as the lacunae and liabilities, of McGurl's foundational intervention. For example, *The Program Era* focuses only on American fiction and the American university, and one objective of this collection is to expand and examine its insights in terms of other genres and sites. Postwar poetry, in particular, has been neglected as a product of the Program Era, even though it is, arguably, a purer example, since poets now depend almost entirely on the patronage of the university. But nonfiction, drama, screenwriting, graphic novels, and electronic literature have increasingly become part of the creative writing curriculum, and work still needs to be done to understand the ways in which the form and content of these genres and modes have been influenced by this development. Similarly, the expansion of creative writing programs has now become unquestionably global, and the Program Era needs to be considered in a more transnational frame. Finally, McGurl's claims, while compelling and already nigh canonical, require the kind of interrogation that all intellectual transformations provoke. His arguments illuminate much, but what might they exclude or obscure? This anthology hopes to answer some of these questions.

First, however, it is necessary to situate *The Program Era* itself in the historical and institutional contexts from which it emerged. McGurl's work can be considered representative of the recent "sociological turn" in literary studies generally but more specifically in the academic study of modernism, a development that came to a certain maturity with the founding of the Modernist Studies Association (MSA) and its official journal, *Modernism/Modernity*, in 1998. The mandate of the MSA was, on the one hand, to diversify the authors and texts considered "modernist" beyond the canonized geniuses and masterpieces of the interwar years and, on the other, to apply the methodologies loosely associated with cultural studies to this expanded canon. Since then, the field of modernist studies, in terms of both archive and method, has grown significantly.

One of the noteworthy aspects of this growth has been a shift from single-author and major text studies to a focus on the various institutions that enabled the publication and reception of literary modernism. Deeply informed by the foundational work of Pierre Bourdieu, scholars of modernism such as Lawrence Rainey, Susan Stanford Friedman, Joyce Piell Wexler, and Leonard Diepeveen began to integrate close readings of individual texts into a more properly sociological consideration of the cultural fields in which these texts circulated. *The Program Era*, in its titular invocation of Hugh Kenner's epochal (and epoch-defining) *The Pound Era*, epitomizes this shift.

Indeed, *The Program Era* establishes the degree to which creative writing programs in the postwar era can be understood to have institutionalized the aesthetic practices and protocols of the Pound Era, preserving rather than displacing literary modernism; it is in this sense that McGurl revises both the generic and periodizing terminology whereby we had previously understood postwar literature. McGurl posits three broad generic categories to "map the totality of postwar American fiction": high cultural pluralism, which "joins the high literary values of modernism with a fascination with the experience of cultural difference and the authenticity of the ethnic voice"; lower-middle-class modernism, which "takes the form of the minimalist short story, and is preoccupied more than anything else with economic and other forms of insecurity"; and technomodernism, "a tweaking of the term 'postmodernism' in that it emphasizes the all-important engagement of postmodern literature with information technology" (32). The effect of this terminology is to displace, if not replace, the blanket designation "postmodernism" with a plurality of institutionalized modernisms embedded within what Langdon Hammer has called "the culture of the school."[2] The success and significance of this revision are illustrated by the degree to which the term "Program Era" seems to be gradually replacing "postmodernism" in both academic and popular parlance.

IF, AS PASCALE CASANOVA has recently claimed, Paris is the Greenwich Meridian of the World Republic of Letters, then Iowa City is its somewhat unlikely heir as ground zero of what McGurl calls a "World Pluribus of Letters," the new global literary space that corresponds to the historical period of the Program Era.[3] This era indisputably begins with the founding of the Iowa Writers' Workshop in 1936, which would establish the basic protocols of creative writing pedagogy and certification, pioneering both the MFA and the creative dissertation.[4] Iowa City may not command the cultural authority once held by Paris—a World Pluribus is by definition decentered—but it possesses an analogous historical significance. This was not by chance. It had been Paul Engle's plan, as he wrote to University of Iowa president Virgil Hancher in 1963, to "run the future of American literature, and a great deal of European and Asian, through Iowa City."[5]

As director of the Writers' Workshop from 1941 to 1965, and then cofounder (with his wife, Hualing) and director of the International Writing Program from 1967 until his death in 1991, Engle was a central architect of the Program Era Pluribus that has effectively displaced Casanova's Paris-based Republic. However, until the publication of *The Program Era* he was little known, even in Iowa City. As James English has affirmed, literary history tends to neglect "the strictly functional middle space between acts of inspired creation on the one hand and acts of brilliantly discerning consumption on the other."[6] And Engle, as I have argued elsewhere, was a middleman—midwestern, middle class, middlebrow.[7] Though he wrote both poetry and criticism, he had no particular talent for either, and aside from his autobiography of his early life, *A Lucky American Childhood*, none of his books remain in print.

Rather, his talent was to recognize talent, and his management of and recruitment for the Workshop was more in the style of a football coach than a department chair. It was Engle who would standardize the practice of recruiting famous figures for brief, and frequently failed, stints as visiting professors. Robert Lowell, John Berryman, Philip Roth, Kurt Vonnegut: Engle recognized early that he could, in essence, leach off the cultural capital and charisma of such figures, raising the reputation of the Workshop with each new recruit, no matter how brief or inconsequential their tenures. Engle was also preternaturally adept at fund-raising, effectively outflanking the hierarchy of the English Department by soliciting donations from both local businesses and national foundations. Unlike so many of his peers, he saw no conflict between culture and commerce. He was, in other words, a cultural entrepreneur and therefore central to the accommodation of art and institution that characterizes the Program Era.

As Stephen Wilbers documents in the appendix to his history of the Workshop, many of the creative writing programs that were launched in the 1950s and 1960s were founded and staffed by Iowa graduates, but as Seth Abramson establishes in his contribution to this book, it is important to qualify the dominance of the so-called Iowa model in the history of creative writing (see Wilbers 137–39). While the workshop format unquestionably continued to dominate creative writing pedagogy, the genres of writing taught, the administrative structures established, and the credentials awarded have varied. Thus, Stanford's program, usually coupled with Iowa's in its inaugural significance and founded in 1946 by Iowa (and Harvard) graduate Wallace Stegner, awards no degree. Rather, it consists in a generous two-year fellowship, granting recipients complete freedom to focus on their writing. Unlike more traditional MFA programs, it does not provide training in or a credential for teaching, though many Stegner fellows do end up in the classroom. And Johns Hopkins's highly regarded Writing Seminars, founded by Elliot Coleman in 1947, initially awarded simply a standard MA and has included an emphasis on journalistic nonfiction writing from its inception. Thus, while the basic practice of workshop pedagogy remains fairly constant across programs, each maintains a discrete structure and identity because of the personality and philosophy of its founder(s) as well as the administrative idiosyncrasies of the department and institution within which it was founded.

As Eric Bennett's recent *Workshops of Empire* (2015) affirms, the inception of the Program Era has to be understood in terms of the Cold War expansion of the American university and the rise of cultural diplomacy in the decades after World War II. On the most general level, of course, creative writing was the beneficiary of Cold War initiatives such as the GI Bill and the National Defense Education Act, both of which put the federal government in the business of subsidizing the expansion of American universities in the service of competing with the Soviet Union. More specifically, in emphasizing the individual over the collective and the concrete over the abstract, creative writing pedagogy as formulated by such pioneers as Engle and Stegner was explicitly conceived as an ideological bulwark against the specter of the collectivist Soviet State and its purported designs for world domination. From the beginning, then, the creative writing workshop was a national institution with international aspirations and attitudes. Long before he launched the International Writing Program, Engle invited writers from all over the world to come to Iowa City, which he saw as representing a much more wholesome version of America than Manhattan and Washington, DC (to which he was, nevertheless, a frequent visitor). By the 1960s, Engle was a major player in the Kennedy administration's cultural Cold War, regularly visiting DC as a member of the National Council of the Arts and American specialist for the Department of State.

Creative writing reached a certain disciplinary maturity with the founding, by Iowa alum and instructor Verlin Cassill, of the Associated Writing Programs (AWP) in 1967. Officially established by fifteen writers representing thirteen writing programs, the AWP was meant to recognize the specificity of creative writing in contrast to (and in some ways in opposition to) the English departments long represented by the Modern Language Association (MLA). Since then, the AWP has both represented and tracked the rise of the discipline of creative writing into the new millennium. And its rise has been remarkable. According to the AWP website, there were 79 creative writing programs in 1975, 319 by 1984, 535 by 1994, 719 by 2004, and 880 by 2012.[8]

In this post-1960s phase of accelerating expansion, programs would emerge in explicit opposition to Iowa's perceived conservatism, absorbing many heretofore anti-institutional and countercultural groups and aesthetics into the university system. Thus, Allen Ginsberg and Anne Waldman founded the Jack Kerouac School of Disembodied Poetics at the Naropa Institute in Boulder, Colorado, in 1974, which awards both a residential and low-residency MFA. And the Language Poets who, like the Beats, maintained an explicitly anti-institutional ethos in their formative period, would enter the academy in force in the late 1970s and early 1980s, establishing beachheads in Buffalo and Berkeley and instituting an alliance with prominent literary theorists and traditional PhD programs that stands in distinct contrast to the mutual suspicion bordering on hostility that frequently characterizes relations between the critical and creative components of many English departments.

As Juliana Spahr and Stephanie Young affirm in their contribution to this book, the Program Era really begins to take off only after 1989, indicating that creative writing has comfortably adapted to, and can be seen as a premium product of, the corporate-financed enterprise university that is currently (and rapidly) displacing the government-funded research university of the Cold War era. If, during that earlier era, creative writers were still somewhat idiosyncratic outsiders, they have now become representative insiders, avatars of the entrepreneurial creative class that Richard Florida has identified as emerging in the late twentieth century.[9] And if, during that era, they were a supplement to, and frequent irritant in, English departments, they now appear to be the only hope for the survival of English in a time of diminishing enrollments in literary studies and a contracting job market for conventional PhDs.

TO BEST APPRECIATE how these developments have affected our overall sense of twentieth- and twenty-first-century literary history, this anthology is organized into three sections. The first section, "Antecedents," considers figures and formations that preceded and anticipated the postwar innovation and expansion of creative writing programs. First, Marija Reiff takes the long view, showing how creative writing must be understood as continuing a long tradition of vocational and humanistic pedagogical practices inaugurated by the Protestant Reformation and, in particular, the Calvinist concept of the "calling." Then, Mike Chasar and Benjamin Kirbach examine two underappreciated figures, poet Vachel Lindsay and critic Malcolm Cowley, as inaugurating a species of institutional itinerancy that both antedated and mediated the establishment of tenured teaching and administrative positions in creative writing.

The second (and largest) section, "Revisions," engages authors, genres, and social formations that are contemporaneous with, and sometimes exceptions to, the developments discussed by McGurl, provoking us to revise and expand some of his central claims. Both Greg Barnhisel and Eric Bennett argue that we need to situate the Program Era more firmly in the context of the

Cold War, while Stephen Voyce reminds us that there were alternative institutions, in his case Black Mountain College, that pursued more collective and politically progressive pedagogies than those that would come to dominate conventional creative writing programs. Other contributors, such as Kelly Budruweit, Matthew Blackwell, Michael Hill, and Simon During, examine figures such as Robert Coover, Gordon Lish, James Alan McPherson, and J. M. Coetzee and modes such as hypertext fiction that McGurl neglects, complicating and supplementing some of his central claims. Juliana Spahr and Stephanie Young, writing in the wake of Junot Díaz's *New Yorker* piece "MFA vs. POC," compel us to take a hard look at the demographics of the Program Era, forcing us to reconsider whether the "aesthetic democracy" that McGurl claims is envisioned by creative writing is more neoliberal ideology than liberal actuality (74).[10]

The third section, "Prospects," looks to the future, speculating on how we might describe or envision an emergent literary period "after" the Program Era or whether it is on the verge of a new phase. Both Sean McCann and Donal Harris tend toward the former; McCann, using the representative work of Russell Banks as an illustration, argues that contemporary social and institutional formations no longer support or enable the type of aesthetic democracy endorsed by *The Program Era*, while Harris sees the emergence of the "peripheral" realism of Jonathan Franzen, Chad Harbach, and others as positioned explicitly in opposition to the institutionalized modernism of creative writing programs. In contrast, Seth Abramson, focusing for the most part on poetry, sees a continuing expansion and accommodation between modernist and poststructuralist protocols in creative writing that he theorizes as an emergent "metamodernism." Finally, McGurl himself provides us with a brief meditation on the various implications of what we're "after" in the title of this anthology.

NOTES

1. Mark McGurl, *The Program Era: Postwar Fiction and the Rise of Creative Writing* (Cambridge: Harvard UP, 2009), ix.

2. See Langdon Hammer, "Plath's Lives," *Representations* 75 (2001): 61–88.

3. Pascale Casanova, *The World Republic of Letters*, trans. M. B. Debevoise (Cambridge: Harvard UP, 2004), 329.

4. For a serviceable, if outdated, history of the Writers' Workshop, see Stephen Wilbers, *The Iowa Writers' Workshop: Origins, Emergence, and Growth* (Iowa City:

U of Iowa P, 1980). The only comprehensive history of the rise of creative writing remains D. G. Myers, *The Elephants Teach: Creative Writing since 1880* (1996; Chicago: U of Chicago P, 2006).

5. Paul Engle, letter to Virgil Hancher, 31 Oct. 1963, University of Iowa Special Collections Library.

6. James English, *The Economy of Prestige: Prizes, Awards, and the Circulation of Cultural Value* (Cambridge: Harvard UP, 2005), 13.

7. Loren Glass, "Middle Man: Paul Engle and the Iowa Writers' Workshop," *minnesota review* 71–72 (Winter/Spring 2009): 256–68.

8. AWP, Jan. 2012, https://www.awpwriter.org/application/public/pdf/AWP_GrowthWritingPrograms.pdf. These numbers include any program offering any undergraduate or graduate degree in creative writing.

9. See Richard Florida, *The Rise of the Creative Class* (New York: Basic Books, 2002).

10. Junot Díaz, "MFA vs. POC," *New Yorker*, 30 Apr. 2014, http://www.newyorker.com/books/page-turner/mfa-vs-poc. See also Jenny Zhang, "They Pretend to Be Us While Pretending We Don't Exist," *Buzzfeed Books*, 11 Sept. 2015, http://www.buzzfeed.com/jennybagel/they-pretend-to-be-us-while-pretending-we-dont-exist#.dkQg5Qwj6.

PART I

Antecedents

CHAPTER 1

The Creative Calling

MARIJA REIFF

Mark McGurl opens *The Program Era* by quoting Vladimir Nabokov's complaint to Edmund Wilson: "I am sick of teaching. I am sick of teaching. I am sick of teaching."[1] Implicit in Nabokov's statement is that there is a better career that he should be pursuing. Though McGurl never uses the term, this drive to seek a meaningful and fulfilling career is often termed a "calling" in a religious sense. Indeed, the belief that there are certain careers that one must pursue in order to be intellectually and artistically fulfilled is deeply embedded in America's Puritan heritage. From before the founding of the United States, the Puritans laid the groundwork for a system of moral education that would teach students how to lead productive and fulfilling lives, and these Puritan values informed the rise of higher education in the nineteenth century. While creative writing programs did not proliferate in the United States until after World War II, the foundational ideals that created them go back much earlier. Though secularized, the modern creative writing program continues the Protestant tradition of discovering and fulfilling one's vocational calling.

Martin Luther was the first theologian to ascribe religious importance to work, and in a 1534 sermon he pronounced,

> See to your vocation. I am called to be a preacher. Now when I preach I perform a holy work that is pleasing to God. If you are a father and mother, believe in Jesus Christ and so you will be a holy father and a holy mother.... These things are none other than holy works to which you have been called.[2]

For the earliest Protestants, no labor was beyond the scope of God's plan, and finding one's calling became a religious imperative. As the Reformation grew and spread, so too did the idea that work is an essential component of religious life.

The Calvinists further clarified this vocational imperative. They believed that God gave "a special command" to every person to fulfill certain duties because "Divine Providence has placed the believer in *this* position" and endowed Christians with certain gifts that they were obligated to use.[3] For the first time in Western history, work became "an end in itself," and thus "the Puritan *wanted* to be a person with a vocational calling" (79, 157, emphasis in original). This idea has come to be known as the "Protestant work ethic," a term championed by Max Weber in his study of Protestant beliefs and their role in the formation of modern capitalism. Because Protestants were "engaged in a task given by God," they were expected to work willingly and diligently, and their work was perceived as fulfilling a moral mandate rather than just an economic imperative.[4]

When Nabokov quit teaching to focus on his writing full time, McGurl writes that he was "release[d] from the prison of the classroom into the richly reflexive freedom of artistic expression" (2). Though McGurl does not describe this as a "calling," it is obvious that writing was what Nabokov felt he was meant to do. Nabokov himself contrasted his loathing for teaching with his passion for writing, averring that "my pleasures are the most intense known to man: writing and butterfly hunting."[5] For Nabokov, writing was one of the most rewarding activities he could pursue. Teaching distracted him from fulfilling his higher calling, and jettisoning it liberated him to pursue his passion.

This desire to fulfill the call is echoed in the language creative writers use to describe their compulsion to write. Thus, James Hynes describes writing as a "spiritual release," and T. Coraghessan Boyle describes an almost mystical power that makes him feel "strong, superior, invincible."[6] Other writers agree. In *We Wanted to Be Writers: Life, Love and Literature at the Iowa Writers' Workshop*, Eric Olsen claims that, for him, "writing's not a choice"; Anthony Bukoski describes how he "yearned" to write; and Gary Iorio describes writing as a "wonderful passion" and an "awakening." Most explicitly, Jayne Anne Philips states, "Writing, or any art, is a calling, rather than a career."[7] Olsen and Glenn Schaeffer more fully explain the writers' call:

> It shouldn't be surprising that many successful writers seem to have some sort of compulsion that keeps them at it, or that *compulsion* seems to be a

> useful trait. . . . This pleasure [writing] becomes for some people an almost mystical experience, leading to the persistent notion throughout Western history that writers have been touched by divinity or the Muse, or touched by something. (16–17)

This "compulsion" that has a touch of the "divinity" is clearly cognate with the concept of the calling. Despite the difficulty of their profession, writers are called to this challenging, rewarding, and mystical activity.

The assertion that writing is a calling is supported by the use of religiously symbolic language when discussing the talent that writers possess. Writers are endowed with gifts or blessings that the average person lacks; as Olsen and Schaeffer note, "We *do* like to think writers are somehow special, gifted—and lots of writers like to think of themselves that way" (17). Because of their talents, writers are hailed as visionaries, prophets, or sages, and their works are supposed to inspire, provoke, and enlighten their readers, the same tasks traditionally assigned to religious texts.

This concept of innate talent can be compared to the idea of "charisma," which Weber defines as "the certain quality of an individual personality by virtue of which he is considered extraordinary and treated as endowed with supernatural, superhuman, or at least specifically exceptional powers or qualities" (216, 241). Thus, to be blessed with charisma is to be gifted with divine or supernatural abilities, and the purpose of the calling, subsequently, is to discover and honor one's talent, a task infused with religious meaning.

This religiously inflected language has been used not only for the writers themselves but also for the MFA programs that nurture their talent. Thus, Paul Engle describes *Midland*, his 1961 anthology of Workshop writing, as the result of a "vision," a word with clear religious evocations; and Robert Frost, who was instrumental in creating the Bread Loaf Writers' Conference, delivered a talk on its fortieth anniversary claiming that writing is one of "the great enterprise[s]" that can "carry the spirit deeper."[8] Loren Glass extends this religious metaphor to the larger sociological framework of the Program Era, claiming that the Iowa Writers' Workshop in its formative years can be understood as a "charismatic community."[9]

It is no coincidence that spiritual ideas and religiously symbolic language apply to both individual writers and the programs that nurture them. The impulse to find and answer the call was never conceived of as a solitary project.

Rather, the Protestants established universities for such purposes, and these educational practices were carried over into the New World. In the nineteenth century, the institutionalization of Protestant-style higher education sowed the seeds for the modern Program Era.

Unlike their Catholic predecessors, Protestants believed that everyone, not just the clergy, needed to learn to read and write and be versed in scripture. This, of course, required an education, and according to Marilynne Robinson, prominent author and mainstay at the Iowa Writers' Workshop, these Protestant activists "established great universities and cultural institutions."[10] In fact, John Calvin is sometimes called the "father of the modern university" because he designed his school in Geneva to be free, open to the public, and based on humanistic learning (Robinson 192). This Protestant propensity for education is one of the primary attributes that Weber believed contributed to the Protestant work ethic and the concomitant rise of capitalism.

Nowhere was this Protestant commitment to education demonstrated more clearly than in the United States. The Puritan founders established a college only six years after their arrival in the New World, and by 1900 more than 450 colleges and universities existed. According to Russell K. Nieli, "[V]irtually all" of these colleges were founded by groups or individuals affiliated with the Protestant church, and even universities that were run by the state "reflect[ed] a general liberal Protestant or Unitarian religious spirit rather than a purely secular or rationalistic outlook."[11] For generations of Americans, education was founded on principles designed by Protestants, even when it was apparently secular.

This liberal Protestantism was evidenced both in the curriculum and the student body of the nineteenth-century university, which was distinguished by its appeal to average middle-class citizens. The Protestant revolution in education began with the mandate for every citizen to read, write, and study the Bible, and it reached its acme in the new republic. The students pouring into colleges in the 1800s were not only wealthy and urban; they frequently came from families of farmers and were "selected as much by individual traits of social ambition and intellectual curiosity as by privileged socioeconomic status."[12] These students were not being trained just to be members of the clergy but also to be businessmen, lawyers, teachers, and government officials. Nor were these new students all white men. This was the age that saw a substantial rise in colleges for women and people of color. While access to higher education was by no means universal, the nineteenth century witnessed a huge leap toward fulfilling Calvin's goal of higher education for all.

This nineteenth-century ideal of democratic education is at the philosophical core of the Program Era. Creative writing workshops democratize authorship by allowing average people to answer their creative calling. According to Workshop historian Stephen Wilbers, creative writing programs act as "an important form of patronage" that permits students, at least temporarily, to write free of financial constraints.[13] This allowed prominent writers to arise from various economic stations, and many of the twentieth century's most celebrated writers—including Raymond Carver, Wallace Stegner, and Sandra Cisneros—were drawn from rural backgrounds or middle to lower socioeconomic classes.

The connection between the nineteenth-century religious university and the twentieth-century Program Era is also apparent in the way modern creative writing programs emphasize self-creation. Almost all of the American nineteenth-century colleges and universities taught what was called the "common curriculum." Unlike the research- and career-oriented schools of today, these institutions taught a comprehensive liberal arts program. The capstone of the college curriculum was usually a course in moral philosophy taught by the president of the college that aimed to connect the various areas of study into a coherent path for ethical living (Nieli 314). The goal of education was moral: to combine classical and contemporary learning to create well-rounded and productive individuals. This objective is explicitly stated in the famous Yale Report of 1828, which claims that education should "maintain such a proportion between the different branches of literature and science, as to form in the student a proper *balance* of character."[14] Moral education aimed to create students who had proper training in all the spheres necessary for personal, spiritual, and vocational growth.

In this era, the arts became a key avenue through which students were taught character, which has ramifications for the modern Program Era. In the nineteenth century, the arts became necessary components of what McGurl terms "autopoiesis," the reflexive creation of the self. It was this goal that the common curriculum of the nineteenth-century university was designed to produce. In the autopoetic occupation of "forming morally earnest Christian gentlemen" (Nieli 314), the arts served an integral function.

There was also an increased stress placed on the *individual* in this type of moral education, which was designed to aid students in discovering their *own* personal calling. In other words, the moral education of the nineteenth century and the contemporary creative pedagogy of writing are both designed to aid the *individual* in becoming his or her own, unique self. Thus, in the twentieth and twenty-first centuries, the arts, including creative writing, occupy much of the same moral space in the university as did the common curriculum of the prior era: they are designed to create self-actualized, well-rounded individuals.

With the rise of the secular and increasingly specialized modern university, creative writing filled the autopoetic void left by the demise of the common curriculum. As McGurl affirms, "The newly dubbed 'creative writing' was promoted as an antidote to rote learning and the conformist genres associated with it. . . . [It] could be understood as a figure of democratized Authorship itself, of the spiritual authority of even the lowliest man or woman to play God in the domain of his or her imagination, if nowhere else" (41). With the waning of the common curriculum, the arts, and particularly creative writing, allowed students to pursue self-realization, and creative writing practices were implemented in the classroom to allow for "student enrichment through autonomous self-creation" (3). And this autopoetic process allowed students to discover their higher calling. In this crucial sense, creative writing is a moral act.

The idea that writing can serve a moral purpose—and indeed is a moral enterprise—is further evident in the mandate to foster empathy. Creative writing leads not only to the development of the individual authorial self but also to the acknowledgment and understanding of the individuality of others. Creative writers understand "that the truth of anything is relative to the position of the observer" (McGurl 399), and according to recent scientific studies, reading literary fiction helps foster empathy by showing how truth changes depending on perspective.[15] Albert Wendland explains, "Reading sensitive and lengthy explorations of people's lives, that kind of fiction is literally putting yourself into another person's position—lives that could be more difficult, more complex . . . [and] that can lead to more empathy and understanding of other lives."[16] Creative writing becomes a moral act insofar as its product encourages compassion for others.

The connection between traditional Protestant values and contemporary creative writing is particularly pertinent for Marilynne Robinson. A professor at the University of Iowa since 1991, Robinson is a key player in the Program Era. But she is also unusual, achieving both popular success and critical acclaim while writing in an old-fashioned poetic style and exploring themes borrowed from nineteenth-century American Romanticism. Moreover, her work, both novels and nonfiction, is steeped in the tradition of theological inquiry. To quote Anne Thurston, Robinson's popularity is "somewhat surprising" because she is "quite countercultural" in her exploration of Protestant concepts such as mystery and grace.[17]

Robinson is not included among the writers that McGurl examines, possibly because she does not have an MFA. In theory, her success as a writer is distinct from the successes enabled by the Program Era. However, Robinson's career is emblematic of the way liberal Protestant values still inflect and permeate the culture. She is "countercultural," but only in the way that she consistently reminds her American readers of their theological roots. More important, Robinson's career reflects how the ethos of nineteenth-century liberal Protestant education informs the creative writers of the twentieth and twenty-first centuries.

Robinson's education is reminiscent of the scholastic practices of the nineteenth century. Furthermore, like many of the newly socially mobile college students of the 1800s, she is from a middle-class, rural background. Robinson was born in Idaho in 1943; her parents were typical of the West: her father worked in the lumber industry, and her mother was a homemaker. However, Robinson was encouraged by her parents to read capaciously; indeed, she has written an entire book dedicated to the books, mostly classical and traditional, that she read as a child. As a high school student in Coeur d'Alene, Robinson was taught in an educational system closer to the nineteenth-century common curriculum than what is today called the "common core." Recalling the influence of her high school education, Robinson says, "I think anyone can see that my style is considerably more in debt to Cicero than to Hemingway."[18] This background in the classics is displayed throughout her works.

Robinson continued her autopoetic growth at Brown University. There she majored in English while frequently discoursing on theological, philosophical, and aesthetic matters with her brother, David. Robinson further pursued her interest in literature in graduate school at the University of Washington, where she received a PhD in English in 1977. Throughout her education, Robinson was, like many students before her, taught a much more classical, much more humanistic curriculum than is often taught now. This education has, in turn, deeply informed her creative sensibility and helped shape her religious and philosophical views.

While Robinson's educational background recalls traditional Protestant scholastic practices, it is in her works themselves that she most fully epitomizes the creative calling. Robinson's works reveal Protestant values in their assertion that we are called to recognize and empathize with the "radical individuality" of others.[19] This connection between religion, radical individuality, writing, and the calling is apparent in her 2004 novel, *Gilead*. The book centers on the aging Rev. John Ames, who pens his reminiscences for his young son. Ames—who claims that his spiritual vocation is a calling[20]—feels that he *must* write. Like the writers featured in *We Wanted to Be Writers*, Ames is compelled to create. He describes writing as his "purpose," and he writes that he cannot die until he has finished his "errand" (118, 135). This errand is to tell his son things he would have told him had he lived (135), and notably, these revelations revolve around the mystery of God, grace, and other people. Indeed, the desire to empathize with and love the unknowable other—to honor the other's radical individuality—is discussed throughout the book. Ames, who has difficulties understanding his fiercely, even violently, abolitionist grandfather and his pacifist father, must actively choose to love them. As he writes, "A man can know his father, or his son, and there might still be nothing between them but loyalty and love and mutual incomprehension" (7). Through his writings, Ames endeavors to teach his son to love and empathize with the mysterious, radically individualized other.

For Reverend Ames and for Robinson, creative writing is fundamental to understanding the radical individuality of others, a quest that is profoundly religious. Ames says this explicitly when he claims that writing "has always felt like praying" (19). Similarly, in the modern Program Era, autopoiesis yields the writer's ability to render the authorial self while empathizing with the individuality of others. Graduates of creative writing programs echo Robinson's goal of discovering and empathizing with the individuality of others, and they also make it a key component of their works. For example, John Irving explains how liking his characters affects his writing (Olsen and Schaeffer 95); T. C. Boyle describes imagining how the world is different for people who are deaf since they have a "special language" of their own (qtd. in Olsen and Schaeffer 107); and Deborah Eisenberg claims that the act of writing, reading, and character building is akin to "learning about life" (Conroy 115). Rita Dove, former US Poet Laureate and professor in the creative writing program at the University of Virginia, goes further by explicitly stating that her goal is to display the individuality of others. She writes, "My feeling, my mission if you will . . . is to restore individual human fates to the oeuvre."[21] In other words, Dove wants the reader to see her characters as distinctive persons worthy of respect and empathy.

This honoring of the individual is highly prized in contemporary culture, yet it is deeply rooted in America's Puritan heritage. For Robinson and other authors, the writer's calling is to foster empathy by making the other more knowable. In this way, the values of the Puritans have been transformed for a secular world. Even today, creative writers are called on to illuminate the mysteries of the human soul, a calling seen as a moral duty. While contemporary MFA programs are almost entirely secular, they have followed America's Protestant forebears in their institutionalized support of a traditionally sacred mission.

NOTES

1. Mark McGurl, *The Program Era: Postwar Fiction and the Rise of Creative Writing* (Cambridge: Harvard UP, 2009), 1.

2. Michael D. Bennethum, *Listen! God Is Calling! Luther Speaks of Vocation, Faith, and Work* (Minneapolis: Augsburg Fortress, 2003), 46.

3. Max Weber, *Economy and Society: An Outline of Interpretive Sociology*, ed. Guenther Roth and Claus Wittich (Berkeley: U of California P, 1968), 93 (emphasis in original).

4. Stephen Kalberg, "Introduction to *The Protestant Ethic*," *"The Protestant Ethic and the Spirit of Capitalism" with Other Writings on the Rise of the West*, by Max Weber (New York: Oxford UP, 2009), 30.

5. Vladimir Nabokov, *Strong Opinions* (St. Louis: Mc-Graw Hill, 1973), 3.

6. Quoted in Frank Conroy, ed., *The Eleventh Draft: Craft and the Writing Life from the Iowa Writers' Workshop* (New York: HarperCollins, 1999), 172, 6.

7. Quoted in Eric Olsen and Glenn Schaeffer, eds., *We Wanted to Be Writers: Life, Love, and Literature at the Iowa Writers' Workshop* (New York: Skyhorse, 2011), 271, 256, 262, 96.

8. Paul Engle, *Midland: Twenty-Five Years of Fiction and Poetry Selected from the Writing Workshops of the State University of Iowa* (New York: Random House, 1961), xxi; Robert Frost, "Cherub Scorn," Bread Loaf School of English, lecture

at Middlebury College, Middlebury, VT, 29 June 1959, Middlebury Special Collections.

9. See Loren Glass, "Middleman: Paul Engle and the Iowa Writers' Workshop," *minnesota review* 71–72 (Winter/Spring 2009): 256–68.

10. Marilynne Robinson, *The Death of Adam: Essays on Modern Thought* (New York: Picador, 2005), 150.

11. Russell K. Nieli, "From Christian Gentleman to Bewildered Seeker: The Transformation of American Higher Education," *Academic Questions* 20.4 (2007): 312–13.

12. Roger L. Geiger, "Introduction: New Themes in the History of Nineteenth-Century Colleges," *The American College in the Nineteenth Century*, ed. Roger L. Geiger (Nashville: Vanderbilt UP, 2000), 4.

13. Stephen Wilbers, *The Iowa Writers' Workshop* (Iowa City: U of Iowa P, 1980), 134.

14. Quoted in George M. Marsden, *The Soul of the American University: From Protestant Establishment to Established Nonbelief* (New York: Oxford UP, 1994), 82 (emphasis in original).

15. Julianne Chiaet, "Novel Finding: Reading Literary Fiction Improves Empathy," *Scientific American*, 4 Oct. 2013, http://www.scientificamerican.com/article/novel-finding-reading-literary-fiction-improves-empathy/.

16. Quoted in Pam Belluck, "For Better Social Skills, Scientists Recommend a Little Chekhov," *New York Times*, 3 Oct. 2013, http://well.blogs.nytimes.com/2013/10/03/i-know-how-youre-feeling-i-read-chekhov/?_r=0.

17. Anne Thurston, "Marilynne Robinson and the Fate of Faith," *Studies: An Irish Quarterly Review* 99.396 (Winter 2010): 449.

18. Quoted in James H. Maguire, *Reading Marilynne Robinson's "Housekeeping"* (Boise: Boise State UP, 2003), 9.

19. Marilynne Robinson, "Preface to the Vintage Spiritual Classics Edition," *John Calvin: Steward of God's Covenant: Selected Writings*, ed. John F. Thornton and Susan B. Varenne (New York: Vintage Books, 2006), xii.

20. Marilynne Robinson, *Gilead* (New York: Picador, 2004), 32.

21. Quoted in Steven Ratiner, ed., *Giving Their Word: Conversations with Contemporary Poets* (Amherst: U of Massachusetts P, 2002), 215.

CHAPTER 2

From Vagabond to Visiting Poet

Vachel Lindsay and the Institutionalization of American Poetry

MIKE CHASAR

Poet Nicholas Vachel Lindsay entered Hiram College in the fall of 1897.[1] He was seventeen years old. His father, a religiously fundamentalist doctor, wanted Vachel to become a doctor as well, but Vachel didn't take to college. According to biographer and fellow "prairie poet" Edgar Lee Masters, Lindsay "hated trigonometry, astronomy, anatomy, French, Latin, chemistry, [and] physics."[2] Despite Lindsay's later fame as a performer of his own poems, he even came out last in the school's oratory contests. This isn't to say that he didn't enjoy his time in Garrettsville, Ohio, however. He played pick-up basketball and ran around campus each night for exercise. He barged in on a girls' sheet and pillowcase party and later bragged, "I am a great friend of every girl in Hiram, have made myself dear to them all, after my famous manner."[3] All the same, he said his studies made his brain feel "like scrambled eggs" and, two years later, wrote what he called his "revolutionary letter" informing his parents of his intention to drop out (Ruggles 64, 66).

In finding higher education unfulfilling, Lindsay was not unlike other poets of his generation. Many of the modern American poets who would become his friends, peers, rivals, readers, editors, and associates thought colleges and universities were not conducive to the writing of good poetry; for them, universities were stifling to creativity—conservative, backward-looking institutions where literature went to perish in the hands of so-called experts.[4] Robert Frost dropped out of Dartmouth and Harvard and became a chicken farmer. Later, he would call the college teacher's approach to poetry "the worst system of teaching that ever endangered a nation's literature."[5] After spending two years at the University of Pennsylvania, Ezra Pound managed a degree from Hamilton College and declared, in a rare understatement, that higher education was not the place for the "unusual young man."[6] Pound did find his first job teaching French and Spanish at Wabash College in Indiana but, after less than a year, was dismissed for having a woman in his room after hours. Edna St. Vincent Millay broke rule after rule at Vassar College and was expelled on the eve of her graduation; were it not for a petition from her fellow students for whom she had written a commencement hymn, she might not have graduated at all. Nor did modernist poets work as teachers in higher education; of the more than seven hundred graduate or undergraduate creative writing programs currently being administered in the United States, not one existed before 1936, at which time Lindsay would have been over fifty-five years old. Thus, William Carlos Williams was a doctor. Wallace Stevens was vice president of the Hartford Indemnity Insurance Corporation. Edgar Lee Masters and Arthur Davison Ficke were lawyers. T. S. Eliot began as a banker and then had a long and influential career in publishing. Louis Untermeyer dropped out of high school and worked for his father's jewelry company.

When not living next to the Governor's Mansion in his parents' Springfield, Illinois, home—a house where Lindsay spent his time writing, illustrating, and printing editions of his homemade, grass-roots publication called the *Village Magazine*; where he would later live with his wife, Elizabeth, and their two children; and where he would commit suicide in 1931—Lindsay supported himself outside the academy too, and fairly well. Today, Lindsay is most remembered as the author of "The Congo"—the highly rhythmic, dramatic, very popular, and racist poem that elicited a storm of criticism and poetic rebuttals by Sterling Brown and Frank Marshall Davis. During his lifetime, though, Lindsay was an extremely well-known and popular performer whose half-chanted, half-sung recitations were in high demand in both literary and popular circles; "The Congo"—described by *Poetry* magazine's longtime associate editor Eunice Tietjens as "perilously near great poetry, broad in sweep, imaginative, full of fire and color, psychological—and very strange"—was an especially frequent request.[7] Outside New England, college- and university-based reading circuits were virtually nonexistent, so for many years Lindsay earned an income by performing for Rotary clubs, women's clubs, churches, libraries, and public schools. He crossed the nation on foot several times preaching what he called the "Gospel of Beauty" and the "New Localism"—visions of what the United States would look like if every small town fulfilled its artistic potential. He won awards from *Poetry*, where editor Harriet Monroe was a vociferous advocate and Pound a vociferous detractor. He wrote what many people consider to be the first book of film criticism, *The Art of the Moving Picture* (1915). He read before President Woodrow Wilson and Wilson's cabinet in 1915. And in 1920 he became the first American poet to read at Oxford University; London headlines reported, "American Poet Thrills Europe," and the *Observer* called him "easily the most important living American poet."

Given this success and popularity, as well as the anti-institutional ethos of much modernist poetry, it's surprising to find Lindsay in Iowa City in 1921, a year after his Oxford and London appearances, reading at the University of Iowa—the school that would launch the first creative writing MFA program in history fifteen years later, thereby initiating what Mark McGurl has called the Program Era. "I enjoy college classes in poetry and scribble clubs," Lindsay told the student newspaper, the *Daily Iowan*, which had been enthusiastically reporting on his visit. "I love the young college students who attempt to write verse and who admit it."[8] Those words weren't off-the-cuff remarks; Lindsay had in fact sent a press kit in advance of his reading that extended his enthusiasm and contained language that might have scandalized Robert Frost. "Many a University Department has become letter-perfect, without a groan or sigh," Lindsay's press kit gushed. "I love them dearly, these English Departments."

Part of this chapter's goal is to account for the change in Lindsay's thinking about American colleges and universities and to suggest that, in the process of that change, he not only pioneered the role of the visiting poet as we now know it but also came up with a rationale for why a modern poet might seek out university audiences. Aided by Baylor University English professor A. Joseph Armstrong, who owned a travel agency (Armstrong Educational Tours) and served as Lindsay's ad hoc agent, Lindsay made many visits to schools in the South, West, and Midwest that effectively extended the American poetry scene beyond the Northeast and into the nation's interior, making it possible for people to imagine that a place as "remote" as the University of Iowa could one day become the creative writing center of the United States as well as a UNESCO City of Literature (a designation Iowa City received in 2008). In telling this history, I want to nuance our understanding of a figure who has been minimized in histories of American literature despite his great impact on it and capture some of the prehistory of the Program Era, which, as McGurl has argued, is one of the most important and singular shifts in literary production and patronage in the history of Western literature. The logic and precedent that Lindsay established in pursuing nationwide university patronage would not only help initiate a rapprochement between poets and universities that paved the way for the more extensive partnerships of the Program Era but would also offer a model that generations of poets have followed in rationalizing their own connections to what has become, according to McGurl, "perhaps the most important patron of artistically ambitious literary practice in the United States."[9]

McGurl has told aspects of this history very well. Nevertheless, *The Program Era* focuses on fiction even when the emergence of that era is most clearly visible via poetry. The first writers-in-residence (Percy MacKaye at Miami University in Ohio and Frost at the University of Michigan) were poets. Paul Engle, longtime director of the University of Iowa Writers' Workshop, who shepherded that program to national prominence, was first and foremost a poet. Crucial Program Era textbooks were forged via poetry and edited by poets, especially *Understanding Poetry*, the 1938 Cleanth Brooks and Robert Penn Warren instructional text that, six years later, spawned *Understanding Fiction*, which McGurl highlights for its historical significance. Even the low-residency creative writing program came into existence via a poet, Ellen Bryant Voigt, who in 1976 founded the Warren Wilson MFA Program at Goddard College. Thus, even as I relate a history of how Lindsay gave up on the established patronage system of his time and decided to cultivate nationwide university audiences instead, I intend this chapter to be something of a corrective as well, standing for the role that poets and poetry have played in shaping the institutional history we have inherited and continue to make.

Vachel Revolts

On November 11, 1913, Lindsay wrote to Arthur Davidson Ficke—a Davenport, Iowa, lawyer, poet, Japanese art specialist, Harvard alum, probable lover of Millay, *Poetry* supporter, and perpetrator along with Witter Bynner of the 1916–18 Spectra Hoax—that he was working on a new poem, what he called "a Congo piece" that aimed to include "[e]very kind of a war-drum ever heard. Then a Minstrel's Heaven—then a glorified camp-meeting. Boomlay Boomlay Boomlay Boom." "I am doubtful," Lindsay went on, "whether this stuff is poetry. But I discover a lot of it in me. One composes it—not by listening to the inner voice and following the gleam—but by pounding the table with a ruler and looking out the window at the Electric signs.... I do not suppose I ever put so much progressive gradually developing polish on anything."[10]

Earlier in 1913, Lindsay's poem "General William Booth Enters into Heaven" had caused a sensation when it appeared as the lead poem in January's *Poetry* magazine, and it became his first popular and critically acclaimed hit. At *Poetry*, Monroe created a special $100 award for it after Pound bullied her into awarding the magazine's first Guarantor's Prize of $250 to William Butler Yeats for "The Grey Rock."[11] Elsewhere, audiences loved Lindsay's half-sung dramatic performance of "William Booth" so much that Lindsay wrote to Ficke, "I have recited the General till my jaws ache—4444 times" (*Letters* 81). But the new "Congo piece," which would appear as "The Congo" in *Poetry* the following year, gained Lindsay even more fame—more than he had bargained for and more than he was ready to handle. On March 1, 1914, he performed "The Congo" at a *Poetry* banquet being held in honor of Yeats's visit to Chicago. In his remarks, Yeats praised "William Booth" for its "strange beauty" and for being "stripped bare of ornament."[12] Monroe was there. Ficke was there. Carl Sandburg was there. "The Congo" took more than seven minutes to recite, and when Lindsay finished, biographer Eleanor Ruggles reports, "The audience burst into applause . . . and there were bravos from Lindsay's fellow Midwesterners" (218). An enthralled Randolph Bourne later remarked in the December 5, 1914, *New Republic*:

> You must hear Mr. Lindsay recite his own "Congo," his body tense and swaying, his hands keeping time like an orchestral leader to his own rhythms, his tone changing color in response to the noise and savage imagery of the lines . . . the "futurist" phrases crashing through the scene like a glorious college yell,—you must hear this yourself, and learn what an arresting, exciting person this new indigenous Illinois poet is.[13]

Popular audiences loved "The Congo" as well, and Lindsay's animated performances of it and "William Booth" catapulted him into stardom. In May 1915, for example, Lindsay visited the coal-mining town of Wilkes-Barre, Pennsylvania, and fifteen hundred people—nearly 5 percent of the population—turned out to hear him read.

Lindsay had tried for years to find and reach an American public—not an elite, New England audience that he perceived to be dominating American arts and letters but a broader national public. Living in New York, Lindsay had gone door-to-door trying to sell his poems to shopkeepers. He gave away copies of the *Village Magazine* for free or for the cost of postage. He had also embarked on mammoth, cross-country walking tours—one from Florida to Kentucky, another from New York to Hiram College, another from Illinois to New Mexico—during which he espoused what he called the "new creed of a beggar" and exchanged his poems for food and lodging. No innocent when it came to branding himself, he titled one of his early books *Rhymes to Be Traded for Food and Bread* and cast himself as "that vain and foolish mendicant"—a description that the press loved and that would later become central to shaping his identity as a visiting poet at colleges and universities.[14] Lindsay became known as "the most perfect modern example of the traditional minstrel who lived for and by song alone." Newspapers called him "a literary hobo," a "tramp poet," "a Peripatetic of Old," "a sort of prophet, a sort of tramp, a sort of wandering minstrel," and "a wandering poet and vagabond." Indeed, a teacher's resource guide for a course on contemporary American poetry being taught at the University of Alabama in 1924 took this identity as fundamental to Lindsay's work, asking students to discuss what it called "the influence of vagabondage" on Lindsay's verse.[15]

Now that the public was there—filling auditoriums, lecture halls, and parlors and clamoring night after night for performances of "William Booth" and "The Congo"—Lindsay found that popular fame wasn't all he had imagined it. Audiences didn't particularly care about the Gospel of Beauty and New Localism; they wanted to be entertained. They didn't want to hear the new verse he was writing; they wanted the poems that had made him famous. He was called "the best American poet" by future British Poet Laureate John Masefield, "a revelation" in the *Yale Daily News*, and "probably the most real and the most American [poet] we have today," but he felt people didn't read his books seriously enough, nor did they take to heart his philosophy about the artistic potential of small American towns; they wanted a vaudeville performance. This is a constant cause of consternation in his correspondence with A. Joseph Armstrong. "I have recited for thousands of people so far," Lindsay wrote on one occasion, "and have seen and autographed a total of about 20 books. People do not want to send for my books, neither do the publishers want to send them! But there is one thing sure, the people want to hear me, nearly every house is packed, and every day takes the limit of my strength."[16] In 1919, he complained to Armstrong, "I assure you the longer I live the more I dislike an audience that makes a curiosity out of me," and a few days later reiterated, "I cannot monkey with people who think I am an entertainer" (*Letters of Nicholas* 8, 15).

But monkey with them he did. First, in one of the larger ironies of twentieth-century literary history, he swore off reciting "The Congo"—the poem we now most remember him by and for which crowds "howl[ed]," he wrote, "till I am ready to vomit"—in favor of continuing other work, especially the *Village Magazine* and *The Golden Book of Springfield*, neither of which has garnered a fraction of the attention that "The Congo" has (*Letters* 267). It's an understatement to say Lindsay swore off reciting the poem, though, for he went on to wage an active campaign against it and "William Booth"—"two pieces that I utterly abhor"—for over a decade (259). In a 1920 letter to Harriet Monroe, he explained, "I do not want to be the slave of past performance or habits," and "I dislike the very name of every poem I have recited very much" (213). Monroe went on to print large excerpts from that letter in the February 1921 issue of *Poetry*, where she herself speculated on "his threat to cease reciting."[17] Four years later, in the preface to his 1925 *Collected Poems*, Lindsay continued to distance himself from his most famous poems. "I do not want to recite 'The Congo,'" he stated. "You can recite it yourself as well as I can."[18] And as late as 1931, nine months before his death, he was complaining about "mobs, tyrannical, ignorant mobs . . . mobbing me for 'The Congo'" and writing to his wife, Elizabeth, via Western Union from Asheville, North Carolina, explaining how audiences there "put on the thumbscrews till I was ready to scream because they could not sweat the Congo out of me. Two more such persecutions and I am a goner for sure" (*Letters* 453, 452).

However, even in the 1920 letter he wrote to Monroe and that Monroe published in *Poetry*—a letter he wrote while preparing the second edition of the *Village Magazine*—Lindsay knew he couldn't simultaneously boycott "The Congo" and proceed with his other projects, since the income he earned by reciting was the magazine's main source of funding. "Paper went up so high," he explained to Monroe, "that the reprint of the Village Magazine cost more than I thought. So I will have to be reciting just a bit off and on, till that bill is met. Then so far as I know I am free" (*Letters* 213). Writing the next year, from the Hotel Brevoort in New York, he again explained, "I have tried several times to quit reciting. . . . But just financially—I cannot afford to quit entirely, so I recite from hand-to-mouth as one may say . . . and then to keep out of debt" (222). To Armstrong he wrote, "I will have to fight it out alone perhaps forever, putting money I make as a reciter into zinc-etchings, probably for a steadily enlarged VM, which will be . . . slowly perfected with each new reprint. . . . Only in this way can I unify all my activities in balanced proportion, and introduce what might be called my genuine *public self* to my little public and keep from being the parrot and ape of what I did yesterday" (*Letters of Nicholas* 27).

In an effort to manage his relationship to the public, Lindsay began printing and distributing a combination of press kit and instructional manual that he sent in advance of his readings to better prime towns for his arrival. In this kit, he asked to have appointed a "personal conductor" who would read and discuss his writing with a small group of like-minded literary folk in order to "alter the public's mind, before I arrive." He even drew up a list of previsit strategies and goals on a large poster titled "The Kind of a Visit I Like to Make." When this intervention didn't work, Lindsay tried getting publicly angry—which *did* work—singling out the pomp and circumstance of women's clubs for special critique in what amounted to a nigh-scandalous attack on one of Progressive Era America's main forms of literary patronage, as well as a foundation of the American family and middlebrow society. He wasn't the only modernist to attack women's taste in poetry. Pound had railed against the "poppycock," "painted adjectives," and "emotional slither" of verse that "Aunt Hepsy liked."[19] Frost didn't like women's clubs either. But Pound was no populist, and Frost didn't bill himself, as Lindsay did, as "a traditional minstrel who lived for and by song alone." Telling a luncheon of businessmen in his hometown of Springfield, Illinois, how he wished he could find hostesses "who do their own work and who also read," Lindsay in 1925 appallingly explained:

> [B]ut the women's clubs hate such people with a deadly hatred. They thrust me among hostesses where there is much tea, a smothering of servants, and if there are husbands present, they are the kind of business men who find their chief nourishment in the full-page advertisements of office supplies in the back of the Literary Digest and Saturday Evening Post and whose

> only idealism is to keep their wives supplied with tea, poets and servants, while they themselves, as good business men keep looking like planks of the Republican platform every minute and attending peppy business men's banquets.

Lindsay had been saying similar if somewhat more muted things for years; in 1920, he had tendered his resignation from the Springfield Rotary Club, citing its "caste hate or condescending patronage of working people" as well as its devotion to "the roller-top desk point of view in life" (*Letters* 196). But the 1925 meeting was different because the Associated Press was present. Their nationally broadcast report began with the pugilistic headline:

> VACHEL REVOLTS
> LINDSAY HITS TEA-SIPPING WOMEN
> "HOBO POET" SNEERS AT FORMER HOSTESSES

We might be sympathetic to Lindsay's explanation today, that he didn't like to be "called upon to ape myself and parrot myself and recite my oldest verse for an audience that has not read anyone's verses, and has not the least idea of reading mine, new or old" (*Adventures* 278). But reporting on New England's response to Lindsay's tirade, Boston's *Evening Traveler* appeared to side with the women's organizations, the high society, and the cultural and regional superiority of the Northeast that those women represented. "Vagabond Poet of Springfield, Illinois," read that paper's headline, "Stands Snubbed by Club-women of Boston."

Singing for His Supper

In December 1921, four years before the Springfield controversy and the same year in which he was distributing copies of "The Kind of a Visit I Like to Make," Lindsay visited the University of Iowa. Both the student newspaper, the *Daily Iowan*, and the city's daily, the *Press-Citizen*, announced Lindsay's arrival on their front pages. Not surprisingly, these articles played up his vagabond reputation—both as an authentic throwback to earlier times and as a modernist iconoclast. "He seems," the *Daily Iowan* wrote, "to have been descended from the wandering minstrels of the time of lords and ladies when they roamed all through the countryside singing of conquests." That article then recaps Lindsay's 1912 walking tour from Illinois to New Mexico, reporting that Lindsay "preferred the highway to the railway ties because he came in closer touch with mankind. Mr. Lindsay would read his poems and distribute his pamphlets as he trudged along."[20] Two days before his visit, under the headline "Lindsay Sings for His Supper," the *Daily Iowan* had called Lindsay "a combined pagan and puritan, minstrel and missionary" and again highlighted his vagabond past, quoting him as saying, "[T]he open road is the symbol to me of opportunity and of the unfolding of life."[21]

If the papers played up Lindsay's nomadic reputation, it was to juxtapose it with the society audiences against which Lindsay would rail in Springfield four years later. The *Daily Iowan* reported that Lindsay "will not speak before business men or women's clubs" and quoted a description of Lindsay from *Century* magazine. "Ethically and spiritually," that article went on, "[Lindsay] represents the revolt against 'the roller top desk' side of American life" ("Large Crowd" 1). It's worth considering how Lindsay, despite his publicized distaste for men's and women's clubs, would nevertheless go on to read "'The Congo,' and other products of his genius" for those same audiences for years.[22] Judging from materials like "The Kind of a Visit I Like to Make," he was less interested in simply abandoning the public—which would have been a financial as well as a public relations nightmare—than he was in reforming it. This isn't especially surprising; to a large extent, Lindsay's stance against women's clubs served to heighten his authenticity as genuine performer and poet, casting him back into the role of outsider and nonconformist yet making him even more desirable by women's clubs for that same reason. What's more surprising about Lindsay's Iowa City visit is that we see him appealing to not just the university and higher education but English departments in particular as an alternative model of literary engagement and patronage—the same English departments that Frost accused of using "the worst system of teaching that ever endangered a nation's literature."

Indeed, during his 1921 Iowa City visit, Lindsay didn't just accept the university as host and personal conductor, but he went out of his way to praise and almost pander to its activity as if he were on campus more for a job interview than for a guest reading. He told the *Daily Iowan*, "I enjoy college and University audiences that are made up of those who have read my poems and prose works or have read some one else's copy of them. . . . I like to talk to people who are interested in poetry and literature, but I am not a public entertainer or amuser. Two groups of people whom I will not meet to talk to are women's clubs at three o'clock and business luncheons at twelve" ("Large Crowd" 1). Billed as "the guest of the University and especially of the English Department," he went on to explain that "[p]eople seem to think that I spend all of my time on the vaudeville stage. I do not. I am a private citizen and not a public amuser. I enjoy college classes in poetry and scribble clubs. I love the young college students who attempt to write verse and who admit it" (1). Lindsay also used the occasion to laud English Department faculty member John Towner Frederick and the regional literary magazine the *Midland*, which Frederick was editing. "I know what it means to continue an enterprise like that," Lindsay said, referring to his *Village Magazine*. "For this reason I have every admiration for the man who can make a success of a magazine such as that of the Midland" (1).

Far from presenting himself as an alternative to the stifling, repressive world of higher education, Lindsay is constructing his public image here as a university insider—defining himself against clubs not associated with the university, praising university students and their professors, and situating his own work as the type of work being done in higher education. Iowa City isn't an isolated example either. In fact, in the press kit he was sending around in 1921, he explicitly praised the work of English departments and directed townsfolk to follow their lead. "Many a University Department," he writes, "has become letter-perfect, without a groan or sigh. . . . I love them dearly, these English Departments." To a certain extent, Lindsay's praise is entirely sincere, since the construction of a small midwestern town around a public, land-grant university realized one vision of the Gospel of Beauty that he had preached while crossing the nation on foot and through which he sought to inspire artistic and cultural centers outside major cities across the continent. The wandering poet and vagabond, it seems, had found an audience that would listen, if not a place to actually settle down.

Creating an Industry

The year 1921 is important in the history of the Program Era and the reconciliation between poets and universities for another reason. As Lindsay was visiting what would soon become the epicenter of institutionalized creative writing, Robert Frost was concluding his first semester as writer-in-residence at the University of Michigan—the second such designated appointment in US history and one that Frank Lentricchia has called "an industry-inaugurating moment."[23] Like Lindsay, Frost had been struggling with the poet's relationship to higher education. He taught at Amherst College a couple of years earlier and had resigned over disagreements with Amherst's administration and general educational philosophy. That experience made him hesitate before accepting the Michigan offer, but he eventually gave in to its five thousand–dollar stipend and the school's promise that he would not have to teach. (That five thousand dollars is the rough equivalent of fifty-four thousand dollars today.) It was from this position that Frost would bring Lindsay to read at Michigan in 1922, as the capstone reading in a series of visiting poets that included Carl Sandburg, Louis Untermeyer, and Amy Lowell. Frost left Ann Arbor after two years but returned permanently when the university extended him an impossible-to-refuse lifetime writer-in-residence position with a salary and no teaching obligations at all.

Was Lindsay thinking of this in December 1921 while in Iowa City? You bet. When an old Hiram College friend—concerned about how Lindsay's constant traveling was adversely affecting his health—helped Lindsay secure a temporary writer-in-residence position in 1923 at Gulf Park Junior College for women in Mississippi, Lindsay described that position in relation to Frost's. "You know the arrangements made for Robert Frost in Ann Arbor the last two years," he wrote to Henry Canby of the *New York Evening Post*:

> I will be here till June 1, 1924 under almost the same arrangements. I will conduct one special class, selected from the forty highest in a stiff examination. After that examination there will be freedom, I hope, for my scholars. They will write and study as they please. . . . So please tell all the brainy *young* women—note the word young—in the United States to come here and try their luck on that terrible entrance examination. They must also be of school age. No women's club presidents need apply. I want to run my own class. (*Letters* 284)

Once again, we see Lindsay viewing higher education not primarily as an alternative source of patronage, as was the case with Frost, but as a way of mediating his relationship to the public and controlling who has access to him, in what ways, and on what terms. Not only does Gulf Park Junior College give Lindsay the freedom to craft his own class, but more important—by way of "that terrible entrance examination"—it offers a merit-based system by which to discriminate among his readers without entirely betraying the populist impulses that motivated him to go door-to-door preaching the Gospel of Beauty years before.

While Frost more or less had his position presented to him in 1921, Lindsay had been trying to work out in theory as well as practice the exact nature of the relationship between poets and higher education for quite some time: How does a modern poet rationalize affiliating with the university without losing his or her credibility as an outsider or iconoclast? In the second decade of the century, poets like Frost and Lindsay did read at colleges and universities now and again, oftentimes as the guest of one academic club or another, but those colleges—and the reading circuit, such as one could call it—were primarily in the "roller-top desk" culture of New England, not nationwide. Lindsay read at Mount Holyoke, Wellesley, Vassar, Syracuse, Smith, West Point, and Yale, for example, but when he went to Bloomington, Indiana, in 1914, he appeared not at Indiana University but at the Withers Public Library. In Indianapolis in 1913, he spoke at a women's club, not at Butler University. In an ambitious visit to Evansville, Indiana, in 1919, he read at Central High School, Francis Reitz High School, the YMCA, and at a noon meeting of the Kiwanis, Rotary, and Real Estate Clubs, but he did not read where we'd most expect a poet to read today—at Evansville University.

In 1919, however, Lindsay began a long relationship with Baylor University English professor A. Joseph Armstrong that would help to permanently change this dynamic by expanding the geographic range of American poetry beyond the Northeast and reconfiguring the relationship between poets and universities on a national scale. Armstrong had been trying to get poets to visit his modern literature classes in Waco, Texas, but few were inclined to come: in the days before plane travel, it was a long and time-consuming trip to speak at a single college in Texas, and many East Coast writers doubted that "culture" could in fact sell in the South and West. To address these obstacles and misperceptions, Armstrong reached out to other colleges in the region to create a necklace of schools willing to host—and pay for—visiting writers, and Lindsay was the perfect figure to help launch such a program and demonstrate that a market for poetry actually did exist in those parts of the country. Having tramped there in his youth and having staked his vision on the possibilities of art in middle and small-town America, Lindsay the "prairie poet" from Illinois wasn't as parochial as East Coast poets (many of whom had been born or raised in the Midwest and West but nevertheless left), and as a well-known performer he had the right amount of crowd appeal. From Lindsay's perspective, the partnership came at exactly the right time. He had been struggling with how to manage his celebrity status, and Armstrong offered an ideal way to self-select and coordinate poetry audiences; Lindsay, in fact, would send Armstrong one hundred copies of "The Kind of a Visit I Like to Make" so that Armstrong could distribute them to "personal conductors" at other colleges and universities. "Believe me," Lindsay wrote at the beginning of their partnership, "I am not so much out for the income or a long list of dates, as I am for a *few very well prepared audiences*" (*Letters of Nicholas* 11).

Over the years, Lindsay read at Baylor fifteen times, and for three years beginning in 1919, Armstrong served as Lindsay's manager and point person in coordinating three rather lucrative "Transcontinental Tours" concentrating on colleges and universities. "Be sure," Lindsay wrote to Armstrong,

> it is the Colleges and High Schools, and Negro Schools I covet, and the rest are merely incidental. I assure you the longer I live the more I dislike an audience that makes a curiosity out of me, and a committee that makes me talk about myself and listens and listens for queer things. The English Departments of High School, College, and University never, never, never do that, bless them. And since there are about one million of them in the United States, let's go after them, and forget the rest. (*Letters of Nicholas* 8)

With Lindsay setting the pace and precedent, Armstrong proceeded to channel more than seventy poets into the new poetry-reading circuit, opening colleges and universities in the South and West—many for the first time—to writers including Frost, Sandburg, and Amy Lowell, and, at the same time, opening American poets to a nationwide face-to-face audience. Baylor and Armstrong benefited as well, using their cut of the business to build Baylor's Browning Library, the world's largest collection of books, letters, manuscripts, and memorabilia pertaining to Robert and Elizabeth Barrett Browning. "We have maintained a very high literary standard," Armstrong wrote, "and we have netted a considerable sum of money." "The creation of this industry outside the Northeast," he later reflected, "was the outgrowth of ideas conceived in presenting Vachel Lindsay to the colleges and universities of America" (*Letters of Nicholas* xi).

Lindsay was not just a happy participant in Armstrong's plan, but he became an evangelist for it too, encouraging Frost, Sandburg, Lowell, and others to follow Armstrong's lead and management. "I hope the Armstrongs can send you and many other English Poets on this University Circuit," he wrote to John Drinkwater in 1922, for example, "which seems now wished on to them by the American poets" (*Letters* 247). Receiving an honorary degree from Hiram in 1931, he would stake his claim to the pioneering role he played in this new source of poetic patronage. "I have since 1912 spoken in every university in America, some of them 7 times," he explained, "yet Hiram looms larger than them all in my eyes." As a 1920 letter to Armstrong indicates, though, Lindsay's motivations were more complex than situating himself personally at the center of the industry:

> I think I wrote you my thought as to Amy Lowell. But here it is again. Send her, at any sacrifice of blood and nerve, in the same path you sent me this Spring and last, and extend it, till she has had a complete education in the South and the West. She will, having acquired that education, proceed to educate the East on the same terms. . . . Move Heaven and Earth to make a westerner and southerner out of her, and believe me she will then proceed to send all Boston and all the aesthetes of England west and south, and believe me, the west and south needs them, and they need the west and south. Each is suffering for the lack of the other. (*Letters of Nicholas* 30)

Here we can see that Lindsay's relationship with Baylor and Armstrong is more than a financial one and about more than simply priming audiences for his own work. Indeed, his goal is the same one that motivated him to hike across the country reading poems in the living rooms of complete strangers, and the same one he'd been promoting in the *Village Magazine*: to dislodge the East Coast from the center of American arts and letters and to bring "culture" to parts of America that didn't have as ready access to it. Ideally, getting poets to essentially go "on tour"—and this is a logic counter to the one that would enable Frost's permanent residency at Michigan—would not just educate America but would educate American poets as well. Armstrong and Lindsay's extension of American poetry into the nation's interior made it possible to imagine that somewhere as "remote" as the University of Iowa could become the center of creative writing education in the United States.

Once you get poets visiting English departments, it's probably a small step to get them hired, teaching creative writing classes, and starting MFA programs, but the temptation of an easy job and financial gain wasn't enough, in and of itself, to lure many modern poets, who prized their autonomy and their disconnection from established institutions, into the academy. For that reconciliation or marriage to ultimately happen and grow into the Program Era, poets had to be assured that they weren't simply selling out to the institution they abandoned and heavily critiqued. For Frost at Ann Arbor, this meant obtaining a promise that he wouldn't have to do anything he didn't want to do in order to draw his paycheck. Such agreements, however, are rare, expensive, and difficult to justify; more like the title of British Poet Laureate, which is conferred for life, they require a deep belief and financial investment in the value of simply having a poet on campus. Frost himself would call this type of arrangement "education by presence."

In adopting the model of the "visiting" poet and appealing to the integrity and outsider status of the vagabond or literary missionary, however, Armstrong and Lindsay offered another, more affordable way to conduct the reconciliation between poets and higher education. This system of patronage worked for everyone involved: it absolved universities from having to provide large amounts of money to support writers who guaranteed little in return other than their presence on campus; it allowed students getting their educations in the middlebrow era of charisma and celebrity to get more poets for their money; and, in casting artists into the role of literary tramp, troubadour, or hobo traveling from town to town, it allowed poets to maintain the particular outsider status essential to their sense of legitimacy—and to *our* sense of their legitimacy—at the same time that it provided them with an income and well-prepared audiences that would listen to and respect them rather than turn them into amusers or entertainers. Lindsay was such a successful figure in establishing the logic of this compromise because he could, in fact, point to a demonstrable vagabond past and a reputation as an itinerant literary hobo less devoted to the commercial truck of everyday life than to the ideals of the art. "I stand ready to beg tomorrow and to the end of the chapter," he wrote in the fourth (1925) edition of the *Village Magazine*, "rather than write a line I do not want to write, recite for a routine audience, or go through any parrot or ape performances." In Lindsay, the distinction between "vagabond" and "visiting poet" was a hard one to make, and no matter how vociferously he resisted being cast as a performer, he performed that role perfectly.

In 1921, Lindsay wrote to Armstrong from Iowa City, advising Armstrong to contact Percy MacKaye at Miami University in Ohio, and saying that MacKaye "has the makings yet of a great aesthetic evangelist" who could help Armstrong "build up a real American University platform prestige for the great body of poets in the American anthologies" (*Letters of Nicholas* 47–48). In the end, though, it was Lindsay, not MacKaye, who helped create the platform prestige that set in motion a new partnership between American poets and universities that would provide the conceptual grounding for the Program Era—an era in which poets (raw and cooked, mainstream and avant-garde, post-avant-garde and quietist) have become so at home in the university that they can no longer be described as outsiders. In such an era, it's all the more intriguing to think about the institution of the visiting writer in particular and consider whether its performance of itinerant outsiderness is all the more important to poets today because it may be the only part of the outside that the insiders have left.

NOTES

1. The Vachel Lindsay Collection at the Lincoln Library in Springfield, Illinois, contains a small archive of Lindsay-related materials to which I refer and on which I rely throughout this essay. Crucial to this archive are two large scrapbooks assembled by Lindsay's "Aunt Fannie"—Frances Hamilton of Indianapolis, Indiana—that collect two decades of newspaper clippings from around the world that report on Lindsay. I depend heavily on Fannie's one-of-a-kind compendium for information about Lindsay's travels, talks, audiences, and controversies. While many of the clippings are dated, many others lack complete bibliographical information; when I do not identify the source of details about Lindsay's tours in this essay, the reader can assume the information came from the articles in these albums.

2. Edgar Lee Masters, *Vachel Lindsay: A Poet in America* (New York: Biblo and Tannen, 1935), 56.

3. Eleanor Ruggles, *The West-Going Heart: A Life of Vachel Lindsay* (New York: W. W. Norton, 1959), 58.

4. This was not entirely the case, as some poet-critics of the time—notably Fugitive Poets such as Donald Davidson (1893–1968), John Crowe Ransom (1888–1974), Allen Tate (1899–1979), and Robert Penn Warren (1905–89)—did find university life hospitable. Nevertheless, it is fair to say that writers typically characterized as "modernist" did not make the teaching of creative writing or literature a career choice.

5. Robert Frost, *Selected Letters of Robert Frost*, ed. Lawrance Roger Thompson (New York: Holt, Rinehart and Winston, 1964), 146.

6. Anthony David Moody, *Ezra Pound: Poet* (Oxford: Oxford UP, 2007), 16.

7. Eunice Tietjens, "Vachel Lindsay's Books," *Little Review* 1.8 (Nov. 1914): 57.

8. "Large Crowd Hears Poems of Lindsay," *Daily Iowan*, 11 Dec. 1921, 1.

9. Mark McGurl, *The Program Era: Postwar Fiction and the Rise of Creative Writing* (Cambridge: Harvard UP, 2009), 22.

10. Vachel Lindsay, *Letters of Vachel Lindsay*, ed. Marc Chenetier (New York: Burt Franklin, 1979), 81.

11. Monroe would get her revenge on Pound two years later when—much to Pound's consternation—she awarded *Poetry*'s 1915 Levinson prize to Lindsay, choosing Lindsay's "The Chinese Nightingale" over T. S. Eliot's "The Love Song of J. Alfred Prufrock."

12. "Poetry's Banquet," *Poetry* 4.1 (Apr. 1914): 25.

13. Randolph Bourne, "Sincerity in the Making," *New Republic*, 5 Dec. 1914, 26.

14. Vachel Lindsay, *Adventures While Preaching the Gospel of Beauty* (New York: Mitchell Kennerley, 1914), 15.

15. Carl Carmer, *An Outline Course in Contemporary American Poetry* (Tuscaloosa: University of Alabama Extension Division, 1924), 6.

16. Vachel Lindsay, *Letters of Nicholas Vachel Lindsay to A. Joseph Armstrong* (Waco: Baylor UP, 1940), 45.

17. Harriet Monroe, "Notes and Queries from Mr. Lindsay," *Poetry* 17.5 (Feb. 1921): 264.

18. Vachel Lindsay, *Collected Poems* (New York: MacMillan, 1925), xlv.

19. Ezra Pound, "A Retrospect," *Literary Essays of Ezra Pound*, ed. T. S. Eliot (1918; Norfolk, CT: New Directions, 1954), 12; Ezra Pound, *How to Read* (1931; New York: Haskell House, 1971), 10.

20. "Lindsay a Poet and Missionary," *Daily Iowan*, 10 Dec. 1921, 1.

21. "Lindsay Sings for His Supper," *Daily Iowan*, 8 Dec. 1921, 5.

22. "Jottings about Town," Iowa City *Press-Citizen*, 12 Dec. 1921, 2.

23. Frank Lentricchia, *Modernist Quartet* (Cambridge: Cambridge UP, 1994), 106.

CHAPTER 3

Institutional Itinerancy

Malcolm Cowley and the Domestication of Cosmopolitanism

BENJAMIN KIRBACH

In the spring of 1950, the *Western Review* sent out a list of queries about the recent proliferation of writing programs in the United States. Malcolm Cowley was one of a handful of recipients. When asked if he had any advice for young writers, Cowley responded:

> My chief advice to a young writer today, if he wants to be really good, is to cut loose and take chances. Too many youngsters of the present generation are playing safe and taking courses in creative writing. I can imagine no better way for a creative writing program . . . to become inbred and useless. The instructors in the course should be writers and not graduated students of writing.[1]

Cowley had spent a good chunk of his own youth cutting loose and taking chances. His studies at Harvard were interrupted by World War I, during which he drove ambulances and munitions trucks for the French army. He graduated in 1920, then returned to Paris to rub elbows with the likes of Ernest Hemingway, Gertrude Stein, F. Scott Fitzgerald, Ezra Pound, and other expatriates of the Lost Generation. The sense of deracination that informed these Americans abroad deeply affected Cowley's appreciation for the necessity—and risks—of artistic freedom. In his memoir, *Exile's Return*, Cowley recalls that "our whole training was involuntarily directed toward destroying whatever roots we had in the soil, toward eradicating our local and regional peculiarities, toward making us homeless citizens of the world."[2] A similar rejection of a nationalist ethos is found in Cowley's advice for young writers: the true writer doesn't play safe, doesn't ensconce himself or herself within the academy but must first depart on a bohemian pilgrimage. In a 1959 letter to Richard Fariña, Cowley writes that "[o]ne has to lead a sort of monastic life of poverty and obedience, though not chastity, only nonpaternity, in order to be truly independent. Who's willing to do that now in the washing-machine era?"[3] Cowley consistently opposes artistic progress to bourgeois conformity. The "washing-machine era" is shorthand for the affluent consumerism of the postwar United States, but we might wonder whether it could also designate the Program Era—when institutional patronage could spare one from the hardscrabble realities of the unaffiliated writer.

A "writer" is not the same as a writing program graduate, Cowley argues. Yet by the late 1950s, Cowley would go on to teach writing himself. While he held posts at numerous universities, scholars have largely overlooked Cowley's involvement with creative writing programs. They most often emphasize his role as a chronicler of the Lost Generation, his leftist politics, or his illustrious editorial career at Viking Press. Cowley did not produce fiction; it is therefore no surprise that he is mentioned only twice, and in passing, in Mark McGurl's *The Program Era*.[4] He was also never a lasting fixture in any particular program. He taught at Yale, Stanford, California at Irvine and Berkeley, Hollins, Michigan, Minnesota, Washington, and Warwick in Great Britain, among other places, but never maintained a full-time position. Cowley thus personifies the oxymoronic figure of the "permanent" visiting professor. One might call this a deliberate *institutional itinerancy*, and I argue that it represents a way of reconciling modernism's cosmopolitan ideal within the constraints of the academy. Cowley's vision of the writer's parabolic trajectory—as one who departs, becomes "homeless" in the world, and only then returns to teach—also maps adjacently to McGurl's appropriation of systems theory and his coinage of the term "autopoetics." Construed as the formal or thematic reflexivity characteristic of modernist literary tradition, autopoetics refers both to the problem of the author within the larger matrices of "systematic creativity" and to the fallout of the recursive injunction to "write what you know." Cowley gives voice to the anxiety that a program becomes "inbred and useless" by shorting the autopoetic circuit and substituting imitation for experience.

The pattern of exile and return central to Cowley's life and work illustrates his concern for the writer's place in what Pascale Casanova calls the World Republic of Letters—a transnational literary space whose capital Cowley saw coagulate incestuously into the folds of the "program." A middleman of

American letters, Cowley was best known as an editor, poet, historian, and translator; as the critic whose *Portable Faulkner* (1946) helped pave the way toward Faulkner's Nobel Prize; and as the editor who all but single-handedly ushered Kerouac's *On the Road* (1957) to press. Thus, while Cowley may not have been one of the most preeminent *producers* of American literature, he was no doubt a preeminent *facilitator* of that production. He occupied a unique position in the circles of twentieth-century literary, political, and academic life. A perpetual interloper whose home was everywhere and nowhere, Cowley embodies an insider-outsider dialectic crucial to linking the university to the publishing industry during the emergence of the Program Era.

McGurl's study of postwar fiction is more precisely a study of how modernism was institutionalized, when the imperative to "make it new" became, he argues, "another form of original research sponsored by the booming, science-oriented universities of the Cold War era" (4). McGurl names the act of authorship in the Program Era the "autopoetic process." In his diagrammatics, three primary values undergird autopoetics: creativity (imagination, fantasy, "find your voice"), craft (revision, technique, "show don't tell"), and experience (authenticity, memory, "write what you know"). The rhetoric of institutional creative writing after World War II frames each of these as "the psychic and symbolic resources upon which a writer draws in the act of writing" (23). McGurl adapts autopoetics from "autopoiesis"—the idea that any system is a network of processes, the products of which realize the very network that produces them. Francisco Varela, the Chilean biologist-philosopher who invented the term, writes of autopoiesis that it is "a logical bootstrap, a loop: a network produces entities that create a boundary, which constrains the network that produces the boundary."[5] For Varela, autopoiesis is the process by which a living cell differentiates itself from the surrounding environment, how the cell membrane maintains an "inside" separate from an "outside." Slavoj Žižek would have it that autopoiesis is also evident in the ontology of the human subject. The "self" is purely virtual, he argues: an "Inside which appears only when viewed from the Outside."[6] For Žižek, subjectivity is merely a "surface-effect" of the body (206). In a systems-model, autopoiesis names the virtual gap necessary for a self to (seem to) appear.

We would suppose autopoetics to therefore encompass the twin processes of authorship in general—meaningful coherence, like the "self," emerging from a primordial ooze of experiential data—as well as what McGurl identifies as the paradoxical concept of "systematic creativity"—that writing, as a form of free artistic expression, is something that can be "taught" in the first place. That a work of fiction recapitulates its own creative process is perhaps evident in the high modernist technique of, say, a Joyce or a Stein. But once the Parisian café had migrated to the college classroom, the phenomenon became part and parcel of progressive pedagogy. McGurl argues that literary production within the university generates fictions that dramatize the very autopoetics they draw on (in metafictional "campus novels" like Barth's *Giles Goat-Boy* [1966] or, to a lesser extent, Pynchon's *The Crying of Lot 49* [1966]). Reflexivity is therefore symptomatic of a culture of self-expression; the act of reflection as the basis *for* writing is re-presented in the very products *of* writing. "[E]ncouraged to 'write what you know,'" McGurl continues, "the novelist eventually is driven to represent his intimate knowledge of the writing process and its consequences, to address the fact of fiction making" (53).

For Cowley, the tripartite process of creativity/craft/experience is not so evenly balanced. The perceived conformity incubated by an American liberal education is perhaps implicit in the counterintuitive notion that one can teach writing at all in the university. What can one truly teach beyond craft? McGurl questions whether the advent of writing programs was an antidote to this perceived conformity or whether it instead effectuated a leveling of aesthetic form across all MFA-produced fiction. Cowley himself claims in an interview with journalist John King, "The experience I had supporting myself for 30 years before getting involved in university life was a good thing. . . . [Today] [y]ou have students learning writing from professors who joined the faculty as soon as they got out of graduate school. They teach creative writing and never *do* anything."[7] Cowley does not equivocate when he suggests that good writing necessarily draws on life outside the classroom. When Wallace Stegner invited him to teach at Stanford in 1955 (where he would return again in 1956, 1958, and 1959), Cowley wrote about the sort of course he would like to design:

> [T]he present writing programs are either suffused with artiness and yearnings toward Creative Self-Expression, or else they are actually courses in critical analysis. . . . I'd like to see a writing program that was a *writing* program and not . . . a treatise on how to masturbate on the typewriter in ten easy lessons. (*Long Voyage* 507)

The kind of writing these programs both facilitate and encourage is, Cowley suggests, either masturbatory or inbred. In either case, the implication is that institutionalized writing replicates the same ideas—portable tricks of craft—without risk or innovation. The bona fide writer instead comes from outside the system. Cutting loose is thus analogous to the "cut" in systems theory: "the primary distinction," McGurl writes, that "initiates [the system's] very existence" (54). Without first escaping the confines of the academy (or, indeed, of the culture at large), the writer has no recourse to a primary distinction, no way to differentiate himself or herself from the surrounding environment. Output is fed back immediately as input, and a unique authorial "self" fails to materialize. The program cannot but extol craft over experience, and for Cowley, the result is a loss of authenticity. He therefore constructs a myth of exile and return as a kind of sociologically (if not geographically) reflexive loop. Like Žižek's "Inside which appears only when viewed from the Outside," the writer can't see his or her place within the literary world without first separating himself or herself from the parent culture. Call it the "autopoetics of exile": without such a virtual loop, the graduated student of writing is all form and no content.

Donald W. Faulkner claims that, by the late 1950s, the surge of baby boomers into the university left many young American writers struggling to construct a sense of regional identity: "Am I a city writer who's trying to be a country writer? Am I basically a country writer who's trying to be a city writer?" and so on.[8] Faulkner, based on feedback from Cowley's former students, asserts that Cowley had been instrumental in pointing them toward a "cosmopolitan world of writing" (207). Cowley claims that, at the time, he was profoundly interested in a "Republic of Letters," the idea that writers could belong to "a confraternity of writers all over the world" (qtd. in Faulkner 207). Envisioned as a "denationalized" space, as Cowley once, in 1927, described the expatriate experience itself (*Long Voyage* 150), the Republic of Letters exceeded the "regional peculiarities" and myopic nationalism that had been responsible for the Great War. Writers everywhere were instead part of a "world" system that could transcend (and perhaps even resist) state power. Pascale Casanova describes such an idea in her *World Republic of Letters* as the international field, both real and imagined, in which literature is produced, circulated, and legitimized. But, contrary to Cowley, Casanova challenges the view of a Republic of Letters as "an enchanted world, a kingdom of pure creation, the best of all possible worlds where universality reigns through liberty and equality."[9] She calls this a utopian fiction, one that obscures the underlying—and unequal—economy of geographical and cultural centers, literary prestige, translation, world markets, and so on. Paris, for example, had become the epicenter of the Republic of Letters in the late eighteenth century due to its literary prestige but also, in Cowley's day, to Europe's political and economic upheaval in the wake of World War I. Extended stays in Paris became not only possible but also quite affordable for middle-class Americans. Moreover, the shadow of revolution ran long over Parisian culture. It promised a response to the drab, businesslike quality of American politics in the 1920s. A hub of liberal internationalism, Casanova writes, "Paris therefore became the capital of those who proclaimed themselves to be stateless and above political laws: in a word, artists" (29).

If Cowley harbored a naïve faith that an imagined Republic of Letters could transcend real-world geopolitics and the ills of capitalism, he at least felt the cultural influence of Paris begin to wane by the outset of World War II. Europe's decline into another total war meant that the internationalist promise of the 1920s had been forsaken. In a 1940 letter to John Crowe Ransom, Cowley confides that New York had become "almost the last refuge of the international culture that used to flourish in Paris, Munich, Vienna, Berlin, Madrid, Petersburg, even Bucharest" (*Long Voyage* 265). After the fall of France to the Nazis, a disillusioned Cowley resigned as editor for the *New Republic*, which he had previously steered in "a resolutely communist direction."[10] While Cowley was never officially a member of the US Communist Party, he had been affiliated with it since his return from Europe in the late 1920s. He had been exposed to Dada and Marxism during his travels, and the first edition of *Exile's Return* (1936) put forth a distinctly Marxian interpretation of history. When fellow leftist Archibald MacLeish was appointed director of the War Department's Office of Facts and Figures in 1941, he offered Cowley a job as an analyst. Cowley's politics quickly came under fire from Martin Dies and the House Committee on Un-American Activities. Dies denounced Cowley on the floor of Congress, claiming that he belonged to "seventy-two communist-front organizations" (Benfey). This number was certainly an exaggeration, but Cowley had no recourse to deny it. He resigned in 1942 and withdrew from virtually all outspoken political activity. He would later refer to these as "the worst two years of my life."[11]

Cowley's unsuccessful foray into politics fits a structure not unlike the homelessness of his expatriate days—only this time he was an outsider on American soil. But he nevertheless remained invested in the revolutionary potential of the author. In 1944, he accepted a position with Viking Press to work on the newly minted *Portable Library.* Ironically, the series began in 1943 with *As You Were: A Portable Library of American Prose and Poetry Assembled for Members of the Armed Forces and Merchant Marine.* Cheap paperback reprints, the *Portable Library* was developed specifically for service personnel to capitalize on the recent uptick in wartime readership. Cowley was able to reappropriate this propagandist emphasis on a national literary tradition to focus on what were, in his esteem, underappreciated writers. Brought on board to edit the Hemingway volume, Cowley departed in his introductory essay from earlier critical assessments of Hemingway as emotionally sparse and overly masculine. Framed instead as essentially a tortured and submerged gothic writer, Cowley's re-evaluation is the dominant critical view today. And Hemingway's signature tip-of-the-iceberg style has perhaps become the most emulated in writing workshops. Representative of what McGurl calls the "pathos of understatement," Hemingway's name is now all but synonymous with "the value of craft as represented by the practice of multiple revision" (244–45). *The Portable Hemingway* (1944) sold tremendously, so much so that Cowley was able to convince Viking to publish a *Portable Faulkner* in 1946. At the time, Faulkner was all but out of print and slipping into literary obscurity. Cowley's introduction repositioned Faulkner as a kind of internal émigré, spiritual counterpart to his Lost Generation brethren. Robert Penn Warren calls *The Portable Faulkner* "the great watershed" moment in Faulkner's reputation, and many scholars have traced a fairly clear line between its publication and Faulkner's Nobel Prize in 1949.[12]

Cowley's success in the publishing world led to a career in academia. In his first book of poetry, *Blue Juniata*, Cowley describes his as a "wandering, landless, uprooted generation."[13] He was able to cultivate a similar sense of cosmopolitanism in the classroom. Donald W. Faulkner suggests that Cowley helped students in his workshops overcome their crises of regional identity, partially due to his expatriate past but also because he showed relatively little institutional fealty. "Perhaps I did give [the students] an outside perspective on what they were doing," Cowley says. "I had this advantage in teaching that class at Stanford, that I wasn't trying to do anything for myself. . . . [T]hey liked that idea of a friendly outsider" (qtd. in Faulkner 207). Yet Cowley writes in a 1957 letter to James Thurber that he felt like a "spy and interloper" in the academy (*Long Voyage* 506). One reason is that he deliberately avoided full-time positions. The idea that a writer could support himself or herself by teaching sporadically was a relatively new cultural development. In a 1982 interview with the *Paris Review*, Cowley says: "In many ways things are easier now for writers. Sixty years ago there were no such things as writing fellowships; there were no Guggenheims . . . very few prizes. There were almost no teaching posts for writers."[14] In the same interview, Cowley cites Robert Frost as pioneering in the sense that he was able to subsist on a mixture of poetry, teaching, and public engagements. "Frost managed to support himself after *North of Boston* by readings, and by lecturing at universities," Cowley says. "He rather blazed a trail in that respect" (qtd. in McCall). The tenet of nonpaternity surfaces here in Cowley's willingness to teach only when necessary. To domesticate the cosmopolitan was to dodge permanent institutional commitments. But it also meant that a writer could eradicate his or her regional peculiarities by entering into a pervasive "denationalized" space, of which Cowley was an evanescent emissary. The role of a Republic of Letters might therefore hint at a kind of modernist workshop ideal—a global community of writers bound by unpunctuated dialogue, not institutional happenstance. As a figure both inside and outside the university system, Cowley could purvey a kind of cosmopolitan "workshop" not unlike the fluid expatriate communities of the 1920s.

The Program Era nevertheless initiated shifts in the geopolitical fabric of the Republic of Letters. Casanova writes that the "capital" accumulated by a national literature attests to its collective wealth and influence—often due to the historical depth of a literary tradition but also to the economy of literary "prestige." Prestige, she argues, is produced by "an interested aristocracy or enlightened bourgeoisie" and is materialized in salons, publishing houses, reviews, awards, academies, schools of literature, and so on (15). By the mid-twentieth century, the American university had begun to absorb the credentialing authority for professionalized writing. Cowley seemed almost seismographically aware of this. He was able to navigate issues of canonicity and mass readership with a level of expertise inaccessible to academics and publishers who had hitherto operated within separate spheres. Hans Bak writes that Cowley "forge[d] a bridge between the academic critics, who had a thorough knowledge of the literary past but barely any feeling of the present, and the literary journalists, who [had] a sense of commercial and cultural trends but no feeling for historical perspective."[15] On the publishing end of this bridge, Cowley was keenly attuned to trends in readership. "[K]eep an eye on what the colleges are assigning, [and] I'm sure we will come to have a larger share of that very considerable demand for trustworthy texts," he wrote (qtd. in Travis 13). On the academic end, he was able to rely on his connections at Viking and elsewhere to assist, directly or indirectly, in the careers of writers like Ken Kesey, Larry McMurtry, Peter S. Beagle, Wendell Berry, and Tillie Olsen. The reputation he built at Viking also enabled Cowley to publish a revised edition of *Exile's Return* in 1951. He now emphasized the *return* of the exile as a necessary step toward reestablishing a culture's solidarity: "the old pattern of alienation and reintegration, or departure and return, that is repeated in scores of European myths and continually re-embodied in life," he writes (289). And further:

> During the years when the exiles tried to stand apart from American society they had pictured it as a unified mass that was moving in a fixed direction and could not be turned aside by the efforts of any individual. The picture had to be changed after the Wall Street crash, for then the mass seemed to hesitate like a cloud in a cross wind. Instead of being fixed, its direction proved to be the result of a struggle among social groups with different aims and of social forces working against one another. The exiles learned that the struggle would affect everyone's future, including their own. (290–91)

Cowley's essay "Invitation to Innovators," which appeared in the *Saturday Review* in 1954, suggests that not enough young American writers had followed this exile-return pattern and thus not enough young American writers had the requisite vantage to see their role in the cultural struggle. "Invitation to Innovators" is a screed against the perceived social conformity of the 1950s. "It seems to me that a good deal of American writing after World War II, including most of the serious novels and not a little of the poetry, has been essentially pseudomorphic," Cowley writes.[16] The term is mineralogical; when a rock formation is hollowed out by erosion, crystals of a different mineral can sometimes form inside. But the external shape remains the same, stifling the new crystals' growth. Cowley borrows the term from Oswald Spengler, who uses "historical pseudomorphosis" to designate cases in which a younger generation can't escape the expressive forms of the older and is therefore unable to fully realize its own self-awareness. Imitation replaces innovation, and after a culture has passed its apogee (as Spengler's *Decline of the West* [1918] suggests ours has), such a culture is incapable of generating emancipatory aesthetics.

For Cowley, the autopoetics of exile is necessary to view one's parent nation as anything other than a fixed "unified mass." The parabolic arc of the exile is the virtual gap necessary for a "self" to appear—or, in this case, a sense of rejuvenated national identity. In *Exile's Return*, Cowley suggests that the prolonged detour through Europe had "an unexpected effect on most of [the American expatriates]: it taught them to admire their own country" from afar (289). In this sense, the pseudomorphic enclosure of a national culture is not dissimilar from the pseudomorphic enclosure of the writing program. The workshop, thought as a microcosm of the "nation," delimits the range of artistic expression. Autopoetics' experiential input becomes ossified; writing becomes "inbred and useless." As an editor, Cowley was thus always on the lookout for more radical expressions of the literary. He was a tastemaker—resuscitating the status of writers like Faulkner, Hemingway, and even Whitman (in 1959, he oversaw the re-release of the original 1855 edition of *Leaves of Grass*)—but he also had a broad aesthetic palette, championing variety and experimentation. And he welcomed literature associated with subversive lifestyles. Cowley uses Kerouac as an example in "Invitation to Innovators," writing:

> There is one fairly large group that refuses to conform and has waged a dogged sort of rebellion—against what it is hard to say, because the group has no program, but possibly against the whole body of laws, customs, fears, habits of thought, and literary standards that has been accepted by other members of the generation. The rebellion is individual and nihilistic; each of the rebels simply refuses to accept any model, in literature or life, that older people ask him to emulate. . . . Last year they talked about being "underground" and called themselves "the beat generation"; it was John Kerouac who invented the phrase, and his unpublished long narrative "On the Road" is the best record of their lives. ("Invitation" 39)

"I like and respect the new writers as a group," Cowley says further. "My one complaint against them would be that they aren't yet producing new works of literature" ("Invitation" 39). This comment is telling of an autopoetic loop yet to be realized, that new writers still needed to convert raw experience into creative output. It also telling, though, that Kerouac's "unpublished long narrative" was still three years away from shelves. Cowley fought to get *On the Road* published at Viking when no other publishing house would touch it. While Cowley seems to have encouraged Kerouac to pare the sprawling transcontinental romp down to a more coherent narrative, he claims to have insisted on no further editing.[17] It is evident from "Invitation to Innovators" that Cowley saw in Kerouac the refusal to "accept any model" as a struggle against pseudomorphosis. And perhaps he even saw a glimmer of his younger self. Indeed, critic Adam Gussow writes that, "[i]n Malcolm Cowley and Jack Kerouac, it might fairly be said, the Lost Generation and the Beat Generation were meeting for the first time—and discovering in each other an unexpected resemblance" (296). Kerouac was emblematic of the insider-outsider, exile-return dialectic Cowley viewed as crucial for the advancement of literary art. While he had been more or less silenced politically since the 1940s, one sees in Cowley's efforts to align artistic progress with rebellion a still vibrant opposition to bourgeois conformity.

Casanova writes that, as a "prisoner of a particular point of view, [the individual author] glimpses a part of the structure of the literary world without, however, seeing it whole" (10). Viewing the authentic writer to come from the outside (outside the workshop; outside the nation), Cowley's myth of the exile dramatizes a way of trying to see the whole literary world. Autopoetics plays out ideologically in the myth of the exile, but it also plays out thematically in Cowley's frequent writing about the isolated status of authors themselves. Cowley remarks in numerous essays about this peculiar brand of alienation. In a 1975 essay titled "Privatation and Publication," he writes:

> I think most authors feel an immense contrast between the writing of a book, which is a private undertaking, and its exposure to the judgment of whoever is willing to read. Publication: there should be another word to set against it, "privatation," as describing an earlier stage of authorship.[18]

Cowley was thus keenly attuned to the fact that all writing is a kind of self-imposed exile. Writing draws on the "monastic life" of forced isolation to see one's culture, or oneself, from the outside in. What the Program Era initiated was perhaps a further mediation—the "workshop" in between publication and privatation. But what the Program Era replaced—or threatened to, in Cowley's view—was the initial risk taking that privatation necessarily feeds on. Without it, the autopoetic loop is liable to snap back on itself. In this way, the workshop environment can sometimes produce a tendency toward what Cowley calls (and what program graduates no doubt recognize as) "self-enhancement, self-aggrandizement, [and] putting down your rivals so that you will be top dog." As an instructor, the goal, he says, was instead to "build up the builder-uppers and put down the putter-downers, then the class would be successful" (qtd. in Faulkner 205). Indeed, when Cowley taught Ken Kesey at Stanford and was later instrumental in getting *One Flew over the Cuckoo's Nest* (1962) published at Viking, Kesey recalled:

> The greatest thing Cowley taught me was to respect other writers' feelings. If writing is going to have any effect on people morally, it ought to affect the writer morally. It is important to support everyone who tries to write because their victories are your victories.[19]

These shared victories are indicative yet again of the Republic of Letters, Cowley's professed camaraderie between the single, isolated writer and all writers against the backdrop (or in the exiled interstices) of industrial capitalism. Circumventing the knot of institutional authority embodied in the full-time professor, Cowley found a way of reconciling his cosmopolitan ideal within the changing eddies of twentieth-century literary production. Cowley's itinerancy—his seemingly effortless movement between universities and the publishing industry, between writers individual and collective—played a crucial role in institutionalizing modernism in the beginning of the Program Era.

NOTES

1. Malcolm Cowley, "The Teaching and Study of Writing: A Symposium," *Conversations with Malcolm Cowley*, ed. Thomas Daniel Young (Jackson: UP of Mississippi, 1986), 29.

2. Malcolm Cowley, *Exile's Return: A Literary Odyssey of the 1920s*, rev. ed. (1936; New York: Viking Press, 1951), 27.

3. Malcolm Cowley, *The Long Voyage: Selected Letters of Malcolm Cowley, 1915–1987*, ed. Hans Bak (Cambridge: Harvard UP, 2014), 531.

4. Mark McGurl, *The Program Era: Postwar Fiction and the Rise of Creative Writing* (Cambridge: Harvard UP, 2009).

5. Francisco Varela, "The Emergent Self," *The Third Culture*, ed. John Brockman (New York: Simon and Schuster, 1996), 212.

6. Slavoj Žižek, *The Parallax View* (Cambridge: MIT Press, 2006), 206.

7. John King, "Cowley: He Found the Lost Generation," *Conversations with Malcolm Cowley*, 215 (emphasis added).

8. Donald W. Faulkner, "A Conversation with Malcolm Cowley," *Conversations with Malcolm Cowley*, 207.

9. Pascale Casanova, *The World Republic of Letters*, trans. M. B. DeBevoise (1999; Cambridge: Harvard UP, 2004), 12.

10. Christopher Benfey, Review of *The Long Voyage: Selected Letters of Malcolm Cowley, 1915–1987*, by Malcolm Cowley, ed. Hans Bak, *New Republic*, 28 Feb. 2014, https://newrepublic.com/article/116499/long-voyage-selected-letters-malcolm-cowley-reviewed.

11. Quoted in Trysh Travis, "The Man of Letters and the Literary Business: Reviewing Malcolm Cowley, " *Journal of Modern Literature* 25.2 (Winter 2001–2): 5.

12. Robert Penn Warren, "Introduction," *Faulkner: A Collection of Critical Essays*, ed. Robert Penn Warren (Englewood Cliffs: Prentice-Hall, 1966), 10.

13. Malcolm Cowley, *Blue Juniata* (Norwood, MA: Plimpton Press, 1929), 50.

14. John McCall, "Malcolm Cowley: The Art of Fiction No. 70," *Paris Review* 85 (1982), http://www.theparisreview.org/interviews/3137/the-art-of-fiction-no-70-malcolm-cowley.

15. Hans Bak, "A Many-Windowed House: Malcolm Cowley and American Culture at Mid-century," *Predecessors: Intellectual Lineages in American Studies*, ed. Rob Kroes (Amsterdam: VU UP, 1999), 161.

16. Malcolm Cowley, "Invitation to Innovators," *Saturday Review*, 21 Aug. 1954, 40.

17. Adam Gussow, "Bohemia Revisited: Malcolm Cowley, Jack Kerouac, and *On the Road*," *Georgia Review* 38.2 (Summer 1984): 291.

18. Malcolm Cowley, "Privatation and Publication: A Memoir of the Year 1934," *Sewanee Review* 83.1 (Winter 1975): 144.

19. Robert Faggen, "Ken Kesey: The Art of Fiction No. 136," *Paris Review* 130 (1994), http://www.theparisreview.org/interviews/1830/the-art-of-fiction-no-136-ken-kesey.

PART II

Revisions

CHAPTER 4

Modernism and the MFA

GREG BARNHISEL

In the fall 1937 term, a college junior named James Laughlin took English A-3, Harvard College's closest offering to what we might call "creative writing." A-3, as its name suggests, was the third-year writing class—an elective for advanced students, as opposed to English A-1, the first-year writing class that all Harvard men had to take.[1] Laughlin's teacher was Theodore Morrison, a longtime instructor who had just been promoted to assistant professor.

Harvard's writing faculty had just undergone a generational transition. Robert Hillyer, the conservative poet who had overseen the writing classes for years, had accepted the Boylston Chair in Rhetoric and Oratory, and his deputy Morrison succeeded him as writing director. In the mid-1930s, an impressive array of young instructors taught English A-1: Delmore Schwartz, John Berryman, Wallace Stegner, Mark Schorer. English A-3, on the other hand, had been the province of the popular historian Bernard de Voto, who used it to train writers in his mold.

Morrison was a poet, and in his A-3 class he allowed his advanced students to write poetry. Laughlin's work for English A-3, housed in the Laughlin archive at the Houghton Library, shows him starting to employ the poetic style and subject matter that would characterize his poetry for the rest of his life: short lines, simple vocabulary, topics that centered on romantic love or close observation of small interactions between people and the world. William Carlos Williams and Catullus were his inspirations. This was a major swerve from the juvenile poetry he had written while at Choate, which was very much in the Pound/Eliot high-modernist vein: allusive, fragmented, pessimistic, ironic.

Nevertheless, Morrison found Laughlin's poetry unbearably Eliotic and demanded in his comments that Laughlin go his own way and let Eliot go his. In the end, Laughlin did just that, although he never let go of Pound. The publishing house he started that same year, New Directions, became Pound's primary American publisher soon after and remains so. Laughlin made himself into the most important American publisher of modernism and the most influential figure in carrying on and expanding the legacy of high modernism to postwar American writers, readers, and students.

But as odd as Morrison's judgment seems to a contemporary reader, it does illustrate one key point: what the writing faculty at Harvard considered "Eliotic" was quite different from what we consider to be "Eliotic," or modernist, today. Even today, of course, what actually counts as "modernist" is very much at issue. But antimodernists like Morrison and Hillyer saw the practices and techniques of this new poetry—which, it is important to note, was not widely called "modernist" until well into the 1950s—as a pervasive threat. For them, the threat of Eliotism, or "the new poetry," or what later came to be known as modernism, was everywhere.

In *The Program Era*, Mark McGurl does something like what Morrison did with Laughlin's poems. What he calls "modernist" in the long first chapter of his study is so broad and encompassing that it lacks definition, and in fact his modernist tradition could include even the writing that came from the *anti*modernist countertradition of institutions like Bread Loaf. In other words, what McGurl calls the modernist tradition in American fiction, incubated in and disseminated from MFA programs, isn't particularly modernist as the term has come to be used in the last decade or two. In fact, the same aspects of Program Era fiction that for McGurl epitomize the triumph of modernism were common in even the most conservative and traditional writing programs, such as Harvard's.

McGurl's loose use of the term "modernism," though, reflects the *redefinition* of modernism accomplished by what I call "Cold War modernism," which refers to the 1950s defanging of the once-radical modernist movement, accomplished by any number of separate but aligned groups and institutions: the New Critics, the New York Intellectuals, the trade publishing industry, universities, museums, foundations, and even the cultural-diplomatic agencies of the US government. Sometimes separately, sometimes in concert, these people and institutions processed modernist art and literature (much of which had been deeply oppositional, experimental, and antinomian) into high cultural artifacts suitable for consumption by the cultural elite and even the American middle classes.

I don't have enough space here to explain fully all the means by which this process was accomplished, and many other critics and scholars (such as Hugh Wilford, Joan Rubin, Serge Guilbaut, Eva Cockroft, and Cathy Turner, just to name a few) have made important contributions to this investigation. A few operations and developments, though, are central here. First of all, the "aestheticization" of modernism was crucial. Artworks, influential critics of the 1940s and 1950s insisted, must be viewed as aesthetic artifacts, and the social or political ideas those artworks forwarded should not enter into an evaluation of them as artworks. Second, consumer culture and even product design began to incorporate modernist techniques such as abstraction, fragmentation, streamlining, and reflexive self-awareness. In addition, critical discourse explaining what modernism meant and how it worked seeped into high culture, facilitating modernist artworks' entry into major museum collections, trade publishers' lists, and university syllabi.

Cold War imperatives were also hugely important. Once modernist art gained cultural prestige, it could be used as evidence of cultural achievement—and US cultural agencies did just that. As a rejoinder to European prejudices and Soviet propaganda holding that the United States lacked real culture, American institutions such as the Museum of Modern Art, the US Department of State, Voice of America, and the Ford Foundation offered the work of Jackson Pollock, William Faulkner, George Gershwin, and others.

How these institutions *framed* these works made modernism into Cold War modernism. Before the Cold War, critics and intellectuals and even the broader public understood the nature of the movement that was to be known as modernism to be "making it new," ceaseless experimentation, bohemian rejection of bourgeois conventions, or social and political radicalism. But these cultural-diplomatic efforts explained that these attributes were secondary, outward expressions of the *real* core meaning of modernism: the freedom of self-determined individuals to create and express themselves in any way they choose. Modernist art, emptied of its politics and radicalism through aesthetic autonomy and then *refilled* with vague liberal-humanist meaning, became the manifestation of the individualist freedoms of the West.

I would like to map Cold War modernism and its institutional components onto McGurl's modernism. "The Program Era" is McGurl's term for the period in American fiction roughly beginning with the end of the Second World War and whose dominance, at least in prestige literary fiction, continues today. Its reliance on modernist practices makes the "Program Era"—

a term meant to evoke Hugh Kenner's designation of the high-modernist period as the "Pound Era"—the inheritor of the modernist tradition. But the modernism that McGurl sees at the heart of Program Era literature is essentially Cold War modernism, institutionalized and tamed modernism, the liberal-humanist isotope of a volatile tradition.

For McGurl, Program Era fiction comes in three varieties: "lower-middle-class modernism," "technomodernism," and "high cultural pluralism." "Technomodernism," he explains, is most characterized by "systematic experimentation with narrative form" but is also concerned with "the scandalous continuity of literary *techne* (craft) with technology in the grosser sense—including, most importantly, media technology."[2] "Lower-middle-class modernism," which has become the emblematic iteration of Program Era fiction, "defines itself against the cultural forms actually consumed by the lower middle class against which it struggles to separate itself" but also against "the flagrantly intellectualist experimentalism of technomodernism" (67). Finally, "high cultural pluralism" expresses the point of view of a marginalized or disadvantaged population group in "self-consciously crafted and/or intellectual substantial products importantly distinct from mass culture or genre fiction" (57). High cultural pluralist pioneer Philip Roth "join[ed] the modernist literary sophistication of his higher educational training with the ethnic specificity of his upbringing—the late modernist version of writing what you know" (58), a path followed by later writers from Ha Jin to Sandra Cisneros to Junot Díaz to Maxine Hong-Kingston to Jamaica Kincaid to Jhumpa Lahiri to Dorothy Allison.

In one of his most perceptive observations, McGurl points out that although we commonly think of MFA fiction as overwhelmingly, even prescriptively or oppressively realist, realism and experimentalism are in a "classically dialectical struggle in which opposing sides begin, despite themselves, to interpenetrate" (33). Even lower-middle-class modernism, the most grittily realist of his three types of Program Era fiction, exhibits the self-reflexivity of the experimentalist strain in the sense that it is "rife with reflexive consideration of writing as an occupational and existential condition" (33).

Given his explanation of the three strains of Program Era fiction, McGurl's modernism boils down to two primary attributes. The first is a rejection of the popular marketplace, particularly the cultural artifacts typically consumed by members of the writer's social class (middlebrow products, for the bourgeois;

genre and popular entertainments, for the lower-middle-class or pluralist writers). The second is a self-reflexive concern with the act of writing—manifested in experiments with narration, which are "one of the earmarks of modernism" (50)—and the identity of being a writer. "The portrait of the artist," McGurl says, "is not only an important single book and an important genre, but also a name for one of the routine operations of literary modernism" (48). He calls this last trait "autopoetics."

McGurl's "autopoetics" is similar to aesthetic autonomy in that both suggest that artworks are fundamentally about artworks. Furthermore, both—like Program Era fiction itself—appear to have been sustained by, even in some cases generated by, the university. Indeed, notoriously hidebound Harvard helped pave the way for modernism in the academy. As D. G. Myers writes in *The Elephants Teach*, Harvard was the first university to teach "creative writing" and did so as early as the late nineteenth century. These early writing classes "sharply differentiated" the academic study of writing from philological research, at the time the only type of literary study in the university. Harvard's early adoption of such writing classes showed "that literature could be used in the university for some other purpose than scholarly research."[3] Advanced writing teachers at Harvard, particularly Barrett Wendell, pioneered what would later be called "creative writing."

This idea that literary writing was valuable as something more than raw material for philological investigation spread beyond Cambridge and influenced what would become New Criticism. Later in the century, the critics who then ensconced themselves in English departments (Yvor Winters, Cleanth Brooks, John Crowe Ransom, R. P. Blackmur, and others) approached literary works as autonomous aesthetic artifacts. For them, literature classes should promote the appreciation of literature, not philological or historical or biographical investigation (Myers 129). McGurl sees the same evolution. For him, "the pedagogy of New Criticism" meant "rescu[ing] literature from the exhumations of the philologists to elevate literature's status as a *living art*" (23).

This development helped modernist literature enter university curricula. "In the thirties," Myers writes, critics and writers friendly to modernism "took control of the institutions of American literary life, starting with the English departments of many universities" (138). Then, in the 1940s and 1950s, as McGurl points out, "the ways and means of interwar literary modernism" were "codified in the pedagogy of New Criticism and then disseminated to a range of student populations previously underrepresented in the writing profession" (50).

As Myers shows, some of the displaced faculty saw this as a "modernist grab for power," a takeover of literature departments by a group of aestheticists whose intent was "to break out of the purely literary domain and carry literature, *studied purely as literature*, into a social and cultural institution—the university." In doing so, they displaced a "middle generation" of leftist writer/teachers who endorsed and practiced a more socially engaged form of writing (138). Ironically, given the general Western understanding of modernism as radical, this "middle generation" objected to modernism precisely because—just as the Socialist Realist critics of the USSR did—they saw it as decadent aestheticism.

But McGurl and Myers both get this wrong by using the term "modernist" to characterize both works of literature *and* the New Critical pedagogical method. While New Critics and aestheticists may have been ensconcing themselves in English departments in the 1930s, for the most part they were not teaching Pound and Joyce. Alfred Barr is sometimes given credit for offering the first American college course focusing on modernist visual art (at Wellesley in 1927), and Harvard's Ted Spencer has been identified as the first professor to teach Joyce in a college class, but as late as the 1940s Norman Holmes Pearson feared that teaching modernist authors threatened his chances for tenure at Yale (Goldfarb Marquis; Mark Bernstein).

Nevertheless, the New Critical method of criticism and pedagogy in the pre–World War II period proved very adaptable to modernist works when they did start to appear on university syllabi, a development that owed much to the invention of the trade paperback. And this aestheticization of modernism was a crucial precursor of Cold War modernism, as it effaced the works' often-radical political or social content.

While McGurl's autopoetics has interesting parallels with the aestheticization that made Cold War modernism possible, it is even more closely related to the ultimate message of Cold War modernism: the centrality of the individual. All strains of Program Era fiction are grounded on, and most interested in, the exploration of the unique and autotelic consciousness of an individual. This pervasive concern with the individual consciousness mirrors the Cold War modernist valorization of the individual.

Cold War modernism had an ideal adversary in Socialist Realism, the style prescribed for Soviet writers after the 1930s. Socialist Realism asserted that it concerned itself primarily with objective, material facts and events in the world and held that the sociopolitical message of an artwork was the central measure of its value. We are all familiar with trite jokes about novels and paintings and plays depicting striving peasants and tractors and benevolent Stalins, and the earnest, tendentious pieties of Socialist Realism offered an appealing punching bag for Western critics of the 1950s and 1960s.

Communist critics, though, gave back as good as they got. In official English-language publications like *VOKS Bulletin*, cultural commissars attacked the very notions of "individual" and "freedom" and "innovation" as used in the West. Orthodox Marxism, of course, rejects the primacy of the individual and (in the words of the *Dictionary of Marxist Thought*) "postulates that individualistic theories and modes of thought, especially those couched in terms of abstract individuals . . . conceal the underlying social relations (above all relations of production) that in turn explain individual thought and action." Equating "personal freedom" with the "anarchic, rampant individualism in modern bourgeois decadent art" is ludicrous, because

> [i]t is just this individualism and this false pretence that the artist is independent of society that really make for the disintegration of the personality, for the death of the artist, and of art as a whole. It is the "freedom" of the man slipping down the chasm of ideological decay and political reaction.[4]

Whereas Cold War modernism held that the diversity of styles and techniques of modernism showed the fertility of a society foregrounded on individualism and freedom, Soviet critics saw only legerdemain. In a 1952 article, Soviet art critic V. M. Zimenko argued that the "individualism" in "formalist" (modernist) art was illusory: "[I]ndividual differences never go beyond superficial tricks in the handling of form. . . . [T]hey have drastically limited their creative possibilities by disregarding realities and distorting the foundations of art."[5]

An autonomous, aestheticized literary work, using sometimes-opaque forms of narration, whose ultimate concern was the consciousness of the individual creator: the attributes of modernism that McGurl sees as defining Program Era fiction are precisely the attributes of modernism that Socialist Realism rejects and thus the attributes that Cold War modernism embraces.

I would go further than this and point out that McGurl's "lower-middle-class modernism" and "high cultural pluralism" result from the extension and evolution of Cold War modernism. A society predicated on freedom and individualism, Cold War modernism implies, gives all of its individual members equal opportunity to self-expression. In these two strains, individuals belonging to groups marginalized by social class, gender, ethnicity, or language tradition successfully claim the voice and authority of prestige literature.

So if Program Era fiction and Cold War modernism both draw on quintessentially modernist autopoetics, what of McGurl's other primary indicator of modernism: a self-conscious rejection of popular or commercial cultural products? This is in fact a precursor of aesthetic autonomy. Although Kant, in *Critique of Judgment*, first develops the notion of aesthetic autonomy in the late eighteenth century, Terry Eagleton, Andreas Huyssen, Raymond Williams, and others have all argued that the "ideology of the aesthetic" became more common in the increasingly capitalist mid-1800s as writers grew resentful of being evaluated by the market. Early modernism made "no compromise with the public taste" (as the slogan of the *Little Review* put it) and defined itself against popular entertainment.

The market's pervasiveness only grew in the twentieth century, but in the West, institutions stepped in to support high culture as patrons. Among these institutions were museums, foundations, magazines, governmental agencies, and, with the great expansion of higher education in the United States after World War II, universities. Insular writers' colonies like Bread Loaf, Yaddo, and MacDowell "were attempts to subsidize and give sanction to the life of art," Myers suggests, "but at best they were temporary accommodations. After the Second World War the university stepped forward to become the permanent center of artistic activity in America" (148). "The university stepped forward in the postwar period," McGurl points out,

> both to facilitate and to buffer the writer's relation to the culture industry and market culture more broadly. . . . Once perceived as the stuffy enemy of modernist innovation in the arts . . . the university has . . . become perhaps the most important patron of artistically ambitious literary practice in the United States. (15, 21–22)

As the institutions supporting oppositional artists became more established and respectable, modernism became more comfortable with the establishment. From the belligerent *Little Review* to the Rockefellers' Museum of Modern Art (MoMA) to the State Department, modernist patrons became part of the bourgeois cultural establishment modernism had birthed itself by rejecting. Cold War modernism and Program Era fiction both arise from modernism's retreat into the embrace of the institutions it once reviled.

The publishing industry also contributed. Small-press and coterie publishers from Hours Press to Black Sun to Shakespeare and Company shielded early modernist writers from the unforgiving market through unearned advances, loans, and costly fine editions that never recouped their printing expenses. In the 1920s and 1930s, that relationship spread beyond the insular world of the literary underground when a few for-profit publishers protected modernist authors from the market. At Scribner's, for instance, the profits generated by mystery writer S. S. Van Dine allowed Maxwell Perkins to provide F. Scott Fitzgerald with endless advances on royalties that he would never earn, and Anita Loos's *Gentlemen Prefer Blondes* permitted Horace Liveright to underwrite modernist authors like T. S. Eliot and Ezra Pound. James Laughlin, at New Directions, operated much the same way, his personal wealth providing a cushion for his small publishing house. And in the 1950s, Laughlin, Alfred A. Knopf, and several other major trade publishers involved themselves in Cold War modernist undertakings like published anthologies of American literature by the US Information Agency (USIA), a Ford Foundation–funded modernist cultural magazine, and sweetheart subsidiary-rights deals for publication of American authors abroad.

Publishing was even more important in helping Program Era fiction keep a denatured modernism alive and bring it to middlebrow readers. Laughlin's New Directions and Barney Rosset's Grove Press—both occupying a space between large trade literary publishers and underground presses—published their share of MFA students and teachers, but many of the key works and writers of the Program Era appeared from major publishers: Raymond Carver's *Will You Please Be Quiet, Please?* (McGraw-Hill, 1976), Flannery O'Connor's *Wise Blood* (Harcourt Brace, 1952), John Gardner's *Grendel* (Knopf, 1971), John Barth's *Giles Goat-Boy* (Doubleday, 1966), and Bobbie Ann Mason's *Shiloh* (Harper and Row, 1982). But the symbiotic and parasitic, or perhaps just codependent, relationship between MFA programs and the American trade publishing industry reached its apotheosis in the 1980s, when Knopf editor and creative writing teacher Gordon Lish became famous for his championing—

and, it came out later, very intrusive editing—of MFA titan Raymond Carver, and another Knopf editor, Gary Fisketjon, created the Vintage Contemporaries series. One of the first Vintage Contemporaries, *Bright Lights, Big City* by Fisketjon's college friend (and Carver's student) Jay McInerney, was a brilliant modernist experiment (the first major novel in second-person narration) that sold three hundred thousand copies. By the end of the 1980s publication as a paperback original Vintage Contemporary had become the mythic reward that MFAs sought.

So Cold War modernism and the modernism that McGurl sees at the roots of Program Era fiction are close siblings—twins, even. But in his nebulous use of the term "modernism," McGurl occludes another of modernism's central attributes, one that did survive as a kind of countertradition to the MFA program and Cold War modernism as well. Modernism arose out of an implacable hostility to bourgeois institutions: churches, school systems, governments, the market, middle-class morality. This hostility manifested itself often in antinomianism and nihilism; Irving Howe claimed that modernism is "a revolt against [the] prevalent style, an unyielding rage against the official order."[6] However, at other times modernist experimentation and rebellion against middle-class society took the form of the totalizing ideology, the movement, the program. The panoply of early modernist "isms"—cubism, futurism, Dada(ism), surrealism, absurdism, imagism, vorticism—demonstrates how prone modernist artists, in their rejection of bourgeois institutions, were to propose an all-consuming response. "If only we all followed this set of rules and rejected traditional ways of seeing and doing things, we can remake the world and how we see it," modernism too often proposes. For this reason, fascism and Nazism and communism are often seen as deeply modernist. Cold War modernism purposely stripped modernist art of this attribute, and McGurl's Program Era modernism certainly lacks any totalizing ideology, except perhaps aestheticism.

A modernist tradition that retained its original utopianism did survive to the 1950s in a few small redoubts and outposts. Notable among these is Black Mountain College in North Carolina, examined much more fully elsewhere in this anthology. Many of the early faculty members did develop modernist aesthetics, and the school presented art as a complete way of life, an approach to everything. Charles Olson, the poet-scholar who headed Black Mountain in its last years, carried the spirit of high modernism forth into the 1950s.

His famed "Projective Verse" essay revives some of the dicta of Ezra Pound's early works of poetic theory. In "A Retrospect," Pound insisted that lines be composed on the principle "of the musical phrase, not in sequence of a metronome," and Olson echoes this in his belief that lines should be composed on the principle of breath.[7]

Olson was also susceptible to the totalizing impulse of modernism. Vincent Katz describes his Black Mountain years as an attempt "to encompass everything in a mind-boggling attempt at universality . . . a grand cultural theory, incorporating anthropology, archeology, psychology, Heisenberg's uncertainty principle, theatre, performance, the act of the word in the moment of literary creation."[8] He was a friend and admirer of Ezra Pound and sought to keep alive the modernist project of renewing the world through art.

Ironically, though, Olson had also been involved in the effort to adapt modernist artistic techniques as a defense of the liberal state. In World War II, he worked in the Office of War Information with other modernists (and Black Mountain faculty) such as Ben Shahn. Neither option—the destructive totalizing of high modernism as it confronted its dead ends or the glib mainstreaming of Cold War modernism—suited him. The modernist project of making it new through experimental and at times revolutionary art, as opposed to Cold War modernism's humanist stylizations, continued with Black Mountain writing teachers like Robert Duncan, Denise Levertov, and Robert Creeley—who, like the early modernists, published with oppositional small presses like City Lights and the Jargon Society and the school's own journal, the *Black Mountain Review*.

So I would agree with McGurl that modernism survived in MFA programs and that MFA programs contributed to modernism's endurance. But MFA modernism is a denatured modernism, altered both due to the needs and imperatives of the programs themselves and in response to the larger transformations of modernism occurring because of the Cold War and the liberal cultural consensus behind it. "Modernism declines into the Program Era due to the conduit of craft—but is this 'fall' into institutionality really so unfortunate?" McGurl asks rhetorically in the caption to the last of his curious diagrams (409). But I think McGurl has this backward. The preoccupation with craft wasn't what drained the energy and innovation and rebellion from modernism and made modernism suitable for our universities and MFA programs. Instead, it was Cold War modernism—the deployment of modernist art on behalf of political and cultural institutions and the accompanying redefinition of modernism as pure technique—that resulted in the Program Era's overwhelming concern with craft.

NOTES

1. Kelly Ritter, *Before Shaughnessy: Basic Writing at Harvard and Yale, 1920–1960* (Carbondale: Southern Illinois UP, 2009), 102. English A-1 was the standard first-year writing course; English A-2 was "a more advanced course in writing," and English A-3 was the advanced composition course.

2. Mark McGurl, *The Program Era: Postwar Fiction and the Rise of Creative Writing* (Cambridge: Harvard UP, 2009), 42.

3. D. G. Myers, *The Elephants Teach: Creative Writing since 1880*, rev. ed. (Chicago: U of Chicago P, 2006), 40–46.

4. "Against Formalism in Soviet Music," *VOKS Bulletin* 54 (1948): 11.

5. V. M. Zimenko, "Socialist Realism and the Artist's Individuality," *VOKS Bulletin* 74 (1952): 42.

6. Irving Howe, "The Idea of the Modern," *Selected Writings 1950–1990*, ed. Irving Howe (New York: Harcourt Brace Jovanovich, 1990), 140–41.

7. Ezra Pound, "A Retrospect," *Literary Essays of Ezra Pound*, ed. T. S. Eliot (New York: New Directions, 1968), 3.

8. Vincent Katz, *Black Mountain College: Experiment in Art* (Cambridge: MIT Press, 2002), n.p.

CHAPTER 5

Flannery O'Connor, the Cold War, and the Canon

ERIC BENNETT

The economic logic of Europe and the United States passed a tipping point by the mid-nineteenth century, give or take twenty years, depending on the nation. The old habit of measuring affluence in land and bullion had given way to the new premium on speculation and earnings to come. Adam Smith's theories, which excoriated royally sanctioned monopolies, had won the day by Waterloo, and in the ensuing era, with no small help from David Ricardo, factories, governments, and entrepreneurs, the future rather than the past was where the money was.

The transition from a retrospective and landed paradigm for prosperity to a prospective and speculative one—from gold to stocks—stretched across the decades before and after the height of the Industrial Revolution. But habits of thought and the language that conveys them often catch up, in sudden lexical efflorescence, with what people who are set in their ways fail to theorize—and so it was 150 years ago. "In the 1860s a new word entered the economic and political vocabulary of the world," Eric Hobsbawm writes: "capitalism."[1] And for a century following that emergence of capitalistic self-consciousness, the arts, with increasing velocity, changed too, from instantiations of value retrospectively constituted to instantiations prospectively acclaimed. Much of modernist art and literature reflect at the aesthetic level the liquidation of economic realities and, by the twentieth century, patronage, with all else, got prospective.

Yet circa 1900, old notions of literary longevity still haunted American writers, including devout republican ones who sympathized with socialists and did a steady business in belles lettres. "What Longfellow's place in literature will be, I shall not offer to say," William Dean Howells wrote eulogistically, "that is Time's affair, not mine."[2] Meaning a poet, even in an industrialized United States, still would have to stand the test of time. Howells, who died in 1920, nevertheless was well aware of the dawning of a new order. In 1915, Van Wyck Brooks blamed canon hygiene—in which death was a prerequisite to greatness—on "a peculiar twist in the academic mind" and mocked those who believed that the quality in literature that "makes it literature only comes out, like the quality in wines, with age."[3] It was Brooks's vision of a contemporary canon that was ultimately to win the day.

The widespread admission of contemporary American literature into a canon of revered works was to take another thirty years and is a story that implicates commerce, journalism, academia, and the balance of international power. About these dimensions I have more to say in the body of this chapter. But my central thesis is that after 1945 the emerging MFA programs in the United States ensured the final liquidation of the long-standing habits of cultural capital that the United States inherited, sans aristocracy, from Europe; that MFA programs did so by bringing to fruition trends that had been growing since World War I but that flourished after World War II; that those overseeing this liquidation honored or, better yet, half-honored the principles of a retrospective canon, using the recent and distant past as collateral for future loans of prestige; and that Flannery O'Connor, more powerfully than any other single author, embodied in her narrow career multiple dimensions of the change. In the years of her adult life—from the mid-1940s to the mid-1960s—one can behold a moment of teetering between traditional and speculative prestige, a moment as revolutionary in the history of literature as the 1860s are in Hobsbawm's narrative of capital. O'Connor entered a canon elite and nostalgic in ethos and did so via an institution so antielite that it almost seems Soviet—a creative writing program at a state university in the Midwest expanding with help from federal funding. She gave that program a luster of excellence that has outlasted, in collective estimation, the cultural necessity of a canon. More than any other workshop writer, she performed the double duty of making fiction appear eternal and stately and showing that it can be manufactured at the university, sold, and fast succeeded by a new product line.

By the end of her life, O'Connor assumed the stature of an author who had stood the test of time—without much time having gone by. She appeared in numerous textbooks and anthologies on which so many Americans were to base their lifelong sense of what literature was.

TABLE 1. A living O'Connor enters the anthologies

Year	Anthology	Editors	O'Connor work included
1952	*New World Writing*	Arabel J. Porter	"Enoch and the Gorilla"
1953	*The Avon Book of Modern Writing*	William Phillips & Philip Rahv	"A Good Man Is Hard to Find"
1955	*New World Writing 8*	Arabel J. Porter	"You Can't Be Any Poorer Than Dead"
1959	*Acts of Violence*	William Kozlenko	"A Good Man Is Hard to Find"
	An Introduction to Literature in Four Parts	Herbert Barrows, Hubert Heffner, John Ciardi, & Wallace Douglas	"The Displaced Person"
	Understanding Fiction, 2nd ed. (1st ed., 1943; student text for O'Connor)	Cleanth Brooks & Robert Penn Warren	"A Good Man Is Hard to Find"
1960	*The House of Fiction: An Anthology of the Short Story with Commentary*, 2nd ed. (1st ed., 1950)	Caroline Gordon & Allen Tate	"A Good Man Is Hard to Find"
1961	*New World Writing 19*	Stewart Richardson & Corlies M. Smith	"Everything That Rises Must Converge"
1962	*The Forms of Fiction*	John Gardner & Lennis Dunlap	"A Good Man Is Hard to Find"
	Reading Modern Fiction, 3rd ed. (1st ed., 1952; 2nd ed., 1957)	Winifred Lynskey	"A Good Man Is Hard to Find"
1963	*Eight Great American Short Novels*	Philip Rahv	*Wise Blood*
	The Expanded Moment: A Short Story Anthology	Robert Gordon	"The Artificial Nigger"
	Modern Short Stories	M. X. Lesser & John N. Morris	"The Artificial Nigger"

In 1952, O'Connor was twenty-seven years old; in 1963, the year before her death, only thirty-eight. Particularly notable is her inclusion in a second edition of Brooks and Warren's *Understanding Fiction*, as the first edition served as her textbook at Iowa. She was also included in the second edition of Tate and Gordon's *The House of Fiction*, having received the essence of the earlier version, published in 1950, through her correspondence with Gordon.

Perhaps no Iowa alumna is claimed more enthusiastically by her alma mater, and many beyond Iowa City recognize her importance to the history of creative writing programs. For McGurl, O'Connor rivals Paul Engle as the key figure at Iowa. In *The Program Era*, she symbolizes a kind of disciplinary masochism that McGurl places at the heart of the MFA experience. In my argument, too, O'Connor opens a window on an institution. In this case, the context is the Cold War, and at stake is the endgame of aristocratic practices of evaluation.

In 1945, as Mary Flannery O'Connor was settling in in Iowa City, influential American writers, critics, scholars, and philanthropists were embracing with unprecedented urgency the belief that new American art and literature were as good as old European works. The campaign reflected developments far beyond English departments and stemmed from shifts in the world order. The nations of Western Europe had just committed infrastructural suicide. Cities from London to Belgrade were crippled or obliterated, and with basically one industrialized nation left standing, world currencies were newly pegged against the US dollar. Political influence, technological capacity, and even human capital now centered on North America, and cultural consequences rivaled material and economic ones. Displaced professors from Europe found homes on American faculties, and they joined their new colleagues for a postmortem on the cataclysm.

The vacuum of power in Western Europe inspired policy decisions in Washington and Moscow that produced a polarized globe and heightened the mood of seriousness on American campuses and beyond. Europe was to be propped up and Russia resisted, and the propping and resistance took fantastic forms. The wartime Office of Strategic Services (OSS), staffed not inconsiderably by men with literature degrees from the Ivy League, dissolved to be replaced by the Central Intelligence Agency (CIA) with its campaigns of cultural subterfuge beginning in 1950. Alfred Kazin and F. O. Matthiessen lectured on American literature amid a smoldering Austria. Henry Luce's magazines, the boards of the Whitney and Museum of Modern Art (MoMA), and essays in the *Partisan Review* appointed Jackson Pollock to succeed Pablo Picasso. Malcolm Cowley and Robert Penn Warren boosted Hemingway to the world stage and caught America up with France's high esteem for Faulkner; both Hemingway and Faulkner, and also T. S. Eliot, won Nobel Prizes. Paul Engle initiated a three-decade crusade to import foreign poets and fiction writers to Iowa City to tempt them from communism. Private individuals cooperated with philanthropic foundations, such as the Rockefeller and Ford Foundations, and with the federal government through the State Department and its US Information Agency (USIA).

If the Soviets were the object of animosity, then non-Russian Europeans were the object of flirtation, courtship, and resentment. Cold warriors aimed not only to demonstrate American superiority to Moscow and St. Petersburg but also to earn the respect of London, Paris, Rome, and Berlin. This meant fitting American narratives of modernity and modernism into the longer European story of post-Renaissance humanism. It meant affirming from abroad precisely those traditions that Americans, even in the act of affirmation, wished to rival and supplant. It meant talking liberal capitalistic democracy out of one side of the mouth and high culture out the other. It meant insisting on an American canon as formidable as the European one. It's worth stating explicitly what a confused project this was.

In fact confusion—interrogation, questioning, open-ended soul searching—is what Mark Greif's recent study, *The Age of the Crisis of Man*, identifies as a central feature of the period. A question asked again and again, Greif shows, was, What is the nature of Man?[4] The unprecedented scientific and social scientific powers of modernity suggested to many observers that recent changes resisted comprehension and might spell the doom of the species. Those who interrogated the nature of Man, in Greif's telling, didn't seek answers so much as desire to sustain an exercise whose continuance was regarded as existentially prophylactic. It was the asking that mattered. Greif's study captures the (by current standards) almost unimaginable ponderousness with which Cold War critics argued for the importance of literature. Modern fiction, better suited to pose big questions than to solve big problems, might save us all. There had been too much already of solving big problems in the abstract in Hitler's Germany, Stalin's Russia, and the Manhattan Project.

Central to the salubrious maieutic were two possibilities existing in tension, which those involved believed needed to be explored at length. One was that "Man" really was unchanging in his nature, meaning that social science and dreams of planning and reform had merely obscured and heightened age-old problems of evil. The other was that modern conditions had wrought changes to social reality so deep and so terrible that persevering human nature appeared nevertheless under threat. Totalitarianism was a new thing—or not?

To Greif's thesis one could add that this collective questioning, prolix going on tediously unreadable, was a boon for Americans who wanted both to join the European cultural party and to supersede it. To facilitate the transatlantic shift in influence, the verities of the Renaissance and the Enlightenment had to remain living but not *too* living, timeless yet in need of modification from the outside. For, if Europe in 1945 differed little from Europe in 1914 or 1815, then American writers and artists would remain, even after Potsdam, only at the periphery. But if, instead, modernity threatened to alter the essential nature of "Man," then the United States had important contributions to make to the conversation.

Clement Greenberg, writing about the visual artists, suggested simultaneously a continuity of human spirit and the radical unfamiliarity of new conditions. "The School of Paris rested on a sufficient acceptance of the world as it must be," he wrote, "and it delighted in the world's very disenchantment, seeing it as evidence of man's triumph over it. We [meaning Americans] confronted more immediately by the paraphernalia of industrialism, see the situation as too overwhelming to come to terms with, and look for an escape in transcendent exceptions and aberrated states."[5] Witness the terms in tension: the transcendence of European apprehensions; the aberration of the new—which Americans could speak to with at least as much authority as Picasso and friends. For Greenberg, Jackson Pollock and David Smith offered innovative responses to unprecedented problems, yet responses that fit into that older tradition of the "world as it must be."

O'Connor's fiction, as countless critics have argued, rendered images of modernity that also pitted aberration against transcendence—monstrous novelty against the world as it must be—with transcendence, specifically Christian salvation, bloodily winning the day. Greif argues that O'Connor played a subversive role in the discourse of the Crisis of Man as that discourse was winding down. Her fiction exposed the limitations of the maieutic. I would add that O'Connor replicated deeply established patterns of European thought, earning a place at the Cold War table, yet appeared unmistakably American, therefore new, therefore newly necessary, despite all the seeming eternity redounding from her pages. For, again, on what authority can the new displace the old? As long as the putative excellence of culture derives power from the longevity of culture, it's an uphill battle for such an outlier, so young and so weird, as the United States. But the bombs that razed cathedrals and the camps that exterminated populations put the whole notion of European culture under such duress that a culturally ambidextrous United States had an in. O'Connor, writing with one hand episodes that felt ancient and with the other hand bracing modernist sentences, did such double work.

American intellectuals would have had trouble storming the world stage after 1945 starting on V-J Day from scratch. But the postwar moment brought to fruition trends, attitudes, aspirations, and methodologies that had lived on the margins in earlier decades. Before the war the groundwork for the changing balance—from Europe to America and from past to present and future—appeared, in the United States, in at least three spheres: commerce, journalism, and academia. Understanding O'Connor's role in the 1950s involves appraising this background.

The story of commerce and the canon is famously thorny. Avant-garde writers, in France but also, in lesser form, in the United States, had long tended to position themselves in opposition to the bourgeois marketplace. They could do so all they wanted, but this positioning often belied commercial acumen. Even before the iconoclastic 1920s, American publishers were betting on the new and making a tradition of the antitraditional. "No, no!" cries Fulkerson, the literary publisher from William Dean Howells's *A Hazard of New Fortunes* (1890), selling his collaborators on unconventional means of promotion. "You don't catch on to the business end of this thing, my friends. You're proceeding on something like the old exploded idea that the demand creates the supply, when everybody knows, if he's watched the course of modern events, that it's just as apt to be the other way."[6] By the turn of the century, as Loren Glass has shown, the commercialization of literary prestige and its prospective logic were common enough to get satirized. Glass points to *Bookman*'s facetious 1901 "Interview with Nobody," which imagines an author who has sold half a million copies of a book not yet published. Nothing exists to stand the test of time. "But in this new corporate calculus," Glass writes, "the value of the text is judged purely by the context of its corporate promotion, which precedes actual publication and operates independently of anyone ever actually reading the book."[7] Over the next four decades, savvy publishers, clever advertisers, critics valorizing novelty, and Americans hungering for a viable avant-garde gave rise to a type of literary celebrity distant in its relationship to the poems, novels, or stories on which it was based. An American in 1941, as John Raeburn has shown, could know Hemingway backward and forward without having read a word.[8]

The premier example of American businessmen banking on Parnassus were the *Ulysses* censorship trials in the early 1930s, which are worth reviewing briefly. After the European publication of *Ulysses* in 1922, Random House wanted to add the title to its Modern Library, alongside ancient texts and other works of European modernism. But the putatively obscene excerpts of *Ulysses* published in the *Little Review* in 1918 had gotten that journal into serious trouble. To avoid similar consequences, Random House staged a legal battle by loudly importing a copy. The US Tariff Act prohibited the importation of obscene books but made an exception for classics, and Random House argued that *Ulysses* was one. Congress had intended "classics" to mean racy stuff by dead authors. But in multiple trials the attorney for the defense convinced judges that *Ulysses*, despite its author's still-pulsing blood, was for the ages. To get around the courtroom ban on expert testimony, Random House pasted testimony in the hard copy of the book itself—what we would call blurbs. The courts ruled in favor of the modern classic as a meaningful concept. In the early 1930s, this move was not new to publishing (as Glass's *Bookman* spoof makes clear) but was new to the law.

Within a generation, curricula at colleges and universities had followed the courts. Barney Rosset's remarkable career at Grove Press, which thrived on the revolution in paperback technology after World War II, marked the convergence of avant-garde literature, commercial viability, and college syllabi. Outsider texts of the 1950s became campus mainstays by the 1960s, a story captured in Glass's *Counterculture Colophon: Grove Press, the "Evergreen Review," and the Incorporation of the Avant-Garde.* Without question, business interests helped open the academy to contemporary literature, and the Iowa Writers' Workshop was yet another bellwether for the tacit commercialization of the classroom. In 1953, Paul Engle made a scouting arrangement with Doubleday to receive commissions on work the company, on his recommendation, accepted for publication. In 1955, he established another arrangement with a television production company looking for screenplays. During her tenure at Iowa, O'Connor received $750 from Rinehart & Company. "This is the only example in the United States of a commercial publishing house offering such prize money to a single university class," Paul Engle boasted in 1947 to newspaper readers in Des Moines, proud of his student and untroubled by the partnership.[9]

If market forces, bolstered by new laws, eased contemporary literature into college classrooms, so too did the journalism of those who despised market forces. Left-wing writers attained new public prominence in the 1930s, and they tended to believe that poetry and fiction had to catch up with the economically abysmal times. Malcolm Cowley at the *New Republic* put out the call for living relevance and tried to redirect modernist literature away from its internal preoccupations to external ones that might figure in the life of the nation. "Artists used to think that the world outside had become colorless and dull in comparison with the bright inner world they tenderly nourished; now it is the inner world that has been enfeebled as a result of its isolation; it is the outer world that is strong and colorful and demands to be imaginatively portrayed. The subjects are waiting everywhere."[10] Cowley was proud that *Scrutiny* had praised the *New Republic* for its emphasis on contemporary literature and bragged that his magazine was "not handicapped by the belief general in England that no useful service can be served by trying to assess the importance of contemporary literary figures" (158). After the war, Cowley-the-pro-Soviet-journalist became Cowley-the-pro-American-college-professor. He brought to Stanford his belief that new literature had a vitality that old literature didn't.

As a Rhodes Scholar in the 1930s, Paul Engle mingled at Oxford with W. H. Auden, Cecil Day-Lewis, and Stephen Spender and adopted their Marxist views. When he returned to the United States, he preached this gospel on the lecture circuit. Left-wing poetry, Engle enthused, reported on the world around it. "These poets talked about things which verse up until then had avoided: airplanes, the radio, politics, and economics."[11] Engle welcomed into poetry "machinery, psychology, and sociology."[12] Universal conscription gave a poet reason to be interested in "an armament bill in Washington or Westminster and in the foreign policy of his own and all other nations" and also in the industrial economy ("Poetry" 436). By the early 1940s, Engle had dropped his communism, but until his death in 1991 he never lost interest in the contemporary.

Van Wyck Brooks, so irritated by glacial professorial standards in 1915, belonged to the Left, as did C. F. Calverton and Granville Hicks, Marxist critics and authors of surveys of American literature who would join the postwar veneration of the contemporary. In *Creating American Civilization*, David Shumway chronicles the emergence of American literature as an academic discipline and captures these left-wing contributions. But he also makes clear that the rise of an institutionalized national literature transcended the left-right split. "If the United States has not developed a Shakespeare or a Milton," Howard Mumford Jones told the Modern Language Association (MLA) in 1935, speaking from the political center, "Great Britain has not developed a Whitman or a Mark Twain."[13] Positing such an equivalency at the MLA would have been inconceivable before World War I. In the address, Jones extolled Henry James, alive within living memory, and from there it was a short step to canonizing the living.

Again, the conservatives were also on board. Shumway gives pride of place in his history to Norman Foerster, the torchbearer of the conservative new humanism of Irving Babbitt and Paul Elmer More. Foerster rejected the positivistic methodology of the interwar English departments—their preoccupation with sources and biographies—and centered the study of American literature instead on ideal thematic categories. Not until "Puritan traditions," "the Frontier spirit," "Romanticism," and "realism" replaced objective historical periodization did the field cease to seem like dry local history and acquire a kind of mythological intensity out of time. Such idealism, so much more than a record of facts, would greatly serve the cultural Cold War and its devotion to American studies.

Foerster mattered as much to the discipline of creative writing as to the story Shumway tells. In the early 1930s the new humanist scion instituted the reforms at the University of Iowa that led to the creation of the creative writing program there. Foerster was troubled by the migration of American literature from the academy to the newsroom and, like Babbitt, by the increasingly scientific spirit of the humanities. The new humanism posited Man as the starting point for all knowledge, extolled the freedom of the will, emphasized personal responsibility, and eschewed the deterministic overtones of American naturalism. Drawing writers back into the lecture halls would improve literature and faculty alike. At Iowa, Foerster mentored Engle, and a dozen years later, Engle mentored O'Connor.

The new humanism, if only through a nostalgia for a world order its proponents had never experienced, was antimodern and even antiliberal. The liberalism it opposed was the liberalism of left-wing reform, in which dreams of economic equality undermined the sanctity of private property, in which the admission of deterministic forces distracted people from pressing concerns of individual responsibility, and in which easy humanitarianism edged out aristocratic compassion and the putatively salutary energy of cultural differences that came with caste. Babbitt, in the spirit of Burke, believed that the individual should "respect the general sense, the accumulated experience of the past that has become embodied in the habits and usages that the superficial rationalist would dismiss as prejudice."[14] Babbitt, More, and Foerster did not create the postwar vogue in such orientations—Lionel Trilling and the editors of *Life*, who shared them, mostly got them elsewhere—but the new humanists did indeed add to the manifold textures of conservatism after World War II and nurtured the brand of conservatism prevailing at Iowa and Stanford.[15] O'Connor's private library indicates that she read Babbitt and Foerster at Iowa under Engle, and her lampooning of foolish intellectuals would have delighted Babbitt.

O'Connor, like the new humanists, believed that the wrong kind of cerebration is more likely to make somebody idiotic than wise. Her texts radiate an abiding respect for doing things as they are done—and not as they should be done according to abstract notions of justice. Scholars have commented at length on the recurrent figure of the benighted intellectual in her fiction: the daughter home from college, the son aspiring to write important things, the failed philosopher, and the violently well-intended atheist. Where O'Connor declines to dramatize her opprobrium against these types, she states it in letters and essays, and these statements were very much of her age. In the 1950s, visions of reform—including, in O'Connor's case, the civil rights movement—inspired, in those who held these attitudes, skepticism and often hostility. Outside meddling, in O'Connor's view, was at best rude and at worst catastrophic.

Of course the wellspring of O'Connor's conservatism was her faith in the Roman Catholic Church. Thomas Aquinas and his modern popularizers provided O'Connor with strangely fertile grounds for her instincts as a caricaturist. Jacques Maritain, an especial influence, revealed in a high theoretical register the potential for modernist art and writing in the Catholic spirit. Maritain believed that the anti-illusionary and antinaturalistic techniques of painters like Gauguin and Cézanne captured more of ultimate reality than slavish nineteenth-century academicism did. "Gauguin, in affirming that it was necessary to renounce *making what one sees*, formulated a primary truth which the masters have practiced from the very beginning."[16] Straying from the literalness of the eye allowed one to paint the beyond, as painters had done in the medieval period. In order for the artist to make "radiances shine in his work, and therefore to be truly docile and faithful to the invisible spirit that plays in things," Maritain argued, "he can, and he even must, distort in some measure, reconstruct, transfigure the material appearances of nature" (60). O'Connor said the same thing in simpler language. She embraced the grotesque because its distortions upset the smugness of a mind sold on materialistic accounts of reality. A devout writer was always "looking for one image that will connect or combine or embody two points; one is a point in the concrete, and the other is a point not visible to the naked eye, but believed in by him firmly, just as real to him, really, as the one that everybody sees."[17] Too much fidelity to the naked eye—for O'Connor and Maritain both—and an artist produced an immanently godless surface. Transcendence and aberration—the bounty that America had to offer Europe—permeated O'Connor's oeuvre.

O'Connor met the challenge of seeming both ancient and new. That she was self-conscious about trying to do so is clear. It delighted her when George Clay said "that the best of my work sounded like the Old Testament would sound if it were being written today."[18] The religious energy of her stories was a millennial throwback, but there was nothing antique about her technique. Like Maritain's vision of successful modernist painters, she employed radical methods for traditional effects. She wrote sentences unimaginable before the crystalline distillations of late nineteenth-century innovations in literary style. She was unself-consciously of the school of Pound and Hulme, absorbing by cultural osmosis the unostentatious strains of post-Hemingway prose style, so in accord with her anti-intellectualism.

The sun was behind
the wood, very red,
looking over the paling of trees
like a farmer inspecting his own hogs.[19]

That's a typical sentence from an O'Connor story. The free-verse lineation allows one to set it beside "Autumn" by Hulme, a constitutional poem of the imagist ferment:

> I walked abroad,
> And saw the ruddy moon lean over a hedge
> Like a red-faced farmer.[20]

In Hulme's poem a lyrical speaker projects onto disenchanted nature a fullness of sensation that characterizes the speaker more than it describes the world. The poem holds charm because one both sees, and fails to believe in, the moon like a farmer. O'Connor built stories in like language but vested such repletion in a reality beyond the observer. She believed in God and labored to trace his numinous aura. You sympathized with creation, not the foolish protagonist.

The Program Era attends to O'Connor's Catholicism, but for McGurl what matters is how the faith prepares O'Connor for the masochistic psychodynamics of Paul Engle's workshops. McGurl conjures a woman who cherished the smarts and lashes of draconian authority and taught others how to. "Discipline meant obedience to rules, and rules were established and maintained by institutions; and to submit to the authority of these institutions, while painful, was also a source of great potential pleasure, aesthetic and otherwise."[21] Institutional authority originates in church and king in Western Europe, but "as it unfolds in her work the aesthetics of institutionalization becomes applicable to various secular entities including the school, the family, the community, and the state" (135). McGurl's O'Connor, the displaced Catholic, was "not only one of the first major figures of what I am calling the Program Era, when American writers in large numbers made their first awkward professional embrace of institutions like the Iowa Writers' Workshop, but also one of the prime rhetoricians of the transformation of literary modernism into a discourse of institutional being" (136).

No doubt secular research universities have inherited the epistemological hegemony once held by Rome. I'm less convinced, though, that O'Connor played the role in the history of the discipline in which *The Program Era* casts her. O'Connor never couched her religious faith in terms of pleasure, and I have trouble making up the difference by psychoanalyzing the mind that appears in the letters and published writings. O'Connor made a point of insisting on the objective reality of the sacraments regardless of what a person felt in the face of them. She discounted emotions as the least trustworthy part of going to Mass. Nor did she seem keen on being a conventionally obedient Catholic. Her commitment to dogma and to the observation of the sacraments in fact emboldened her (with help from a strong ego) to take or leave the all-too-human humanity of priests and nuns. McGurl suggests that O'Connor effectively established "what we might, after one of her own phrases, call the habit of institutional being" (156). But inserting "institutional" in "the habit of being," a cherished phrase of O'Connor's, does violence against her well-documented theory of art making, which reflected the needs of the story to be excellent rather than the will of an established order to be heeded.

Drawing on Aquinas's notion of semiautonomous goods, O'Connor believed that the *thing made*—for her, the short story—was the source of the discipline. The discipline that McGurl invokes—doing what other people tell you to do because there's pleasure in obedience—is no doubt a real phenomenon, not least of all in writing workshops. But O'Connor left no trace of feeling pleasures like that. To the contrary. She irked gads of Catholics in her lifetime and took obvious delight in doing so. And she appears to have been quietly humoring Paul Engle and the other boys and men of Iowa City as they told her what to do. If anything, she was a circumspect sadist waiting to graduate and keep to herself.

Regardless of these differences of interpretation, O'Connor's Catholicism surely contributes to her importance to the history of Iowa in the 1950s. And O'Connor suited her moment in many other ways. It was helpful that she dropped "Mary" for the androgynous "Flannery," letting the Crisis of Man continue to be the Crisis of Man. It was helpful that she wrote religious stories in an era collectively dedicated to contrasting godless communism with a United States "under God" and willing, for once, to brook antidemocratic caste for the sake of artistic excellence. It was helpful (as McGurl points out) that her stories followed the aesthetic preferences of the New Critics, so influential on campuses at the time. It was helpful that she radiated decorum and propriety in an era of containment, when bohemianism and romantic artistry called to mind the left-wing ferment of the 1930s. It was helpful that her circumspection, her sarcasm, her scoffing attitude toward her modest celebrity, her feigned inability to perform literary criticism on her own work, and even her poor physical health made her seem, in a way, already interred. Her stories did not hang off her body as, say, Norman Mailer's fiction hung off his. She strikes one as roughly as ageless in her adolescence as in her adulthood and literary afterlife.

People in the moment saw that O'Connor suited the moment. They sponsored her, supported her, and put forth her image in the service of the cultural Cold War. In the early 1950s, the Humanities Division of the Rockefeller Foundation underwrote a schedule of grants in support of fringe movements in the humanities at campuses and journals across the continent, hoping at once to diminish the scientific atmosphere of literature departments, raise the national level of cultural literacy, and start a world conversation. Attuned both to the local developments of American letters and to the campaigns of soft diplomacy overseas, the Rockefeller Foundation represents a concrete link between O'Connor and the broader themes of this chapter.

In 1952, the *Kenyon Review* announced a three-year fellowship program. Each year, new fellows in fiction, poetry, and criticism were to receive enough money to live on modestly. The foundation provided the funds, and John Crowe Ransom, the editor at *Kenyon*, awarded O'Connor the first one in fiction. "The Life You Save May Be Your Own" appeared in the spring 1953 issue, and Ransom asked the Rockefeller Foundation to renew O'Connor's funding that fall. She was the only writer to win the fellowship two years running. In those years, O'Connor was producing some of the best fiction of her career and writing faster than she would later on. When the foundation asked O'Connor about the effect the fellowships had had on her career, she answered that "with the financial assistance of the fellowship I felt free to write stories instead of a novel."[22] If true, this reflects an instance of the foundation's direct influence on American literary history.

O'Connor was also useful to the Iowa Writers' Workshop (itself a beneficiary of Rockefeller Foundation money). "The Life You Save May Be Your Own," first published in the *Kenyon Review*, was reprinted in the O. Henry Prize Collection in 1954, an annual anthology of the best American short fiction. The series had existed since 1919 but ceased in 1951. Paul Engle helped revive it in 1954, and suddenly many of the annual honorees had Iowa affiliations. In fund-raising campaigns, Engle pointed to such acclaim as proof of Iowa's excellence. O'Connor became a standard and a mascot.

Neither the O. Henry collection nor the *Kenyon Review* nor the Rockefeller Foundation deserve all the credit for the recognition that O'Connor's work received. But O'Connor's career, from very early, unfolded within the network of cultural sponsors for whom establishing an empire of letters for the Pax Americana was a top priority.

Was the Cold War a battle of ideas or a contest of market mechanisms? As far as modern canons go, the question doesn't matter much. Both the United States and the USSR were world-historical juveniles more interested in things to come than in things past. A cultural establishment that valued stuff that lasted—whether poems or family names or chemically stable applications of oil paint—had gasped its last hale breaths around 1914. The USSR and the United States battled on behalf of historically innovative dreams and of the economic structures that went with them. Whether you preferred a free market or the egalitarian utopianism of a command economy, land and bullion, like the test of time, looked quaint. Yet, as the party to the right battling a left-wing Moscow, the United States couched its Cold War initiatives in deference to European traditionalism. This was true even as those doing the couching invented a lot of that tradition.

Rendering a fictional universe whose themes and realities feel positively Old Testament, hailing from a South not quite ashamed of its two-century experiment in legal hierarchy based on race, and practicing a faith that drew on two millennia of apostolic succession, O'Connor became part of this conservative Cold War establishment. Yet by deftly handling literary techniques no older than her mother, by feeding with hermeneutically perplexing short fiction the discussion of the Crisis of Man, and by being among the first crop of graduates from a new academic discipline, O'Connor also bolstered the radically contemporary. The radically contemporary, so much more than the traditional, is her legacy today, even as she continues to endow the creative writing discipline with a trace of the memory of aristocratic prestige. She remains, as she was during the Cold War, a conservative figure in an egalitarian democracy that nurtures a semisecret appetite for conservative reprimand. She continues to do the bidding of a reactionary kind of cultural nostalgia but also of our institutions of writing, which could not be much less tied to the past.

In November 2014, St. John of the Divine Episcopal Cathedral in New York City added a memorial tile to its Poets' Corner (America's poor cousin to the stones in Westminster Abbey). O'Connor, by grace of an early death, will probably be the last inductee from the cultural era of American modernism. When John Updike gets a stone, or (may they live long and prosper) Philip Roth, Toni Morrison, or Thomas Pynchon, the addition will change the mood. As of now, the canon feels historical and settled. Nobody earlier than Phillis Wheatley and Washington Irving and mainly, thereafter, the names you would expect.

O'Connor might have lived much longer than she did. At the time of this writing, she quite plausibly could still have been with us, tenaciously entering a tenth decade, damning with smirk or apothegm the ever-gathering hubris and weakness of a world on which her fiction never came down on the secular side. Whether the years between 1964 and 2014 might have entailed the production of more great stuff from her typewriter or reputation-wounding redundancy, who knows. That she would have outlived a moment of ponderous equilibrium is certain. Half retrospective, half prospective, the United States, throughout the 1950s and early 1960s, made huge cultural claims for itself with noteworthy help from the early creative writing programs—and then it never looked back.

NOTES

My research on O'Connor would not have been possible without the generous support of the National Endowment for the Humanities and the brilliant scholars I met at the NEH Summer Institute on O'Connor in Milledgeville in July 2014.

1. Eric Hobsbawm, *The Age of Capital: 1848–1875* (New York: Vintage, 1996), 1.
2. William Dean Howells, *Literary Friends and Acquaintance: A Personal Retrospect of American Authorship* (New York: Harper and Brothers, 1900), 211.
3. Van Wyck Brooks, *America's Coming of Age* (New York: B. W. Huebsch, 1915), 4–5.
4. The indifference to the question of gender was hardly least among the features of the discourse that today appear astonishing.
5. Clement Greenberg, "The Present Prospects of American Painting and Sculpture," *Horizon* 93–94 (Oct. 1947): 24.
6. William Dean Howells, *A Hazard of New Fortunes* (New York: Penguin, 2001), 258.
7. Loren Glass, *Authors Inc.: Literary Celebrity in the Modern United States, 1880–1980* (New York: New York UP, 2004), 13.
8. See John Raeburn, *Fame Became of Him: Hemingway as Public Writer* (Bloomington: Indiana UP, 1984).
9. Paul Engle, "How Creative Writing Is Taught at University of Iowa Workshop," *Des Moines Sunday Register*, 28 Dec. 1947, 9.
10. Malcolm Cowley, *Think Back on Us: A Contemporary Chronicle of the 1930's*, ed. Henry Dan Piper (Carbondale: Southern Illinois UP, 1967), 62.
11. Paul Engle, "New English Poets," *English Journal* 27.2 (Feb. 1938): 90.

12. Paul Engle, "Poetry in a Machine Age," *English Journal* 26.6 (June 1937): 431.

13. Howard Mumford Jones, "American Scholarship and American Literature," *American Literature* 8.2 (May 1936): 120.

14. Irving Babbitt, *Democracy and Leadership* (Boston: Houghton Mifflin, 1924), 101.

15. Wallace Stegner, who directed the writing seminars in Palo Alto, was also a student of Foerster's.

16. Jacques Maritain, *Art and Scholasticism and the Frontiers of Poetry* (New York: Charles Scribner's Sons, 1962), 59.

17. Flannery O'Connor, *Mystery & Manners* (New York: Farrar, Straus and Giroux, 1969), 42.

18. Flannery O'Connor, *The Habit of Being* (New York: Farrar, Straus and Giroux, 1979), 111.

19. Flannery O'Connor, "Revelation," *Collected Works* (New York: Literary Classics of the United States, 1988), 652.

20. T. E. Hulme, "Autumn," *The Collected Writings of T. E. Hulme*, ed. Karen Csengeri (Oxford: Clarendon Press, 1994), 3.

21. Mark McGurl, *The Program Era: Postwar Fiction and the Rise of Creative Writing* (Cambridge: Harvard UP, 2009), 135.

22. Flannery O'Connor to John Marshall, 12 Sept. 1955, Record Group 1.2, Series 200, Box 359, Folder 3246, Rockefeller Archive Center, Tarrytown, New York.

CHAPTER 6

Alternative Degrees

"Works in OPEN" at Black Mountain College

STEPHEN VOYCE

Since the founding of the Iowa Writers' Workshop in 1936, no fewer than 1,269 degree-granting writing programs have opened across the nation. Hence, there is little doubt regarding Mark McGurl's central thesis in *The Program Era* that the MFA has become the single most powerful institution shaping American literature. Its lasting contribution is a set of defining guidelines for the postwar program fiction author: (1) write what you know, (2) show don't tell, and (3) find your voice. Discussion of these principles appears elsewhere in this edited volume; suffice it to say that *The Program Era* argues for a demonstrable relationship between the formation of cultural institutions and the production of literary forms.[1]

Yet we should also ask, as Fredric Jameson does, "[W]here are the poets?"[2] McGurl's praiseworthy study eliminates in advance both the poetry of the Program Era and the critical attention to it. Jed Rasula's watershed *The American Poetry Wax Museum* (1996), Hank Lazer's *Opposing Poetries* (1996), Christopher Beach's *Poetic Culture* (1999), and Libbie Rifkin's *Career Moves* (2000) offer several fine examples, all of which situate the rise of the MFA program amid a network of award/prize systems, publishing industries, anthology wars, and state- and private-funding models that codified literary canons at midcentury. Indeed, the social and pedagogical contexts for American literature are varied and numerous: How might we document, for instance, the historical influences of the anarchist free schools, artists' and writers' colonies, John Reed Clubs, and prison workshops? How might we attend to the different approaches of academic programs like the Writers' Workshop, Naropa, or the Buffalo Poetics Program alongside organizations such as the St. Mark's Poetry Project, Kootenay School of Writing, San Diego Factory School, or Durruti Free Skool?

This chapter is modest in scope—a single case study intended to signal alternative histories weaving in and out of the creative writing program's varied pedagogical contexts. I trace the relationship between an experiment at Black Mountain College (BMC) and the co-creation of a poetic practice variously called projective verse, open form, and "works in OPEN." Like McGurl, I argue for a demonstrable relationship between institutional structure and poetic form, such that a sociological account of Black Mountain tells us a great deal about one of the most important accomplishments of midcentury poetry: the collaborative and interdisciplinary milieu of the college shaped Olson's theory of what a poem should do. And herein lies an essential difference between the atmosphere at Black Mountain and that of the Writers' Workshop: whereas Engle saw the Workshop's aim to nurture individual talent by giving writers a "community . . . to try out the quality of their gift," Olson was less preoccupied with teaching craft and much more intent on creating collaborative environments for interartistic exchange.[3] Olson envisioned BMC as a community of co-creators who invent new artistic forms.

First and foremost, Black Mountain is the name of a college that opened in the isolated environs of southwestern North Carolina in 1933. For literary scholars, the term marks the era of the college between 1951 and 1956,[4] at which time Charles Olson acted as its rector, and a number of poets transformed the institution into a central site of poetic experimentation—in particular, the development of "open form" or projectivist writing. Sharing its namesake with the *Black Mountain Review*, the term is also a metonym for a little magazine edited by Robert Creeley and a variety of allied publishing venues that include Jonathan Williams's Jargon Press, Cid Corman's *Origin*, and Creeley's own Divers Press. Despite these associations, perhaps the most lasting of its connotations refers to a category in Donald Allen's groundbreaking anthology, *The New American Poetry, 1945–1960*. Hence, these various uses of the signifier speak simultaneously to a set of personal relationships, organizing institutions, and canonical categories. In contrast with the Writers' Workshop, students and faculty at Black Mountain placed less emphasis on the pedagogical role of the classroom, instead treating it as one important component among these other activities typically associated with avant-garde culture.

In an essay titled "Advance-Guard Writing" composed for the *Kenyon Review* in 1951, Paul Goodman argues that the role of the avant-garde must shift: "society" has become "'alienated' from itself, from its own creative development, and its persons . . . estranged from one another"; thus, "the essential present-day advance-guard is the physical reestablishment of community."[5] It is difficult not to attribute these assertions, at least in part, to the trauma of the world wars, the extent of the Second World War's horrors still coming into view while Goodman was writing; likely, however, he is also speaking to a specifically American set of sociopolitical concerns: the suburbanization of culture, the beginning of the Cold War, and a commodity fetishism that Marx could not have fully anticipated. These historical trends lend some context to one of Creeley's most famous poetic lines of the 1950s: "the darkness sur- / rounds us."[6] The line break bifurcating the word "surrounds" seems to emblematize simultaneously the feeling of being encompassed by binaric ideologies of East and West, Left and Right, communism and capitalism. The speaker of Olson's *The Maximus Poems* declares similarly:

> In the present go
> nor right nor left;
>   nor stay
> in the middle[.][7]

Of course, Olson's declaration begs the question: Go where, then? The issue of social organization persists throughout *Maximus*:

> the problem then is whether
>   a Federal organization
> or organization at all except as it comes
> directly in the form of
> the War of the World
> is anything[.] ("13 vessels" [1963], *MP* 2:198)

Not only were the democratic institutions of modernity at stake but the very configuration of the political sphere as such. Goodman's proposed revision of the avant-garde speaks to a set of collective concerns among the poets and artists who congregated at Black Mountain: Could the avant-garde still be relied on to forge an alternative society?

Those who worked at BMC during the early to mid-1950s did so during a time in which the (inter)national was being reconfigured. The establishment of the World Bank (1945) and the International Monetary Fund (1944) inaugurated a new era of capital, the final revisions of the Geneva Conventions

(1949) sought to formalize the role of the United Nations, and the convention designating a new "status of the refugee" (1951) was introduced to respond to diasporas across the planet. Olson's theorization of "polis" in *The Maximus Poems* and Creeley's preoccupation with friendship in *For Love* speak to an emergent politics related to these configurations. It would be more accurate to say of Black Mountain that it exists in a historical moment "sur-rounded," as Creeley puts it, not merely by conservative 1950s culture but by a notion of totalizing governmentality at national and international levels. Community, Olson remarks, "needs now to be as wholly reconceived & newly created as does the concept of Self (& whatever is coming as 'Society'—the present Totalitarian State only a stage of passage)."[8] Olson's note affords greater optimism than in his poem just cited; it also clarifies the historical and philosophical context for the literary-artistic experiments at Black Mountain. The multi-authored development of field composition, the early writings that emerge from these developments, in addition to the interdisciplinary experimentation undertaken at the college are consciously conceived within this milieu of a new collectivity in response to totality.

It is for this reason that one should begin a study of BMC with a reference to Paul Goodman. He had written his essay on the renewed demand for advance-guard community shortly after teaching at the college during the 1950 summer session. Goodman had also just completed a book with his brother Percival titled *Communitas* (1947), a study of American urban space, which endorsed a "commune" model of social organization as an alternative to modern utopian city planning. Reading the book in conjunction with his essay, it is clear that he considered experimental artists' enclaves as possible testing grounds for his vision of community; hence, there is good reason to suspect that he had hoped the place would be a concrete expression of the *communitas* he had theorized in his book. Although Black Mountain was by the standards of 1950s America a quite radically progressive institution, there were questions about Goodman's "ostentatious" bisexuality.[9] Olson's own attitude to homosexuality is not entirely certain, but Edward Halsey Foster records that the poet, in addition to being active in the antiracism Common Council for American Unity during the 1940s, was also amenable to gay liberation and forged friendships with gay teachers and writers like F. O. Matthiesen. Ultimately, however, like many cultural and political movements of the 1950s and 1960s, BMC members often combined radical critiques of capitalist society with predictably conservative attitudes to gender equality and sexual orientation. In recent years, critics such as Michael Davidson, Rachel Blau DuPlessis, and Libbie Rifkin have examined open form poetics in relation to heterosexist concepts of gender and the relationship between masculinity and the Cold War.

Certainly the women at Black Mountain recognized in its social structure what DuPlessis aptly observes in Olson's poetry: "a radical critique of humanist logos" expressing simultaneously a "subtext filled with conventional gender ideas."[10] Assessments of the college by female artists, students, and staff challenged the sentimentalizing and celebratory recollections typical of their male counterparts. Hilda Morley described mixed feelings about "Olson's boys," an apt phrase that would form the gendered exhortation in "Projective Verse": "go by it, boys."[11] Francine du Plessix Gray recounts that Olson was at once "iconoclastic and dictatorial." Yet Olson's "militant" rebellion against traditional literary forms involved a demonstrably altered stance toward literary history in contrast with the early twentieth-century avant-gardes; she discerningly remarks that "he did not so much engage in Oedipal rebellion against contemporary fathers" but instead conveyed a "gigantic, archeological curiosity for all forms of 'immediate' discourse, past and present." Yet she too found herself deeply disappointed with the college's male bravado, finding "much redneck yahoo posturing in this Harvard-educated scholar" who routinely sermonized that one could not attain "freedom" until cleansed of all Western bias.[12] Olson had undoubtedly influenced countless women writers of the past half century. We should say unequivocally, however, that Black Mountain was both an advancement and a failure of egalitarian politics and art. Open form poetics signaled a collectivist social project in opposition to the possessive individualism of 1950s consumer culture, while it failed to extend fully its principles of self-determination, local autonomy, and collective organization to women.

There is no question that those who worked at the college at midcentury found it a productive environment. BMC attracted some of the most important poets, artists, dancers, composers, and architects of the 1940s and 1950s (most of whom were not yet recognized): among them, John Cage, Merce Cunningham, Robert Rauschenberg, Hilda Morley, Josef Albers, Willem de Kooning, Ed Dorn, Buckminster Fuller, Michael Rumaker, Joel Oppenheimer, Franz Kline, Robert Motherwell, Robert Creeley, Francine du Plessix

Gray, Robert Duncan, Katherine Litz, and Stefan Wolpe. By 1950, Olson and Creeley had already begun one of the most significant correspondences in American letters, an exchange that would ultimately bring Creeley to the college; and the method of "field composition" detailed in Olson's famous "Projective Verse" essay emerged from these letters as a theory codeveloped by both poets. It was at BMC that Olson composed the first twenty sections of *The Maximus Poems*, in addition to several of his most important early works collected in *Archaeologist of Morning*. He also wrote a copious number of his most significant manifestos and essays, including his lectures titled *The Special View of History*, "The Present Is Prologue," and the majority of essays compiled in *Human Universe*. Between the time Creeley first began writing to Olson and his eventual sojourn at BMC from 1954 to 1956, he would pen the majority of small volumes and chapbooks assembled in *For Love*—two of which involved collaborations with painters also working at the college (Dan Rice and Fielding Dawson). He also acted as editor of the *Black Mountain Review*, producing the first volumes from Mallorca, Spain, before arriving in North Carolina. Robert Duncan, too, engaged in fruitful correspondence with various members of the BMC community, arriving at the college first in 1955 and then again a year later to teach in the spring and fall terms. It was at this time that he worked on several poems later published in *Letters* and *The Opening of the Field*, two volumes whose titles reflected his growing interest in projectivist methods.

Although scholars often make mention of Creeley's interest in abstract expressionism, other critical instances of interdisciplinary experimentation at BMC have frequently gone unnoticed. Olson's exposure to dancers like Litz and Cunningham and his participation in several theatrical productions renewed his interest in these art forms. The intimacy of the college facilitated several important intermedial collaborations, including an early adaptation of Olson's poem "Glyphs" for a performance piece with Litz, Harrison, and Ben Shahn. Cage, however, organized the most significant example of intermedial performance at the college, and Olson, along with the artist Rauschenberg, pianist David Tudor, and a host of others, took part in its demonstration.

From the beginning, the institution's opposition to mainstream pedagogy shaped its key principles of organization: there was no system of accreditation or board of trustees, and the instructors voted democratically on all issues pertaining to educational policies and procedures. A rector was elected among the faculty to administer and lead meetings, but he received a single vote like all other members. No doubt these procedures would have frustrated Paul Engle, who presided as director of the Iowa Writers' Workshop with the autocratic mandate of a benevolent dictator, "taking it upon himself to hire and fire creative writing instructors as he saw fit."[13] In exchange for greater creative and pedagogical equity, however, BMC faced severe monetary constraints, since the faculty received little compensation for their teaching, and students who attended the college did so with full knowledge that they would receive no degree for their work. During the era of the college in which Olson served as rector, the administrative structure that John Rice had envisioned at the height of the Great Depression was largely similar, yet Olson, Creeley, Duncan, and others increasingly conceived of the institution as an alternative to a condition of 1950s consumer culture and postwar nationalism. Just as the GI Bill had extended postsecondary education to working-class Americans, it had also swelled university enrollment to numbers that threatened to homogenize approaches to creative learning. Engle imagined "[t]he university [a]s the Greenwich Village of the twenties diffused across the country, made more orderly, more efficient."[14] Olson would have rejected this claim as a contradiction; for a bohemian community, if nothing else, constitutes the unique lived relations of its participants. Black Mountain thus sought to combine the accessibility of the postwar public institution with the intimate setting of a small arts community, and, in this regard, Olson shared Paul and Percival Goodman's vision of *communitas.*

Prior to joining BMC, Olson had worked during the war as an associate chief in the Office of War Information (OWI) and then later accepted a potentially lucrative job in the Roosevelt administration. He resigned from the first position apparently in protest of the government's censorship of war reporting and abandoned the second after concluding that the artist could make no social impact in the modern market state. In a letter written to his former colleague at the OWI, anthropologist Ruth Benedict, he admits, "I regret we are not city states here in this wide land. Differentiation, yes. But also the chance for a person like yourself or myself to be central to social action at the same time and because of one's own creative work."[15] Olson's career path moved in virtually the opposite direction of Engle's, who, after his term as director of the Writers' Workshop, became increasingly involved in Kennedy's Cold War cultural front, serving on the National Council on the Arts and as "specialist" for the Department of State. Just as Olson took up the rectorship at BMC, Engle had accepted funds from the State Department and the Rockefeller Foundation. It is enticing to interpret Olson's choice to become a poet commensurately with his retreat from the political sphere, but Olson refutes this notion of writing as divorced from social action. In an early poem announcing his departure from government, he makes the point concisely: "The affairs of men remain a chief concern."[16] Elsewhere, in one of Olson's last poems, the speaker of *Maximus* echoes this project: "the initiation / of another kind of nation" ("I live underneath" [1969], *MP* 3:228). The proclamation here and Olson's letter to Benedict bear a striking resemblance to Goodman's call to the avant-garde.

During the 1950s, Black Mountain retained the basic structure of a creative writing and arts program but functioned more like an artists' colony. It was arguably most effective during its "summer sessions," when artists working in several fields congregated to engage in "short period[s] of intensive work and experimentation . . . in the setting of the Black Mountain community." The aim was to build a "co-operative work program" that expressed artistic exchange as a practice of living.[17] In an open letter to the members of Black Mountain, Olson described this project as "an assembly point of acts," stressing the convergences of ideas and heterogeneous artistic methods.[18] Members of the Black Mountain community frequently characterized the college in terms of a changing collective identity. Just as Creeley remarked that "[p]eople were always drifting through, coming back, coming for the first time," Ed Dorn proclaimed that the "value of being at Black Mountain was that very able people and very alive people were there, back and forth and off and on and through it. . . . I always thought of the place not as a school at all, but as a climate in which people work closely together and talk."[19] Comparable sentiment comes from a diverse consortium of attendees at the college. It is compelling that John Cage believed the aims of BMC were commensurate with his anarchistic principles, citing the college as the most significant experiment in collaboration and experimental pedagogy he had ever encountered.[20]

Olson had become preoccupied with the shared potential of the poem and the college to express alternative forms of collective life. In "Letter to the Faculty of Black Mountain College," he elaborated with an evocative analogy:

> The puzzle in general terms is one of *structure*. We understand a good deal about the *behavior* of electrons, neutrons and protons (for BMC, substitute,

> "man"). But we have no *structure* for them ((Apply, here, BMC & "MAN," likewise)). . . .
>
> We are finding out, moreover, that what we are forced to call elementary particles retain *neither permanence* nor *identity*. That is to say, *they are always capable of change, one into the other*. ((DITTO, BMC, "man"—right?))[.] (29)

Anticipating a concern he would take up in *The Maximus Poems*, Olson was searching for a more adequate language in which to engage the collective subjectivity of communities and the institutions to which they commit themselves. It is clear that Olson deliberately avoided words like "individual" and "society" to denote the identities and relations that structure human interaction at the college:

> we who throw down hierarchy,
> . . .
> do not fail to keep
> a sort of company[.] ("Maximus, at Tyre and at Boston" [1953], *MP* 1:94)

Yet what this "explanation / leaves out," the speaker insists, ". . . is / that chaos / is not our condition" ("Letter 22" [1953], *MP* 1:96). That is, there is a danger in sentimentalizing the "open community." If poets associated with Black Mountain celebrated the nomadic and protean milieu of the college, then this was most certainly also due to the college's limited resources. The idea of a provisional community is the consequence of needing to make do. This is an important yet often overlooked element of open form writing. Projectivism emphasizes immediacy, a writing that responds to a continuously changing environment in which the poet works with the resources available within her field of action. "Working in OPEN," as Olson called it, does not refer to an infinite expanse but a makeshift capacity to adapt to the immediate conditions that a given circumstance demands. Duncan derives from Olson: "The poem is . . . an area of composition where I work with whatever comes into it."[21] If Olson was right that living and writing are one, then open form is local.

As early as 1949, Olson's correspondence indicated a shared vision for Black Mountain and projective verse. Two documents aptly express the origins of Olson's thought: the "Black Mountain Catalogue," a mission statement for the college (1949), and Olson's letter to W. H. Ferry,[22] outlining its interdisciplinary possibilities (1951):

> At the middle of the 20th century, the emphasis—in painting as well as in political theory—is on what happens between things, not on the things themselves. Today the area of exploration, the premise underlying systematic thinking, is that of function, process, change; of interaction and communication. The universe . . . is seen, in microcosm and in macrocosm, as the continuously changing result of the influence that each of its parts exerts upon all the rest of its parts[.] ("Black Mountain Catalogue," qtd. in "Letter to W. H. Ferry" 11)

> What happens *between* things—what happens between *men*—what happens between guest faculty, students, regular faculty—and what happens *among* each as the result of each: for i [*sic*] do not think one can overstate—at this point of time, America, 1951—the importance of workers in different fields of the arts and of knowledge working so closely together some of the time of the year that they find out, from each other, the ideas, forms, energies, and the whole series of kinetics and emotions now opening up, out of the quantitative world. ("Letter to W. H. Ferry" 11)

Continuity exists between these passages and Olson's early essays such as "Human Universe," "The Gate and the Center," and especially "Projective Verse," a document that similarly evoked the bicentenary ("Verse now, 1950") and a "stance toward reality" emphasizing a "kinetic" and nonhierarchical "kind of relation" among objects in the world.[23]

Whether Olson was discussing BMC, his concept of "polis" in *Maximus*, interdisciplinary performance, or the elements that compose the field of a poem, he was interested in how each assembles as a collectivity according to its respective ontological order. Just as poets and artists at BMC are likened to atoms that amalgamate and transform, the field of the poem is a collective of objects that assembles as a social, material, and linguistic constellation. Recall that McGurl in *The Program Era* identifies an MFA aesthetic via analysis of the creative writing program. One might likewise extrapolate a set of poetic axioms from BMC. The goal "at this point of time, America, 1951" was an open form cultural poetics on which "function," "process," "interaction," and "change" would be its guiding principles.

SINCE ITS INITIAL PUBLICATION in *Poetry New York* in October 1950, Charles Olson's "Projective Verse" essay has become a veritable institution whose influence traversed a broad range of literary activities during the 1950s and 1960s, including the frequently overlapping projects of writers associated with Black Mountain, the Beats, the San Francisco Renaissance, the New York school, and TISH. Also referred to as "open form" or "composition by field," Olson's "Projective Verse" introduced some of the most central concerns now associated with mid-twentieth-century North American poetics: his principles of field composition, the function of the typewriter to score the voice on the page, and a stance toward reality that Olson calls objectism. The significant precursors are referenced explicitly: Ezra Pound, W. C. Williams, Ernest Fenollosa, and Louis Zukofsky. Olson's essay has since, unfortunately, become codified as an individual's principal declaration of open form poetics, as critics attempt to delineate linear traditions (and the discrete contributions to these traditions), usually in accordance with a countertradition from Pound to open form, yet field composition was a generative practice invented and transformed by a community of authors over several years. The practice emerged not as a set of principles to be adhered to but as a set of flexible strategies to be adapted.

At the beginning of Olson's essay, the poet made an important—if easily overlooked—remark that composition by field (a practice of writing) is commensurate with what he calls an "objectist" stance (a practice of living). From the outset, Olson associates a system of prosody with the social theory he had been conceiving concurrently. In "I, Mencius," for instance, the speaker insists

> that no line must sleep,
> that as the line goes so goes
> the Nation![24]

The line exists among other elements in a *field*, and the emphasis is on its relation with other variables. Olson explains in "Projective Verse" that "every element in an open poem (the syllable, the line, as well as the image, the sound, the sense)" acts as a "participant" within a social field of action (243). If a writer "works in OPEN," as Olson claims, she must abdicate "inherited line, stanza [and] . . . form" (239). Yet this does not mean that Olson disavows tradition or advocates a poetics of anticonvention for its own sake; rather, the poet should not treat poetic form as the privileged "inheritance" of one's forebears, as one might expect to inherit land or title. The poem is deconstructive and reconstructive; it assembles in the moment of its composition, conditioned by the available elements and contexts that occasion it. More will be said about the concept of field, but it suffices to note at this point that Olson, Levertov, Duncan, and Creeley use the term "field," not "page," because the poem operates as a zone within larger social, political, and technological discursive fields. The task at hand, Olson remarks—both in reference to political organization and line organization—is to determine "what happens between things, not the things themselves" ("Letter to W. H. Ferry" 11). Open form poetics, its process and prosody, needs thus to be read in terms of the social vision that Black Mountain occasioned. It needs also to be read against the poetry that supposedly articulates this social vision.

Early on in "Projective Verse," Olson advances three principles of open form writing, against which we might productively compare McGurl's assessment of Writers' Workshop prose:

(1) The *kinetics*: "a poem is energy transferred from where the poet got it (he will have some several causations), by way of the poem itself to, all the way over to, the reader. . . . [T]he poem itself must, at all points, be a high energy-construct" ("PV" 240).

The concept of "field" that Olson expounds borrows from a materialist-scientific model. The word "energy" is promptly followed by the word "construct" to refute any assumption that he has in mind a quasi-mystical understanding of creative production. This cautionary point aside, Olson's claim seems prosaic enough: that "several causations" imbue the poem with energy. But where does the poet get this creative force? Provided one accepts that Olson disputes the idea of the poem as a rarified, complete object, then the energy comes from an external source that animates language, only to be reanimated by another external force—the reader. Olson's contention that the pressure and duration of breathing can determine the length of the poetic line is often taken to express an organic model of aesthetics, whereby authority is located in voice and/or nature. But for Olson, like the speaker of "The Kingfishers," "[t]he factors are / in the animal and/or the machine" (90). Olson, Creeley, Levertov, Duncan, and others prefer the term "open form" to "voice-based."

(2) The *principle*: "FORM IS NEVER MORE THAN AN EXTENSION OF CONTENT. (Or so it got phrased by one R. Creeley . . . [)]" (240).

Simply put, no predetermined form conditions the act of composition. One should clarify, however, that by "content" Olson and Creeley do not have in mind the sense of the poem as a discrete message or contained unity. The poem is an "energy-construct," and hence "content" refers to the nexus of external forces that bring it into being. The act of composition, being free of predetermined forms, is modular rather than formless, responding to the external world within which writing takes place. Olson cites Creeley's useful formulation, but it is the broader context within which the younger poet makes this assertion that is all the more telling.

The first draft of Olson's "Projective Verse" essay, which he dutifully sent to Creeley, indicates that he was still grappling with a system of prosody to complement the social theory he had begun to conceptualize at Black Mountain. In response, Creeley offered an analogy to jazz: "Miles Davis's group being delighted with the SOUND of a French horn."[25] Creeley would coin his most quotable phrase, "FORM IS NEVER MORE THAN AN EXTENSION OF CONTENT," in a letter nearly two weeks later, but the rudiments of this statement were already present in this earlier letter. That is, Creeley identified in jazz a similar attempt to compose not according to a "form" that "extends" predictably from a predetermined meter but rather a musical rhythm composed in "any given instance" (1:39). Creeley invited Olson to think of the participants within the field of the poem as being akin to the ensemble of instruments in a jazz performance. In both cases, spontaneity should not suggest a random production of sounds but the negotiation between musical elements in the instant of composition. "The job," Creeley states paradoxically, "[is] . . . systematic disorganization" (1:39)—continuously reorganizing the elements of syntax, line, image, and so forth—to reflect the conditions of the present moment.

(3) The *process*: "ONE PERCEPTION MUST IMMEDIATELY AND DIRECTLY LEAD TO A FURTHER PERCEPTION" ("PV" 240).

The "process" may entice the critic to conclude that Olson's is a poetics of cognition, documenting the mental activity of a single consciousness. Rosemarie Waldrop rightly observes that the direction of movement is "outward and physical, toward perceptions rather than ideas."[26] Indeed, Olson remarks in *Human Universe* that "man and external reality are so involved with one another that, for man's purposes, they had better be taken as one."[27] Perception marks not the continuous movement of interior thought but the continuous engagement with external experience—hence, Olson carefully indicates that "one perception" leads directly to another, not "one's perception." Once again, the movement is outward, not inward, traversing the field, negotiating the interaction between emergent variables.

The *kinetic*, the *modular*, and the *processual* combine as the method Olson calls "field composition." Later I give Olson's most candid definition, but one should keep a couple of things in mind: the projective is frequently understood through social/communal analogies. The term "process" is applied very liberally in contemporary studies of poetics to denote poetries that refuse an autonomous status to the art object. Process in Olson's sense clearly does *not* mean a mapping of the interior thought process of a single speaker. It maps the relations and materials involved in the construction of poems:

> It comes to this, this whole aspect of the newer problems. (We now enter, actually, the large area of the whole poem, into the FIELD, if you like, where all the syllables and all the lines must be managed in their *relations* to each other.) It is a matter, finally, of OBJECTS, what they are, what they are inside a poem, how they got there, and, once there, how they are to be used... that every element in an open poem (the syllable, the line, as well as the image, the sound, the sense) must be taken up as participants in the kinetic of the poem just as solidly as we are accustomed to take what we call the objects of reality; and that these elements are to be seen as creating the tensions of a poem just as totally as do those other objects create what we know as the world. ("PV" 243; my italics)

Critics such as Don Byrd suggest that Olson's concept of field is indebted to scientific models; in physics, "field" designates a space affected by an electromagnetic force. Waldrop speculates that Olson came to the idea through Gestalt psychology, which had adapted the concept to designate "a kinetic model of mental states as balances of forces and vectors."[28] But the language Olson employs clearly bears a strong affinity with his descriptions of community at Black Mountain, his statements on interdisciplinarity, his emerging process materialism, and the philosophy of relation that comes to unify these concerns. The field being defined is also quite certainly a *social field*—not a psychological one. The elements of the poem manifest the same logic of relation "as do those other objects [that] create what we know as the world" ("PV" 243). The ontological order is specific to the poetic field, but it bears a logic of relation—an ontology of the "between things"—concurrent with a "stance toward reality" that brought it into being. Just as a nexus of "participants" organize relationally in the field of a poem, objectism denotes a commensurate experience of the subject within the field of reality he occupies and shares with a constellation of other objects: "'objectism' [is] a word to be taken to stand for the kind of relation of man to experience" (247). In an open form poem, any element that enters the social field counts equally. Every element is afforded an unqualified equality among all others.

Although Olson, Levertov, Creeley, and Duncan do not always possess obvious stylistic similarities, they share a commitment to field composition's resistance to hierarchical structures. Levertov's assertion that no one element in composition should "supervise" the others insinuates a critique of the bureaucratic corporatism and militarism of 1950s America. Duncan is even more explicit in this regard: since the advent of the Enlightenment, "in poetry as in government or religion, the goal is system or reason, motive or morality, some set of rules and standards that will bring the troubling plenitude of experience 'within our power.'"[29] The possibilities of projective verse were explicitly linked to an alternative concept of community, "a free association of living things—for my longing moves beyond governments to a co-operation" (90). In a word, Olson, Creeley, Levertov, and Duncan understand that the form of a poem should reflect this axiom of social equality.

In this sense, they are getting at an idea of the poetic that foregrounds its own construction as a social artifact shaped by dynamics of power. The lines of poems are no exception. Consider, for example, the following passage from "I, Mencius":

> we are the process
>
> and our feet
>
> We do not march
>
> We still look
>
> And see
>
> what we see
>
> We do not see
>
> ballads
>
> other than our own. (75–83)

Words like "process," "look," (poetic) feet that "do not march," and the persistence of the social "we" signal the principles of field composition. Olson distributes language across the field of the page by way of a "systematic disorganization" (Creeley's term) of the "march" of the ballad stanza's metered lines:

Mao concluded:
nous devons
nous lever
et agir!
. . . .
not accumulation but change, the feed-back proves, the feed-back is the law
Into the same river no man steps twice
When fire dies air dies
No one remains, nor is, one
Around an appearance, one common model, we grow up many[.][30]

No doubt the reader encounters a surprising amalgam of associations: Heraclitus's ontology of flux, Norbert Weiner's cybernetics, and Mao Zedong's communist directive. The Heraclitian concept of flux is evoked in the very first line of the poem: "what does not change / is the will to change." Ralph Maud and George Butterick both argue that Olson's famous line is likely not a direct translation of Heraclitus's twenty-third fragment,[31] but the subsequent reference to the river aphorism indicates that Olson was aware of the Greek philosopher's crucial intervention into pre-Socratic theories of being and materialism. Objects, Heraclitus argues, are best understood as processes; this idea lays the foundation for Olson's idea of the poem as energy field. Regarding the second of these allusions, Olson learned of cybernetics at BMC during a lecture given by Natasha Goldowski in 1949. The principle of feedback—by which some aspect of the output generated by a system is passed back into the input—is used to explain how systems account for modulation and change. Cybernetics seemed a plausible scientific explanation of Heraclitus's axiom: that the only constant was change itself. As for the third reference, the significance of Mao is potentially more confusing. The phrase "nous devons / nous lever / et agir!" ("we must rise up and act") (51–53) came to Olson by way of a friend, Jean Riboud. Olson retains the French in "The Kingfishers" partly to recognize the debt to his friend and perhaps also to emphasize the proliferation of Mao's message throughout the industrialized world. Notably, Olson finished "The Kingfishers" in 1949. The Cultural Revolution and the Great Leap Forward are yet to be conceived; it would be more than a decade and a half until the Black Panthers encountered Mao's "red book." At precisely the historical moment of Olson's reference, Mao represented to the West both the "red scare" of Soviet communism and a generalized xenophobia toward an emergent Eastern-Orientalist threat. Several of Olson's friends had either been investigated or blacklisted by the FBI. Although Olson was never so explicitly involved in party politics after his departure from the OWI, Black Mountain regularly received visits from the bureau. For Olson, like Riboud, Mao represented the possibility of a subversive energy in opposition to the totalizing project of Western capitalism.

So here, then, are the three references addressed separately, but field composition emphasizes that once an element appears in the field, its relations with other elements will modify its meaning. Mao is Mao only in relation to cybernetic theory and Heraclitian materialism, or as Olson put it, objects do not simply "accumulate": they "change." According to the cybernetic trope Olson advances, each concept might be thought to "feed back" into the others; each element reorients when encountered by another element. With this reflexive assertion in mind, it becomes apparent that all three allusions foreground multiplicity and change—in ontological, technological, and political arenas, respectively. Heraclitus theorizes the flow of material reality; cybernetics explains the interaction of physical systems; and Mao emphasizes the collective form of political action. Notice the complementary approach to the poetic line. Olson represents these concepts, or rather the relation between them, by amalgamating three variations of open form writing: a triadic line in the mold of W. C. Williams, a sprawling prose-poem line, and an indented-verse paragraph. The triadic line, when used to express a phrase from Mao, breaks the directive into discrete actions, the fast-stepping movement of the lines echoing a call for an urgent pace. The continuous flow of the prose-poem line cleverly correlates to the cybernetic theory of feedback. And finally, the indented-verse paragraph incorporates Heraclitus into the fabric of this cybernetic allusion, insinuating a contemporary scientific discourse's reliance on an ancient philosophy of becoming. That Olson's poem blends natural, scientific, and human elements reinforces the premise of objectism; that is, Olson's text exhibits not the interaction between self and other selves (understood in classical liberal discourse as stable, autonomous, discrete entities) but instead how one is never separate from the social environments of which our subjectivity is an effect—that, indeed, subjects share a common world and "we grow up / many" (100–101).

Recall those lessons McGurl draws from the Writers' Workshop: (1) write what you know, (2) show don't tell, and (3) find your voice. Engle's anxiety about teaching literary craft is a problem only insofar as the creation of literature is, for Engle, a resolutely solitary activity. In his introduction to *On Creative Writing*, Engle overtly cites Flaubert's monastic commitment as the preferred model of the ascetic artist. At Black Mountain, in contrast, the artist finds herself in the company of others. Olson remarked, "[D]espite the wearing *closeness* of everything and everybody—the isolation and the common meals, the all-too-aesthetic compression,"

> [Ben] Shahn teaches Olson one hell of a lot about his verse, Kathy Litz picks up clues for pushing her own important advance in dance, Harrison makes music for Abby Shahn and others, Bernarda comes to listen to Olson when she can and shoots in shots of perception about the stuff he reads to the students which opens the eyes of s[ai]d students and lets them find out how to hear[.] ("Letter to W. H. Ferry" 9–10)

Open form poetry's chief task is the invention of new forms of collective life. Yet this account of BMC is in no way meant to disparage the Writers' Workshop, but, rather, at this preliminary juncture, I would urge caution against a unified or singular history of the Program Era. Instead, we should explore creative writing's varied pedagogical contexts and multiple histories, both inside and outside the university proper, by offering rigorously contrastive accounts of literature's institutional sites of activity. In this spirit, let this chapter sit somewhat uneasily in the collection, such that we recognize the complex midcentury cultural formations that shaped and were shaped by the postwar creative writing program.

NOTES

1. Mark McGurl, *The Program Era: Postwar Fiction and the Rise of Creative Writing* (Cambridge: Harvard UP, 2009).

2. Fredric Jameson, "Dirty Little Secret," *London Review of Books* 34.22 (2012), http://www.lrb.co.uk/v34/n22/fredric-jameson/dirty-little-secret.

3. Paul Engle, *On Creative Writing* (New York: Dutton, 1966), xxx.

4. Olson first began teaching at Black Mountain in 1948 but did not become a full-time faculty member until the summer of 1951.

5. Paul Goodman, "Advance-Guard Writing, 1900–1950," *Kenyon Review* 13.3 (Summer 1951): 375.

6. Robert Creeley, "I Know a Man," *The Collected Poems of Robert Creeley: 1945–1975* (Berkeley: U of California P, 1982), 132, lines 5–6.

7. Charles Olson, "The Song and Dance of [1953]," *The Maximus Poems* (Berkeley: U of California P, 1983), 1:54. Hereafter cited as *MP*.

8. Charles Olsen, "West," *OLSON* 5 (Spring 1976): 47.

9. Martin Duberman records in his biography of the college that by 1950 many of the members of the community were openly gay, but Goodman's "ostentatious homosexual[ity] . . . was too much, even for Black Mountain." See Duberman, *Black Mountain: An Exploration in Community* (New York: E. P. Dutton, 1972), 331. Many at the college defended Goodman, including Dan Rice, Robert Creeley, Ed Dorn, and Joel Oppenheimer; nevertheless, the faculty voted against his full-time appointment.

10. Rachel Blau de Plessis, "Manifests," *Diacritics* 26.3–4 (Fall–Winter 1996): 44.

11. Charles Olson, "Projective Verse," *Collected Prose: Charles Olson*, ed. Donald Allen and Benjamin Friedlander (Berkeley: U of California P, 1997), 240.

12. Francine du Plessix Gray, "Black Mountain: The Breaking (Making) of a Writer," *Black Mountain College: Sprouted Seeds: An Anthology of Personal Accounts*, ed. Mervin Lane (Knoxville: U of Tennessee P, 1990), 302.

13. Loren Glass, "Middle Man: Paul Engle and the Iowa Writers' Workshop," *Review* 71–72 (Winter–Spring 2009): 265.

14. Paul Engle, Letter to "Lewis," 27 Feb. 1951, University of Iowa Special Collections.

15. "Letter to Ruth Benedict," 12 Jan. 1945, Notebook, "Key West I, 1945," Charles Olson Papers, University of Connecticut, Storrs.

16. Charles Olson, "The K," *The Collected Poems of Charles Olson*, ed. George F. Butterick (Berkeley: U of California P, 1987), 14, line 8.

17. *Black Mountain College Bulletin* (unsigned), 8.1 (1950–51), Black Mountain College Archives, Raleigh, North Carolina.

18. Charles Olsen, "A Letter to the Faculty of Black Mountain College," *OLSON* 8 (Fall 1977): 28.

19. "*The Sullen Art* Interview," by David Ossman, *Interviews*, ed. Donald Allen (Bolinas, CA: Four Seasons Foundation, 1963), 1–2. See also John Sinclair and Robin Eichele, "An Interview with Robert Creeley," *Contexts of Poetry: Interviews, 1961–1971*, ed. Donald Allen (Bolinas, CA: Four Seasons Foundation, 1973), 69.

20. See Richard Kostelanetz, *Conversing with Cage*, 2nd ed. (New York: Routledge, 2003), 265.

21. Robert Duncan, "Preface," *Bending the Bow* (New York: New Directions, 1968), vi.

22. Charles Olson, "Letter to W. H. Ferry" [7 Aug. 1951], *OLSON* 2 (Fall: 1974):

8–15. A friend of Olson's during his former involvement in the Roosevelt administration, Wilbur Hugh Ferry was the director of public relations for the CIO Political Action Committee and founded the center for the Study of Democratic Institutions in New York.

23. Charles Olson, "Projective Verse," *Collected Prose: Charles Olson*, ed. Donald Allen and Benjamin Friedlander (Berkeley: U of California P, 1997), 239. Henceforth cited as "PV."

24. Charles Olson, "I, Mencius, Pupil of the Master" [1954], *The Collected Poems of Charles Olson*, 318–20, lines 31–33.

25. Charles Olson and Robert Creeley, *The Complete Correspondence*, ed. George Butterick (Santa Barbara: Black Sparrow Press, 1980), 1:39.

26. Rosemarie Waldrop, "Charles Olson: Process and Relationship," *Twentieth Century Literature* 23.4 (Dec. 1977): 470.

27. Charles Olson, "Human Universe," *Human Universe and Other Essays*, ed. Donald Allen (New York: Grove Press, 1967), 9.

28. Waldrop, "Charles Olson," 468.

29. Robert Duncan, "Ideas of the Meaning of Form," *Fictive Certainties* (New York: New Directions, 1985), 102–3.

30. Charles Olson, "The Kingfishers" [1949], *The Collected Poems of Charles Olson*, lines 50–53, 95–101.

31. See Ralph Maud, *What Does Not Change* (Madison: Fairleigh Dickinson UP, 1998), 37; George Butterick, "Charles Olson's 'The Kingfishers' and the Poetics of Change," *American Poetry* 6.2 (Winter 1989): 56.

CHAPTER 7

Robert Coover, Hypertext, and the Technomodern Pedagogy of Fairy Tales

KELLY BUDRUWEIT

Because of his adherence to the myth of the lone writer in the wilderness of narrative, Robert Coover provides an interesting case study in the changing notions of authorship and pedagogy. After years of struggle to avoid teaching as a means of support, Coover, through the rise of hyperfiction in the early 1990s, was allowed to become more involved in a pedagogy that would support both his students' futures and what he saw as the experimental future of narrative. Coover's role as the founder of the first hypertext workshop at Brown University makes him almost a perfect example of Mark McGurl's "technomodernism." Highlighting the continuity between technomodern writing and "the modernist project of systematic experimentation with narrative form," McGurl applies the term to experimental fiction that combines "literary *techné* (craft) with technology in the grosser sense—including, most importantly, media technology."[1] In what follows, I extend McGurl's formulation of technomodernism in order to read the 1996 novella *Briar Rose* as an allegory of Coover's notion of authorship, in which the roles of the fairy, the prince, and the princess stand in, respectively, for the teacher-writer, the student-writer, and the student-reader.

Coover has helped define the technomodern aspects of contemporary fiction. Nevertheless, McGurl makes little mention of him. There are several possible reasons for this. Prior to teaching at Brown, Coover had had an indirect relation to the Program Era. He does not hold an MFA (though he does have an MA in general humanities), and he repeatedly claims that he learned his craft by reading on his own, especially the works of Miguel Cervantes and Samuel Beckett.[2] McGurl also may have excluded Coover's fictions on the basis of their being unnecessary to reiterate an argument that could already be made via similar writers with clearer connections to the university. In technomodern writers who began publishing in the 1960s and 1970s, such as John Barth, Donald Barthelme, and Thomas Pynchon, McGurl identifies the subtext of the university, which leads him to conclude that what had previously been considered "anti-institutional" writing may be less about escaping from institutions and more about revising institutions to become "open systems" (194). In other words, technomodern fictions break down the distinction between the inside and the outside of the institution, arguing for a version of the system that is open to change. To a certain degree, it would be possible to map such an argument onto Coover's work.

On the occasion of Coover's retirement in 2012, Mary Caponegro referred to him as the "founding father" of metafiction, which is the critical label he has favored (or disliked the least) for most of his career.[3] In a 1987 interview, Coover explains that he prefers "metafiction" because the term implies a "more global vision."[4] The pedagogical function of metafiction aligns closely with the Program Era. As McGurl points out, the project of writing about writing has a lot in common with the goal of the creative writing program as a system geared toward the reproduction of the "writer" (49). More specifically, the metafictional unification of the author and teacher functions reflects the inscription of systematized pedagogy, even for those, like Coover, who have endeavored to keep teaching separate from their writing. In terms of the shifting author function, however, metafiction does little to challenge the authority of the writer. The author can be, and often is, portrayed as a hero whose authority is derived not from institutions but from life experiences.

The characterization of the author-as-hero corresponds with the role of the prince in *Briar Rose.* Coover viewed the beginning of his career as a heroic mission in which he "was to sally forth against the stagnant narrative tradition."[5] Furthermore, the prince is out to "make his name," even to find his identity, which is predicated on being "he who will awaken Beauty." Clearly, the awakening of Beauty is a reference to the vocation of being a writer. The prince's vocation, however, is slightly different from that of a mature professional author. A simplistic masculinity drives this hero "to insert himself wholly into that world more than world" and to learn about "the marvelous" that Beauty represents in the person of Briar Rose.[6] The student-writer may be too traditional and naïve, in the modernist sense, in seeking to conquer beauty. Therefore, he is also caught in a dream from which he never quite awakens, tangled in the briar patch, which comes to represent the obscurity of his place in the literary canon: "He feels, oddly, like he is coming home again . . . this flowering briar patch, hung with old bones, wherein he strives. I am he who awakens Beauty, the bones seem to whisper as the blossoms unfold him" (83–84). The hero is one potential writer among others, all of whom have attempted, and failed, to define themselves by storming Beauty's castle. Coover does not suggest a solution for this predicament, though it is clear that the student-writer has yet to break with tradition, and his search for Beauty may be misguided. The fact that Coover does not offer a direct solution for the student-writer corresponds with the idea that writing cannot be taught.

Reading, on the other hand, can be taught, and the princess stands in for the figure of the student as reader. The ending that Briar Rose hopes for is also the familiar, Disney version of Sleeping Beauty, in which the passive, innocent princess will be awakened with a kiss from the hero. As Elizabeth Ly Bell notes, Coover eschews "modern sugarcoated versions" and especially "the Disneyfied ones" in favor of the "ur-forms" of Sleeping Beauty, dating back to the seventeenth century.[7] By subjecting Beauty to nightmares about rape, abandonment, and cannibalism, *Briar Rose* undoes the sanitized versions propagated by the culture industry. More important, so long as the reader stays committed to waiting for a prince, the novella suggests that she will awaken only "to repeated awakenings as though trapped in some strange mechanism" (78). The nightmares suggest that Beauty would do better to manipulate the "mechanism" (i.e., the narrative framework) for herself. To a certain extent, as Marie Bouchet notes, *Briar Rose* might "'awaken' the reader" into an awareness of and resistance to ideology.[8] The gendering of the reader, meanwhile, primarily aims the lesson at female students who are still attached to outworn romantic narratives.

Hypertext disrupts what might so far appear to be a closed system. Up to this point, the pedagogical format of the metafiction reflects the claustrophobia of the more traditional view of authorship. The two dreamers of *Briar Rose* are divided on the basis of gender, the active male author and the passive female reader. In its earlier days, Coover saw in hypertext the future of narrative, a possible extension of his own work in another form. In fact, he garnered a reputation as "something of a hypertext fiction evangelist"[9] for his 1992 essay in the *New York Times*, in which he argued that

> hypertext presents a radically divergent technology, interactive and polyvocal, favoring a plurality of discourses over definitive utterance and freeing the reader from domination by the author. Hypertext reader and writer . . .

> become co-learners or co-writers . . . fellow-travelers in the mapping and remapping of textual (and visual, kinetic and aural) components, not all of which are provided by what used to be called the author.[10]

Hypertext, then, serves a pedagogical function. Readers are co-learners. The new form allows students to become aware of and manipulate the process of knowledge production through creative reading. The author, meanwhile, becomes a more fluid concept. The reader is allowed to step into the place of "what used to be called the author."

Briar Rose enables student-readers to participate in the writing process. The print form is divided into forty-two "lexias," or units of hypertext, describing a narrative arc that starts and ends over and over again. The circularity of the multiple short versions gives readers a degree of agency in determining the "beginning" or the "ending." The role of student choice became even more pronounced when, with the help of Robert Scholes, the lexias were uploaded into an electronic version, which served as a pedagogical tool including discussion sections. The home page of *Briar Rose* invites students to take their own paths in exploring the text: "You do not have to follow our sequence or Coover's. Follow the link you want to follow."[11] Such a format empowers the student-reader. By choosing the sequence, students are invited to become writers.

Coover's reworking of Sleeping Beauty would not have been possible without this third term: the fairy who has cast the spell in the first place. The idea for this story occurred long before Coover was able to realize it: "Years went by. . . . For a while I was using 'briar rose' as a password to my computer, because I wanted to keep telling myself to go back to it. And then one day I found myself thinking about the bad fairy who put Beauty to sleep. . . . And suddenly I had my story."[12] It is the fairy's dual role, as teacher and writer, that makes her so necessary.

The fairy has brought on the curse, but she also entertains Rose with stories to fill up the boredom of one hundred years' sleep. As a writer/spinner of her own stories, the fairy has good intentions. She "recognizes that many of her stories . . . have to do with suffering . . . , probably because she truly is a wicked fairy, but also because she is at heart . . . a practical old thing who wants to prepare her moony charge for more than a quick kiss and a wedding party, which means she is also a good fairy, such distinctions being somewhat blurred in the world she comes from" (60). By telling Rose stories of princesses who awaken to find themselves pregnant, or already having given birth, or being raped, the fairy appeals to a sense of the "real" that opposes the simplistic enchantment of the happily-ever-after. In that sense, Coover's fairy serves the pedagogical function of exposing metanarratives.

The fairy as teacher-writer illuminates how Coover began to embrace his role in the hypertext workshop. Michael Joyce refers to students in Coover's hypertext workshops as "wobbly chicks to his cackling mother hen."[13] In his teaching, Coover embodied what McGurl calls "erotically technologized institutions" (46) in which both the teacher and the technology can be employed as maternal sources of reproduction. At the same time, the notion of the author as the lone male hero is subverted by the collaborative focus of hypertext fictions.

Such challenges to traditional myths about (male) authorship are most prevalent in the work of feminist writers of hypertext, especially Shelley Jackson, perhaps Coover's most famous student. McGurl takes Jackson's *Patchwork Girl* (1995) to be representative of the ways in which technology and the university both allow for the incorporation of women as authority figures. In that text, "the mythical heroic male artist" becomes dislocated from his "craggy mountaintop" (McGurl 46). Coover provided the tools and the setting for Jackson to imagine *Patchwork Girl*, which he later referred to as among "the two or three classic works of electronic writing" from the 1990s.[14] In Coover's own writing, however, the myths about (male) authorship are much more difficult to dislodge. In 1996, just one year after the publication of *Patchwork Girl*, Coover published *Briar Rose*, which might be read as a response to the way that students like Jackson were challenging the myth of the male author.

To a certain extent, Coover does reconceptualize the author as less of a hero and more like the third figure in the story: the fairy who orchestrates the dreams. In the hypertext version of *Briar Rose*, the introduction of the fairy is followed by a photograph of Angela Carter, whose 1979 collection *The Bloody Chamber* has similarly dealt with the violent history of fairy tales. Carter's feminist fictions battle with the misogynist history (and present) of the happily-ever-after. Contrary to the masculine hero cutting through the briar patch of outworn narratives, the fairy is less interested in originality than she is in rewriting and reframing.

Instead of accepting the passive position of the female reader, both the fairy and Briar Rose express fury at the way that the sleeper is bound within the body. The fairy attempts to make Rose aware of her situatedness and even to help her to overcome it: "Castle-bound as the dreamer is, the illusion of boundaries, above all the body, has been one of the fairy's frequent themes, along with . . . the paradoxes . . . between gesture and language" (57). At one point, the fairy comes upon Rose "furiously stabbing herself over and over with the spindle" (80), "hammering away at the center of her pain like some strange mechanism gone amok" (81). The castle and the briar patch are one large body, represented through the circularity of hypertext. The sleeper is trapped in the text, but the fact that Rose stabs herself implies that she might gain control. To return to the "paradox" between "gesture and language," if the sleeper were to realize that the gap between the two is not absolute, the sleeper-reader might find ways of using hypertext to close the gap, to become a writer. In spite of her passivity, the fairy knows that if Rose were to take up the mechanism herself, the spell might be broken: "It's frustrating, she simply cannot, will not learn, and it sometimes makes the fairy, haunting too long this empty head, lose her temper, even though she knows that could she, would she, her own magical ends would surely be thwarted" (32). The ambiguity in the gendered pronouns reinforces the blending of the two women, suggesting that even the passive sleeper might become a writer if she would only decide to make use of the available technology.

When asked whether the fairy might be standing in for the author, Coover responded, "Maybe that does reflect back upon the author's own dilemma, though I hadn't thought of that before. What I think I had in mind when I wrote it, however, was that these eternal reenactments are indeed much like the spells of wicked fairies, and as spells they can be broken."[15] In other words, the fairy performs a function (storytelling) that is similar to authorship, but her purpose is equally to prolong the dream. The ambivalent role of the fairy resonates with Coover's views on teaching, which he sees as "a mistake, even, given my feelings about this vocation, immoral" (McQuade 61). Accordingly, as Gabe Hudson notes, Coover "has always, on principle, refused tenure, and is probably the only chaired adjunct professor in America."[16] If Coover sees himself as part of the Program Era, it is with a large dose of ambivalence.

The fairy represents a sort of teacher-authorship that is more directly implicated in the "bad spells" of what Coover calls the "Consciousness Industry." As Coover explains, "Much of that industry is devoted to sleep and a pampering of the unconscious. Consciousness is an accomplishment which requires enormous effort and so can be maintained only for limited periods, before, with great relief, we sink back into a mindless stupor."[17] As a figure for the teacher-writer, the fairy is caught up in a self-regenerating system that "tolerates the Writer when it is convenient to do so . . . , well aware that the Writer's bad behavior will be industrial fodder a generation on, the stuff of T-shirts and classrooms and bitter laments about the very industry that profits from them" (59–60).

Hypertext allowed Coover to offer his students the tools for getting outside the system. While the growth of the Internet later dampened Coover's initial optimism about the future of electronic literature,[18] he went on to help found the Electronic Literature Organization in 1999 and remained at Brown until his retirement in 2012. Ultimately, *Briar Rose* leaves the task of becoming a writer up to the students themselves. Coover views his own writing as a heroic struggle for "Consciousness," putting an end to the dreams/nightmares of stories that repeat. As a teacher, however, his role in the hypertext workshop suggests that writing might become more collaborative and, via the enchantments of the hypertext fairy, more open to the technological reinvention of the ideologically circumscribed body. Meanwhile, the implication of the teacher-fairy in prolonging the dream wryly suggests that students should perhaps stop listening to their teachers' stories in favor of crafting their own.

NOTES

1. Mark McGurl, *The Program Era: Postwar Fiction and the Rise of Creative Writing* (Cambridge: Harvard UP, 2009), 42.

2. Robert Coover, "Dying Fathers: Stirrings Still," *Kenyon Review* 23.2 (2001): 250–51.

3. Mary Caponegro, "Spanking the Form," *Review of Contemporary Fiction* 32.1 (Spring 2012): 91.

4. "El cómo del cuento," *Quimera: Revista de Literatura* 70–71 (Nov. 1987): 41.

5. Molly McQuade, "Robert Coover: Disturbing the Dogmas," *An Unsentimental Education: Writers and Chicago*, ed. Molly McQuade (Chicago: U of Chicago P, 1995), 251.

6. Robert Coover, *Briar Rose* (New York: Grove Press, 1996), 9, 25.

7. Elizabeth Ly Bell, "Robert Coover's Metaphorical Toy Box: Aleatory—No, Relentlessly Ludic—Yes," *Flashpoint* 15 (Spring 2013): n.p.

8. Marie C. Bouchet, "Between Wake and Sleep: Robert Coover's *Briar Rose*, a Playful Reawakening of *The Sleeping Beauty*," *Fairy Tales Reimagined: Essays on New Retellings*, ed. Susan Redington Bobby (Jefferson, NC: McFarland, 2009), 98.

9. Julian Pindar, "The Codex Unbound: The (Failed?) Promise of the Hypertext Novel," *Philament BOUND* 11 (Dec. 2007): 45.

10. Robert Coover, "The End of Books," *New York Times Book Review* 21.6 (1992): 24.

11. Robert Coover and Robert Scholes, *Briar Rose: A Hypertext Edition*, Brown University, 2007, http://www.brown.edu/Departments/MCM/people/scholes/BriarRose/texts/BRhome.htm.

12. Lydialyle Gibson, "Told and Retold: An Interview with Writer and Tale-Teller Robert Coover, AM'65," *University of Chicago Magazine*, May–June 2012, http://mag.uchicago.edu/arts-humanities/told-and-retold.

13. Michael Joyce, "Introducing Robert Coover (a Mixtape by Request)," *Review of Contemporary Fiction* 32.1 (2012): 169.

14. Robert Coover, "Body Games," *Kenyon Review* 24.1 (2002): 10–11.

15. Susana Pajares Tosca, "Interview with Robert Coover: 'I Am an Intransigent Realist,'" *Espéculo: Revista de estudios literarios* 12 (1999): n.p.

16. Gabe Hudson, "Notes on Craft: Some Instructions for Readers and Writers of American Fiction: An Interview with Robert Coover," *McSweeney's*, 22 June 2004, http://www.mcsweeneys.net/articles/notes-on-craft-some-instructions-for-readers-and-writers-of-american-fiction-an-interview-with-robert-coover.

17. Robert Coover, "Tale, Myth, Writer," *Brothers & Beasts: An Anthology of Men on Fairy Tales*, ed. Kate Bernheimer (Detroit: Wayne State UP, 2007), 57.

18. In a keynote address at a Digital Arts Conference (1999), Coover declared the passing of "the Golden Age of Hypertext," due partially to the effects of the World Wide Web, in which narratives are again linear, if media enhanced, while readers are returned to more passive positions: "in a sense, it's back to the movies again, that most passive and imperious of forms." "Literary Hypertext: The Passing of the Golden Age," *Feed Magazine*, (February 2000): n.p.

CHAPTER 8

What We Talk about When We Talk about Lish

MATTHEW BLACKWELL

In the 2014 film *Birdman*, Michael Keaton plays Riggan Thomson, a former action-movie star desperate to regain artistic legitimacy by writing, directing, and starring in a Broadway adaptation of Raymond Carver's story "What We Talk about When We Talk about Love." Early in the film his script is criticized by Mike Shiner, the star actor he has recruited to act opposite him, played by Edward Norton. Thomson reads lines taken directly from Carver's story: "I'm the wrong person to ask. I didn't even know the man. I've only heard his name mentioned in passing. I wouldn't know. You'd have to know the particulars." Shiner asks him why he is taking four lines to say what could be expressed in one, and Thomson cuts his lines to: "I'm the wrong person to ask. I didn't even know the guy, okay?" This scene sets up the dynamic of these characters' relationship, but it also testifies to the persistence of Carver's reputation as a writer of sparse, minimalist prose—part of the joke is that he is ridiculously ill suited for the melodramatic speeches of the Broadway stage. Carver's characters shouldn't speak; he is a writer renowned for showing, not telling. Even when the dialogue is taken straight from the source, it doesn't sound like Carver until it has been reduced to its barest essence.

This scene will remind those familiar with Carver's biography of the way that "What We Talk about When We Talk about Love," as well as the collection in which it was published, was edited by Gordon Lish. Carver wanted his characters to speak, and Lish silenced them. The 2009 publication of *Beginners*, the original manuscript version of *What We Talk about When We Talk about Love* (hereafter *WWTA*), makes clear the extent of Lish's heavy-handed approach. Lish reduced the length of "What We Talk About" by

50 percent, largely by cutting dialogue.[1] He cut other stories in the collection by upward of 70 percent, as well as changing their titles and even endings. Mark McGurl glosses over the Carver/Lish relationship in *The Program Era*, calling the controversy surrounding Lish's editing "considerably overblown."[2] McGurl instead writes about Lish as a pedagogue, both as a writer of grammar textbooks and a creative writing instructor. "Lish has been remarkable for what he might have been expected to do but hasn't: write a creative writing textbook," McGurl writes. "Instead his teaching is 'live,' conducted in real time, usually over the course of many hours continuously" (293). Moving from the production of grammar textbooks to the teaching of creative writing, Lish skipped the logical intermediary step of producing a creative writing textbook. In his role as editor at *Esquire* and Knopf, however, Lish combined the textual performance of his grammar textbooks with the "live" performance of his teaching by deploying his (in)famously magnetic personality to gain control of the final edits of the publications he chose to print. In this regard, *WWTA* is the strongest evidence we have of the interplay between Lish's overlapping roles of teacher, editor, and publisher.

Lish's editorial practice can be considered within McGurl's analytical framework. Carver's acceptance of Lish's edits was motivated by the "dialectic of shame and pride" (McGurl 284) experienced by those entering academia from lower-middle-class backgrounds. In much the same way that Lish exerted control over his workshop students through his connections in the publishing industry, he manipulated Carver, himself a product of a writing program. Lish met Carver's need for a magnetic personality that would lend him legitimacy in the publishing world. Lish in turn reworked Carver's stories according to his own design, using the cult author James Purdy as a model. Lish has cited Purdy's influence in several interviews, but Purdy has yet to be given a full critical treatment in this context.[3] McGurl calls Carver's politics "a politics of silence—a resistance, perhaps, to media overstimulation or maybe just the silencing, by shame, of the voice of the lower-middle-class worker" (315). This formulation is true of Carver's stories as they were edited by Lish but not as they were originally written. Carver's "politics of silence" results from Lish's transferal of Purdy's style onto Carver's stories. Purdy, as a gay writer struggling to get published in the 1940s and 1950s, often created characters whose inability to communicate dramatized the broader problem of the silencing of racial and sexual minorities. This inability to communicate, when transposed onto Carver's white, straight, lower-middle-class characters, loses its political valence and leaves them simply, and uneasily, quiet. This chapter seeks to account for their silence by mapping the ways that Lish's editorial method silenced Carver himself. Then a comparison of Purdy's story "Man and Wife" with "What We Talk about When We Talk about Love" will illustrate how Carver's seemingly apolitical minimalism is the product of his relationship with Lish.

Carver's deference to Lish led to the adoption of his stories into the curricula of creative writing programs. He was seemingly plucked from the obscurity of his blue-collar background and thrust into the literary limelight single-handedly by Lish through the publication of *Will You Please Be Quiet, Please?* He was then manipulated into accepting the edits for *WWTA* despite his misgivings. It was only after the emotionally draining process of *WWTA*'s publication and his subsequent success that Carver reined Lish in, requesting a lighter edit for *Cathedral.* In interviews he never mentioned Lish's part in the creation of *WWTA*, and his silence on the matter did nothing to discourage his growing reputation as a nearly obsessive reviser. Once we recognize *WWTA* as the product of a collaborative endeavor, though, we can begin to more accurately trace its literary lineage and better position it within the history of minimalism.

The publication history of *WWTA* has been a locus of critical attention since D. T. Max wrote about the manuscript for the *New York Times Magazine* in 1998.[4] Max described the manuscript as containing "pages full of editorial marks—strikeouts, additions and marginal comments in Lish's sprawling handwriting" (1). After Max's article, the project of accounting for the literary, social, and political causes and effects of Carver's minimalism turned into a controversy about Lish's editorial ethics. Richard Ford "feared that any discussion of the archives would 'inadvertently diminish Ray,'" while Mona Simpson downplayed the extent of Lish's involvement, saying, "I think people already assume an editor helps to make the work better. Who would want one who didn't?" (Max 6). This controversy has retained its fascination because it so dramatically illustrates the control that Lish exerted over the writers that he made famous, as well as the equivocal position in which those writers subsequently found themselves. Here we see Carver, Lish's most famous student, submitting to Lish's most manipulative and coercive pedagogical tactics.

Carver was initially eager to publish through Lish's patronage despite his editor's overweening presence. After approving a minor initial edit of *WWTA*, Carver signed a contract for its publication with Knopf. Only after this contract was signed did Lish send the more extreme final edit that was eventually published. In response, a panicked (and now contractually obligated) Carver wrote to Lish on July 8, 1980: "Dearest Gordon, I've got to pull out of this one. Please hear me. Please do the necessary things to stop production of the book. Please try and forgive me, this breach" (qtd. in Sklenicka 257). This letter is telling both in its pleading tone and its naïveté regarding the publication process. Carver signed his contract without consulting an agent or a lawyer, instead relying on his relationship with Lish. It's no coincidence that Carver was beginning his first stable academic job leading up to his acceptance of the contract for *WWTA*. His response to Lish's edits was informed by the dialectic of shame and pride in his new position. Newly arrived at Syracuse in January 1980 after a series of visiting professorships across the United States, Carver felt uncomfortable in his permanent position as full professor in the university's writing program. "I always think they're going to find me out and give me a janitor's job instead," he wrote to his friend Curt Johnson (353). Upon receiving the final edit of *WWTA*, still uncertain and ashamed of his success, he deflected the pride of his accomplishments onto the intervention of Lish, writing in the same July 8 letter to him, "This whole new life I have . . . everything, I owe to you for WILL YOU PLEASE" (357).[5] Unable to proceed with confidence in his own abilities as a writer, Carver instead returned to Lish as the source of his legitimacy. The pride of the publication of *Will You Please Be Quiet, Please?* gave way to the shame associated with upward mobility.

Lish's disregard for Carver's concerns—he told Max that "[m]y sense of it was that there was a letter and that I just went ahead" (4)—was antithetical to Carver's notion of pedagogical ethics. Carver learned through John Gardner, his creative writing teacher at Chico State, that writing short stories is a process of revision:

> It was a basic tenet of his that a writer found what he wanted to say in the ongoing process of seeing what he'd said. And this seeing, or seeing more clearly, came about through revision. He believed in revision, endless revision. . . . And he never seemed to lose patience rereading a student's story, even though he might have seen it in five previous incarnations.[6]

Carver adopted this approach for his own students' stories. Jay McInerney, a student of Carver's at Syracuse, remembers, "Manuscripts came back thoroughly ventilated with Carver deletions, substitutions, question marks, and chicken-scratch queries. I took one story back to him seven times; he must have spent fifteen or twenty hours on it."[7] This account bears more than a passing resemblance to Max's description of the *WWTA* manuscript. The difference is that in actively refusing Carver's input, Lish denied him the "ongoing process of seeing what he'd said." In doing so, he straddled the line between the writing workshop and the publishing world, playing on his teacher-student relationship with Carver to push forward his own designs.

The Carver-Lish relationship illustrates how the power dynamic of the writing workshop can operate outside the classroom, when a writer's entry into the arena of publishing is dependent on the mentorship of an established gatekeeper. Lish is a pivotal figure in the 2014 collection *MFA vs NYC: The Two Cultures of American Fiction* because of his simultaneous operation within both of these writing cultures. In his private writing workshops and seminars at NYU, Yale, and Columbia, Lish was known to groom his students for publication at *Esquire* and Knopf. Carla Blumenkranz, in her contribution to the volume, argues that this power dynamic was sexual. Lish's teaching technique was based on the seduction of his students. In writing workshops, "Actual sex is forbidden—but the most successful workshops (and classes in general) are the ones most charged with erotic potential."[8] Blumenkranz excludes Carver from this eroticized dynamic, arguing, "For cutting most of Carver's best-known stories to half their intended length, turning a deeply traditional writer into a groundbreaking minimalist, [Lish] is remembered as one the most controlling editors on record. But the more characteristic story of Lish as an editor and teacher is not a battle of wills, as was his work with Carver. Rather, it's an emotionally fraught collaboration with a most likely female student" (215). However, if we consider Lish's work with Carver as an example of what Wayne Koestenbaum has called the erotics of male literary collaboration, we can see this battle of wills was its own form of seduction.

In any male collaboration, there is a "writer who keenly feels lack or disenfranchisement, and seeks out a partner to attain power and completion. . . . Both the female hysteric and the man in search of a collaborator were striken [*sic*] with silence and paralysis; each overcame muteness by submitting to a mesmerizing man."[9] Lish's magnetic personality was a factor for Carver as much as it was for his workshop students. Carver, the disenfranchised blue-collar worker, needed a collaborator to give him a voice in the white-collar world, and Lish was more than willing to play the part. After meeting Carver through Curt Johnson in Palo Alto, among Lish's first lessons for his new student was an exercise in sexuality. "Maryann Burk-Carver recalls them walking down a Palo Alto street with Lish asking every woman they passed to sleep with him; he was trying to prove to Carver that you only had to ask to get what you wanted from life" (Max 3). Eighteen months after this meeting, Lish had an editorship at *Esquire* and Carver had his link to the publishing world. Ironically, however, in submitting to Lish's magnetic personality in order to find his voice, Carver simultaneously forfeited control over that voice. Lish's seduction worked, and it gained him the final say in the collaborative endeavor that produced *WWTA*.

Treating *WWTA* as the product of a collaboration allows us to recognize its place in literary history as more complicated than the standard story that casts it as the progeny of Chekhov and Hemingway and the forebear of countless writing workshop hopefuls. The short stories of James Purdy are a crucial part of this history. According to Carol Sklenicka, Purdy's stories "exceed Carver's in the sharpness of the scalpel they use to autopsy conventional emotions. Lish was under the influence of [Grace] Paley and Purdy 'in every respect' and admired Purdy's sense of 'the dark, the unexplained, the uncanny'" (215). Purdy struggled to make a living as a writer, working as a teacher until he could make enough money from his fiction. His stories were initially rejected by many New York publishing houses in the 1940s and 1950s due to their subject matter. Openly gay, Purdy focused on the fringes of society with an unflinching eye—his world is often populated with characters who are marginalized because of their homosexuality, disabilities, or ethnicity. He writes in his "Autobiographical Sketch," "My stories were always returned with angry, peevish, indignant rejections from the New York slick magazines, and they earned, if possible, even more hostile comments from the little magazines. All editors were insistent that I would never be a published writer."[10] Purdy eventually found a successful businessman and Henry James scholar, Osborn Andreas, to privately publish his first short story collection, *Don't Call Me by My Right Name and Other Stories*, in 1956. This volume's cult following led to his first commercially published book, *63: Dream Palace: A Novella and Nine Stories*, the following year. By the mid-1970s, he was recognized as important enough to warrant two critical biographies, but he has generally stayed outside the mainstream. Lish, however, saw that inflecting Carver's stories with the sense of alienation found in Purdy's minimalism would provide an edge to what he saw as his traditional style.

The uneasy silence that permeates *WWTA* has its genesis in the stories Purdy published in the 1950s. Denis Donoghue, in his review of *WWTA*, writes, "In Raymond Carver's stories, it is dangerous even to speak. Conversation completes the damage people have already done to one another in silence. It is not safe to form a sentence or even to speak a name. To say 'Duane' or 'Holly' is to pronounce yet another doom" (*WWTA*, front matter). This anxiety surrounding communication is present in many of Purdy's stories as well, but the political concerns from which it arises are most explicitly foregrounded in "Man and Wife." The story centers on a conversation between Lafe, recently fired from his factory job after being outed as a homosexual, and his wife, Peaches Maud. Sitting in the kitchen of their low-rent apartment, periodically interrupted by the noise of their broken refrigerator, Lafe is trying to explain the cause of his dismissal. Though Lafe's sexuality is clearly the subject of their conversation, Peaches is literally deaf to his explanation. "And for the rest, I don't know what in hell you are really talking about," she says, "and my ears won't let me catch what you seem to be telling."[11] Lafe's sexuality is imbricated with the couple's personal, economic, and social circumstances. They are childless because, according to Peaches, "we could never afford for me to be a mother" (62). They live in an apartment "with nothing but foreigners around us and that busted refrigerator and no ventilation but heat from the roof, but thank Jesus nobody don't know us" (67). It's not until the end of the story that Peaches reveals she knew about Lafe's sexuality throughout their marriage. Ghettoized, racialized, made poor and childless not by Lafe's homosexuality but by their unwillingness to speak of it, the couple in "Man and Wife" have already damaged one another through their silence. In the story's ambivalent final line, their relationship is also consigned to silence. "'Peaches,' he said, and as he paused in his speech, the name he had always called her seemed to move over into the silence and vacancy of the broken refrigerator. 'I will always stand by you anyhow, Peaches Maud'" (69). What standing by her will mean, despite (or because of) their marginalized position, is left to the reader.

The silences before Lafe's final confession are charged with political meaning because the circumstances of the couple's life together—why they live where they do; why they don't have children, why they don't socialize—are predicated on what has been left unsaid up to that point. What is left unsaid by Carver's characters rarely carries this weight, divorced as they are from such social circumstances. "What We Talk about When We Talk about Love," which is titled "Beginners" in Carver's original version, also centers on a conversation around a kitchen table. In this case, however, there are two couples, both sociable, white, straight, economically comfortable, and with children. Mel is discoursing on what (white, straight) love is and is not: it is not the so-called love that his second wife, Terri, had with her abusive and suicidal ex-lover Ed. Terri describes his abuse: "He beat me up one night. He dragged me around the living room by my ankles. He kept saying, 'I love you, I love you, you bitch.' He went on dragging me around the living room. My head kept knocking on things." Terri looked around the table. "What do you do with love like that?"[12] As a contrast, Mel tells a story of an elderly couple whom he treated in his medical practice. After an automobile accident that left them both in the hospital, the husband was depressed not because of his injuries but because he couldn't look at his wife through the eyeholes in his full-body cast. Mel and Terri, along with the narrator, Nick, and his wife, Laura, have been drinking throughout Mel's speech, and the story ends when the alcohol runs out:

> "Gin's gone," Mel said.
>
> Terri said, "Now what?"
>
> I could hear my heart beating. I could hear everyone's heart. I could hear the human noise we sat there making, not one of us moving, not even when the room went dark. (*WWTA* 154)

This ending, which is entirely Lish's invention, finds its power in its abrupt shift to silence, in the question of "Now what?" that is ultimately up to the reader to answer. It remains unknown whether Mel and Terri and Nick and Laura will end like the suicidal Ed or like the exemplary elderly couple. Like Lafe and Peaches, their future is held in this moment of indeterminacy that leaves their respective relationships unresolved.

The only politics to be found here are in the relationships between these four characters. As McGurl notes, in Carver "the politics of gender relations—the personal as the political—is the single vestige of the idea of conflict between groups, between organized, or at least organizable, political interests, that we are ever asked to contemplate" (315). This singular political valence is itself muted by Lish's intervention, however. In Carver's original "Beginners," Mel leaves the kitchen at the end of the story and Terri reveals that she was pregnant with Ed's child during his first suicide attempt. She decided on an abortion, and it was Mel who carried out the operation. She then begins to cry, and Laura comforts her:

> "Terri, sweetheart," Laura said to her tenderly. "It'll be okay, you'll see. It'll be okay."
>
> Laura raised her eyes to mine then. Her look was penetrating, and my heart slowed. She gazed into my eyes for what seemed a long time, and then she nodded. That's all she did, the only sign she gave, but it was enough. It was as if she were telling me, Don't worry, we'll get past this everything is going to be all right with us, you'll see. Easy does it. That's the way I chose to interpret the look anyway, though I could be wrong.[13]

In Lish's edit, Terri's discussion of domestic abuse ends with a question that serves to contain her experience within the abstract: "What do you do with love like that?" In Carver's original, the emotional consequences of her abuse and the question of Mel's complicity in her abortion highlight the complexities of her situation. Her revelation to Laura and Nick, as well as Laura's commiseration with her, suggests the regenerative potential of communication. Laura's sign to Nick, still indeterminate but indicative of the possibility of understanding, anticipates the optimistic tone of the stories in *Cathedral*, published after Carver had learned his lesson about the role his teacher-editor was to take in the production of his stories.

The politics of "Beginners," as limited in scope as they may be, suggest a more general concern on Carver's part for the role of communication in interpersonal relationships. Carver held out hope for communication's redemptive power even as Lish transformed his work into the sparse, workshop-ready stories that came to define minimalism. Traces of Purdy's style can be found in many of Carver's stories of this era. By borrowing the style of stories like "Man and Wife" while disregarding their politics, however, Lish replaced the complexity of "Beginners" with the indeterminacy of "What We Talk about When We Talk about Love," leaving James Purdy an unwitting participant in the depoliticization of Carver Country.

NOTES

1. Raymond Carver, "'Beginners,' Edited," *New Yorker*, 24 Dec. 2007, http://public.wsu.edu/~bryanfry/Beginners%20Edited.pdf.

2. Mark McGurl, *The Program Era: Postwar Fiction and the Rise of Creative Writing* (Cambridge: Harvard UP, 2009), 446 n28.

3. See, for example, D. T. Max, "The Carver Chronicles," *New York Times Magazine*, 9 Aug. 1998, 3; Carol Polsgrove, *It Wasn't Pretty, Folks, but Didn't We Have Fun? Esquire in the Sixties* (New York: W. W. Norton, 1995), 243; and Carol Sklenicka, *Raymond Carver: A Writer's Life* (New York: Scribner, 2010), 215.

4. Max's article provides a useful historical marker in Carver criticism. Critics writing before the article's 1998 publication treat Carver's texts as his own relatively independent productions, while critics writing after this year address Lish's intervention as a matter of course.

5. Sklenicka attributes the tone of this letter to Carver's relatively newfound sobriety, though his move to Syracuse exhibits many of the "opportunities for shame" that McGurl cites through Rita Felski: "geographic and other forms of social mobility, which provide an infinite array of chances for failure, for betraying by word or gesture that one does not belong to one's environment" (qtd. in McGurl 285).

6. Raymond Carver, "John Gardner: Writer and Teacher," *Georgia Review* 55.4/56.1 (Winter 2001/Spring 2002): 128.

7. Jay McInerney, "Raymond Carver, Mentor," *Remembering Ray*, ed. William L. Stull and Maureen P. Carroll (Santa Barbara: Capra Press, 1993), 124.

8. Carla Blumenkranz, "Seduce the Whole World," *MFA vs NYC: The Two Cultures of American Fiction*, ed. Chad Harbach (New York: n+1/Faber and Faber, 2014), 214. Lish finds this reading accusatory and told a *Newsweek* reporter that he considered suing Blumenkranz after her article first appeared. See "An Angry Flash of Gordon," *Newsweek Global* 162.25 (2014): 1–8.

9. Wayne Koestenbaum, *Double Talk: The Erotics of Male Literary Collaboration* (New York: Routledge, 1989), 2, 6.

10. Don Adams, "James Purdy's Allegories of Love," *Texas Studies in Literature and Language* 50.1 (2008): 1–33.

11. James Purdy, *The Complete Short Stories of James Purdy* (New York: Liveright, 2013), 61.

12. Raymond Carver, *What We Talk about When We Talk about Love* (New York: Vintage, 1989), 138.

13. Raymond Carver, *Beginners* (London: Jonathan Cape, 2009), 198.

CHAPTER 9

Timely Exile

James Alan McPherson, the Iowa Writers' Workshop, and Black Creativity

MICHAEL HILL

Daylanne English, in a recent study, concludes that African American writers "are fully *of* their time—or 'coeval,' to use Johannes Fabian's anthropological term." Fleshing out her point, she writes, "This coeval status underlies my argument that many [black authors] have been full, if generally unacknowledged participants in their period's major cultural developments and philosophical debates."[1] Mark McGurl's *The Program Era* affirms English's claim by showing that black writers were key presences in the establishment of creative writing programs. Looking at such programs, McGurl contends that the English departments of America's colleges and universities became sites where an "experiential" economy flourished.[2] His thesis brilliantly captures shifts within a national institution, and by engaging writers like Ernest Gaines, Toni Morrison, and Ishmael Reed, he establishes how black experiences imbricate the phenomenon that he explores. While his analysis grasps the link between changes on campuses and literary production, his neglect of James Alan McPherson, the first African American to win a Pulitzer Prize for fiction, weakens his account of creative writing programs' impact on black artistry. McPherson's studies in the Iowa Writers' Workshop reveal alternative facets of the institutionalization of creativity. More precisely, McPherson's battles with exile underscore the ambivalence that a generation of black writers felt as they achieved the rewards of bourgeois American culture. This ambivalence led them to forge a literary aesthetic that decreased anxieties about combining American values and black cultural autonomy.

McPherson was not the first African American to attend the Iowa Writers' Workshop. In fact, by the time he showed up in 1968, the legacy of black

Workshoppers stretched back thirty years to pioneering first-decade attendees like Margaret Walker (1939–40, 1962–65) and Herbert Nipson (1946–49). McPherson's more immediate predecessors included the poet Michael Harper, who arrived in 1961; the talented Dianne Oliver, who entered in 1965 and died before she received her MFA; and the fiction writer John Edgar Wideman, who matriculated in 1966 fresh off his Rhodes Scholarship. McPherson's Workshop odyssey resembles the journeys of his black forebears in that he was the only African American in the program when he attended and used his University of Iowa (UI) tenure to inaugurate an auspicious career. If he in these ways emblematizes a black norm, then the timing of his arrival at Iowa and the stops he made beforehand show that his representativeness also holds important distinctions.

He hails from the Jim Crow South: Savannah, Georgia. In this he recalls Margaret Walker, a woman raised in segregated Mississippi; however, whereas she came out of Dixie during the Depression and landed at UI by way of Northwestern University, McPherson matriculated in fall 1968 and spent time at Morris Brown and Harvard that conditioned his outlook on the heartland. He left Savannah in the early 1960s to enroll at Morris Brown, a historically black school in Atlanta. After taking an undergraduate degree there, he joined a black cohort who was pursuing training in Ivy League professional schools and studied law at Harvard. This elite episode during the tapering days of the civil rights era contextualized McPherson's Workshop entry and distinguished him from other black creative writing students. By virtue of this distinction, he functions as a complicated allegory in which late twentieth-century mysteries regarding blackness, art, and participatory democracy can be unpacked.

Midwestern Exile

Eugene Garber taught fiction in the Workshop during the 1960s, and as part of his appointment he served on the admissions committee. Describing that service, he wrote, "The fiction workshop had gotten much too big—about 120, as I recall. Applicants of promise were very numerous . . . so we cut down to accepting about one applicant in every 6 or 8."[3] Garber establishes his epoch as one in which the Workshop became more selective. When he comments that this selectivity allowed him to "read the application fiction of many good people," he mentions two examples by name; one of them is James Alan McPherson ("Letter to Steve Wilbers"). McPherson's entry into Iowa's MFA program produces a buzz. Because of his talent, he emerges as a poster child for a cohort of stellar recruits in the Workshop. McPherson embodies that historical reality; however, he also reveals the plight of a black student at an overwhelmingly white institution.

When he stepped on the UI campus in 1968, McPherson entered an environment that bristled with transformative energy. Garber identified the admissions issues that preoccupied Workshop administrators, and without a doubt these preoccupations heralded the consolidation of the creative writing program's status as a mecca for aspiring writers. The Workshop's rising profile reflects its reputation as a space where opportunities flourished. Though McPherson participated in this particular evolution of educational opportunity, he also arrived amid tempestuous historical tides that affected students throughout the university and the nation. The unrest at colleges and universities following the 1968 assassinations of Martin Luther King Jr. and Robert F. Kennedy revealed the anxieties of a young generation struggling to find its moral bearings. Where the wide-ranging results of this crisis impacted all students, the effects on black students proved unique. Black students experienced King's death as a dramatic indication of America's indifference to their reality. Struck by this stubborn ignorance, their calls for black studies increased in volume. As administrators became more receptive to demands that had been gestating for more than half a century, institutions of higher education scrambled to grant the courses, majors, and professors that students required. This situation surfaced at UI; however, it unfolded in a manner befitting the university's special history.

Black students at Iowa emblematize the mixed legacy that defines even the most progressive predominantly white, midwestern public universities. While the school did not practice the crippling racism that kept blacks off the grounds of the University of Missouri, its admission of African Americans nonetheless lacked enthusiasm. This tolerant yet distant institutional posture prevailed well beyond the *Brown v. Board* decision in 1954, but as the civil rights movement captured the country's imagination, the climate at Iowa changed.[4] The emergence of administrators like Phil Hubbard and Willard Boyd signaled the university's embrace of policies that prioritized making minorities partners in creating a community. Garber's focus on McPherson's talent suggests one means whereby such partnering could take place. Black writers like McPherson could contribute to Workshop founder Paul Engle's desire to "run the future of American literature . . . through" Iowa City.[5] Despite McPherson's recognition that he might redeem democratic ideals when he came to UI, he also noted that the post–civil rights era held causes for uncertainty.

During the spring of 1968 when James Earl Ray assassinated Martin Luther King Jr., McPherson was in his final semester at Harvard Law School. He felt King's violent death as a powerful blow to America's social progress, and on a personal level it reinforced his determination to forgo a legal career and become a writer. McPherson had been toying with this path less traveled for more than a year. In his mind, it boiled down to what he elsewhere termed a "problem of fidelities."[6] For the black lawyer, the more liberal social environment put social ascendancy easily within reach. McPherson saw the financial rewards awaiting those who joined the corporate bar, and figures like Charles Hamilton Houston and Thurgood Marshall made it clear that civil rights lawyering conferred immense civic respect. Notwithstanding his chance to have either of these two different brands of bourgeois prestige, he rejected such professional possibilities. This rejection reflected McPherson's belief that the American author could serve the public with the same efficacy as an attorney. By adopting this mind-set, he signaled a faith in writing that produced tremendous consequences for his literary aesthetic. His earliest publications clarify the complex consequences of this faith.

During a six-month spurt from November 1968 to April 1969, the *Atlantic* published three of McPherson's short stories. Thus, decades before Ta-Nehisi Coates vaulted to stardom by gracing its pages, McPherson was the hot, young black author whose career blossomed by receiving the imprimatur of a major mainstream publication. He certainly enjoyed the endorsement of a white creative community; however, he realized that his artistic development would require elements that could not be cultivated in coronations offered by the New York publishing establishment. He sought to find these elements in Roxbury, a black section of Boston. At the same moment that he honed his writing chops by crafting fiction for the *Atlantic*, McPherson also worked for the *Bay State Banner*, a Roxbury newspaper. His newspaper work in some ways marked his embrace of a writer's rite of passage that goes back more than two centuries in American letters. While McPherson would not blanch at that description of his journalistic endeavors, he also craved the newspaper work because his assignments regularly put him in contact with the black community. His sequestering in Cambridge for law school had separated him from such social encounters. Through roaming the nooks and crannies of Roxbury, he once again witnessed the nuances of black social contact. His witnessing textured his outlook on art.

Although the *Bay State Banner* primarily served a local area, McPherson's reporting also engaged national issues. He wrote about one such story in the 1993 essay, "Ivy Day in the Empty Room." Describing an assignment from July 1968, he remarked, "My employer, the editor of *The Bay State Banner* has given his permission for me to do a story for the paper on Resurrection City, a sea of tents occupied by representatives of the nation's poor on the Mall, alongside the Reflecting Pool, in Washington, D.C. Because this black paper is poor and understaffed, I pay my own way to the capitol, and take my own pictures."[7]

The chance to see striking events firsthand provokes McPherson to inconvenience himself. Although race figures in his calculations, since he writes for a black newspaper and some of the poor that he meets are African American, his appetite for covering such events stems from a fundamental conviction about the writer's obligation to a capacious curiosity. McPherson's sense of this obligation entails acknowledging his nation's capacity to honor its creeds even as it often frustratingly failed at fulfilling those lofty goals. Between the *Atlantic* and the *Banner*, he confronted this American attribute in vexing paradoxes of interracial generosity and intraracial revelation. McPherson's contemplation of how these paradoxes circulate forms the intellectual context that shaped his decision to apply to and attend the Workshop. In the same two-year span when black middle-class professionalism, white publishers, and black environments mingle in his ruminations about creating a writing consciousness, he—not coincidentally—strikes up a correspondence with Ralph Ellison.

A crucial basis of McPherson's relationship with Ellison is his conviction that the older man can help him become a powerful writer. In a letter dated January 22, 1970, he tells Ellison that in winter 1969 he was oscillating between writing and the law as a means of making a living. Explaining why he appealed to Ellison, he declares, "When I wrote to you last winter, I indicated that I would like to come to New York for a talk. This was not in anticipation of an article: at that time I had no connection with the *Atlantic*. I merely wanted to talk to you because I recognized that you were an artist, a man produced by my own cultural group, who possessed experiences, insights and an intellect much deeper and far superior to my own." McPherson frets over the moral implications of picking the pen as a way of life. He dealt with this personally; however, in his exchanges with Ellison, he suggested that this was not only a personal dilemma but also a generational conundrum. He comments: "I had accomplished more at 24, in terms of education, experiences and recognition, than my father and his father and his father's father. I had achieved in less than one generation much more than they had in three. . . . I had skipped a generation, perhaps two, and these things bothered me." He continued: I "have made an extremely rapid advancement into some very close proximity to the mainstream. . . . Yet, [I] feel impulses to retreat exclusively into Negro culture, or else [I] feel compelled to join our fellow (but third generation) [white and Jewish] expatriates in the search for something else, even if it is nihilism."[8] McPherson's remarks betray a reckoning regarding his situation that questions the meaning of progress. Evaluating his accomplishments, he admits that his life holds more achievements educationally and economically than the lives of his male elders. This laureling provides little direction, and he casts about for a rudder in the sea of social unrest. Capturing the dilemma of a younger generation burdened by the prize of social possibility, he also limns his creative mood on the eve of his arrival in Iowa City. He eventually solicits Ellison for support as he works through these quandaries; nonetheless, the Workshop emerges as McPherson's first response to a deep-seated confusion. Reaching out to the creative writing program for answers, he validates McGurl's comments about students as clients who seek an experiential commodity in their trip through higher education.

In his January 22, 1970, epistle to Ellison, McPherson cosigns this sentiment, saying that "the university" is "the best place to be, for whatever insights were available" regarding the "alienation" of the age. McPherson defined the alienation of the age by sketching a talented individual who transcended the broader condition of his tribe even as his transcendence owed debts to that very condition. In "You Tell Me It's the Institution: Creative Writing and Literary History," Kenneth Warren expresses how the creative writing program stages and then makes usable such complicated negotiations. He writes, "The ethnic writer who initially believes that her experience lies well outside the boundaries of the literary, the MFA becomes, paradoxically, the mechanism by which the kinds of experience once deemed not fit for literature become instead its essence." Encapsulating this experience, Warren avers, "Alienation produces a sort of psychic repatriation. What one finds in a place far from home are the tools and the authorization to speak for one's aggrieved but resilient people."[9] Warren's statement neatly documents how what McGurl calls "high cultural pluralism" (56) serves as a big tent under which writers from a multitude of ethnicities can gather and receive a blessing from the American educational establishment. While by the 1980s the culture wars routinized heated debates about such transactions, McPherson's exile in and from the Workshop heralds his evolution from an MFA student who was nurtured via absence to a graduate who discovered utopian collaboration. His path from being a student in the late 1960s to being an illustrious alumnus in the 1970s epitomizes the difficulty of wedding democratic possibility and black artistic ambition. I close this chapter by considering the Workshop's place in McPherson's marriage of conscientious citizenship and black creativity.

Art as Public Service

As discussed previously, pregnant events framed McPherson's soul searching as he pondered ways to make writing a viable service profession. He observed conspicuous blows to America's moral commitments, and on the creative front, his allegiances to both the *Atlantic* and the *Bay State Banner* reflected his ambivalence regarding where a socially relevant author should work. He decides to enroll at the Workshop as he ponders these matters, and his decision bears careful scrutiny. McPherson—because he spent his undergraduate summers as a dining-car waiter—is familiar with every part of America from the East to the West. Although his frontier-chasing youth awakened his participation in the national fraternity of masculine self-discovery, his decision to relocate from New England to the Midwest completes a telling triangle, one that connects to archetypal circuits.

McPherson begins his educational odyssey in Atlanta, and during summer 1965, he makes a trip north to Cambridge that aligns him not only with black predecessors propelled by the Great Migration but also with literary luminaries like Quentin Compson, the protagonist of William Faulkner's *Absalom, Absalom!* (1936). Through this relocation, he nourishes the curiosity that blossoms as artistic aspiration and, taking a page from Ellison, discovers the inextricable cultural interrelatedness that binds America together. The move to Iowa City from Cambridge then forms another chapter in McPherson's tour of his nation's psychic geography. From a literary standpoint, his relocation from New England to the Midwest allies him with Jim Burden, the prairie-loving romantic in Willa Cather's *My Ántonia* (1918), and Nick Caraway, the disaffected escapee of elite carelessness in F. Scott Fitzgerald's *The Great Gatsby* (1925). While the literary subtexts of McPherson's movements may seem ornamental, they actually reveal the ways in which a national mythology interconnected with his choices and definitely with his explanations of those choices. If his explanations of his wide-ranging exposure celebrate the Omni-American dimensions of such unpredictable experiences, then upon his arrival at UI much of what McPherson felt was disorientation.[10] His response to that disorientation did not include a dutiful acceptance of the Workshop as an institution that could provoke high cultural writing and naturalize a black man as a legitimate writer; rather, the Workshop served as a literal and aesthetic space of meandering. Beneath this airy conception, McPherson's disposition betrayed the convictions of an exile.

McPherson, as a Workshopper, seems to be equally defined by absence and presence. Later, when he goes to work at the Workshop in the 1980s, he emerges as one of the most eloquent apologists for the spiritual vitality of Iowa City. Such celebrations mark his tenure as an instructor, but on the graduate student front, he straddles the Iowa City that promises to confirm his evolving Omni-American worldview and a sensitivity to the calamitous history that arranged blacks and whites along clenched fault lines in the United States of the late 1960s and early 1970s. His experiences in 1968 prove illustrative. Unlike Michael Harper, who in retrospectives about his time at the Workshop lamented feelings of isolation in Iowa City, McPherson, who never expansively chronicles his experiences as a student in the Workshop, nonetheless juxtaposes the oasis of Iowa City with other spaces roiled by racial conflict. Vivid examples of such juxtaposition are the nonfiction pieces that he publishes in 1969 just months after he arrives at the Workshop. In a two-article series about the Blackstone Rangers, "a street gang" in "the Woodlawn area of Chicago's South Side ghetto," McPherson patiently presents the ambivalent sentiments that the Blackstone Rangers inspire.[11] He meticulously catalogues the complex factors that surround the gang's oscillations between violent criminality and progressive activism. Although McPherson's gripping prose reflects his rapidly maturing nonfiction style, his focus on Chicago, a midwestern city not even four hours away from the Workshop, defines an interesting conflation. Such linkages produce one effect when they surface as he attended Workshop classes; however, their persistence into the later years of his enrollment in the Workshop when he matriculated long-distance produces even more complicated effects.

McPherson's first semester at the Workshop is fall 1968. Since he would have begun classes for the semester somewhere in either August or September, the fact that two years later, by fall 1970, he holds a teaching position at the University of California, Santa Cruz, seems plausible yet noteworthy. Despite the truisms regarding presence as a pretext for learning, McPherson's years at the Workshop feature far more absence than they do actual residency. He road-trips between Chicago and Iowa City conducting research for stories that he will publish in the *Atlantic.* By his third and fourth year when he finally settles down to write the thesis that will allow him to graduate, he leaves Iowa City. What should be made of such a situation? Innumerable Workshop graduates have testified that grueling evaluations in seminars and lively informal exchanges around town form the twin tracks where their artistic education gained the clearest momentum. By commuting to Chicago and relocating to California during his education at UI, McPherson closes the door on making either appearing in the sheets or huddling with respected peers a central part of his Workshop experience. He admits, at least in autobiographies circa 1969, that he held "a post as a teacher of Afro-American literature," yet that avowal of his teaching seemingly constitutes a hollow commitment to sampling Iowa City's fabled treasures.[12] McPherson's exilic consciousness clarifies how a patchwork oscillation around the Workshop eventually surfaces as a prelude to deliverance.

McPherson repeatedly uses the notion of exile to express his position in the world. In a 1987 essay, "Going Up to Atlanta," he states, "Like all permanent exiles, I have learned to be at home inside myself."[13] More than a decade later, his essay collection, *A Region Not Home* (2000), carried the subtitle, *Reflections from Exile.* If multiple travels both intra- and internationally inform McPherson's perception of his exile status, then his tenure as a student in the Workshop shows two revealing facets of this condition. First, McPherson exists as a man banished from home because he is a black student at an overwhelmingly white university. He captures aspects of this situation when he discusses how his refulgent existence allows him to be smarter, more cosmopolitan, and more affluent than his parents. Although he had attended Harvard and thus been exposed to this reality, his familiarity does not obviate the fact that at Iowa for the second time in very short span, he was studying in an environment where he constituted a distinct minority. Second, this physical isolation dovetailed with an experience of psychological disorientation, and in this convergence, we see the genesis of McPherson's evolution regarding the overall efficacy of Iowa City specifically and the Midwest more generally. In some ways, his shift in outlook recalls Ralph Ellison's frontier thesis, a position extolling the spiritual nurturing of the Midwest that the older writer developed in many autobiographical pieces. Ellison called the Midwest home; thus, his perspectives absorbed long and varied conditioning. Before McPherson could be home in Iowa, he first had to experience it as a strange place. His Workshop experiences involve such confrontations with strangeness, and they engage McGurl's hypothesis about the ethnic writer's status as "the outsider inside, the *inside-outer*, if you will" (338). Whereas McGurl believes that this status applies to "all artists on campus," I want to contend that the peculiar conditions a black writer confronted as he entered an MFA program in creative writing during fall 1968 meant that his vocabulary of expression resulted in a distinct kind of creativity. McPherson's peregrinations during his sojourn at the Workshop fueled his discovery of voice in the season that Gil Scott-Heron and Brian Jackson termed "Winter in America."[14] Touching briefly on McPherson's thesis and his award-winning collection *Elbow Room* (1977), I aver that McPherson's Workshop exile proves productive.

Three of the stories that make up McPherson's MFA thesis appear in revised form in *Elbow Room*. While the credential of a creative writing degree signals one aspect of a black writer's triumph over exile, his emergence as the first Pulitzer Prize–winning African American fiction writer conveys an even more decisive creative accomplishment. The Workshop's place in McPherson's artistic development suggests both the merits and limits of a creative writing program's involvement in a black author's creative gestation. Whereas McPherson enrolls at Iowa hoping to infuse bourgeois ascendency with a King-like moral mission, he confronts an institution that is ill equipped for such nuanced negotiations of black artistic identity. The conventions of a high cultural pluralistic aesthetic strike him as technically replete; however, with a skepticism that echoes the sentiments of black practitioners in several art forms, McPherson wonders about the spiritual ethos that animates the Workshop. On the one hand, this surfaces under the familiar heading of alienation and the convenient shorthand of insider-outsider status. This anxiety persists in twenty-first-century debates about minority students on predominantly white campuses, and certainly, McPherson, after his time at Morris Brown, may have wondered about the scarcity of black professors at both Harvard and Iowa. On the other hand, as Hoyt Fuller has noted, McPherson may have resolutely tried to keep the "color part" of his work "in the background" (Fuller 88), yet he does seek out Ellison precisely because the elder writer is both experienced and black. Perhaps, if Ellison had accepted Vance Bourjaily's job offer and become the first black Workshop faculty member in 1959, then McPherson's spiritual suspicions about the Workshop might not have been so acute. Ellison was not a UI professor, and in fact, the Workshop did not have a full-time black faculty member until McPherson himself took a position in 1981. Thus, his school days retained an apprehension about what white spaces could teach him about writing in a world with a black face. While his actions betrayed an exhausting struggle with this reality, his writing reveals a telling shift.

McPherson's first short-story collection chronicles exile as a state of lament. Capturing experiences as varied as a fall from faith to the demise of a service ethos, in *Hue and Cry* he made the individual banished or separated from anchoring rituals a figure of dignified yet wounded resignation. In his thesis stories and his second volume of short fiction, the exile persistently emerges as a symbol of enlightenment. Space constraints will not permit me to undertake the close readings that would show the precise unfolding of this trend in McPherson's work; however, his ability to grow in this way signals an evolving outlook on where the Workshop fits into black literary expression. Whereas McPherson's requests for Ellison's guidance imply that no matter what else it taught, the Workshop could not teach him to be a black writer, his willingness to tinker with exile, a seminal theme in his art, indicates that the institution provoked effective reflection. His presence at the Workshop costs him emotional comfort; nevertheless, it presages how expanded black access to prestigious white educational spaces fuels the paradoxical realities of American democracy in the 1980s and 1990s. UI generally and the Workshop specifically offer glimpses of McPherson's struggle to make the black writer's life a viable civic vocation, and when we place his efforts in the broader context of black literary history in the 1960s and 1970s, we sense why his ideas about blackness and the Midwest illuminate artistic practice.

Morning in America

James Alan McPherson fits into a continuum that runs from Ralph Ellison to Charles Johnson. In many ways, this trio defines a significant yet understudied path in late twentieth-century African American literature. No sane case could be made that Ellison is an invisible figure in contemporary literary inquiry; however, because of his integrative notions about race and culture, many revisionists have read him out of black literature except as a foil for Wright and the Black Arts movement. When Ellison makes a comeback in scholarly conversations about African American literature, he is treated as a shrine where latter-day talents like Jeffrey Renard Allen, Trey Ellis, and Colson Whitehead pray for racially transcendent aesthetics. This account of Ellison threatens to naturalize his ardent resistance to the Black Arts movement as either a textbook case of self-hating racial betrayal or a reified oracle whom people mined for permission to declare a postracial utopia. McPherson wrote to Ellison because the elder writer endured painful episodes where these kinds of determinations were being debated. Through his musings on exile, his matriculation at the Workshop, and his experience of mainstream acclaim, McPherson clarifies the ways that black male writers' refusal to repudiate their interest in blackness or American identity not only challenged the manifest text of black literary expression but also signaled their eloquent acknowledgment that an inability to honor the nation's loftiest ideals should not invalidate the nourishing possibilities of American democratic consciousness. McPherson gleaned this insight in his Workshop sojourn.

McGurl correctly identifies how creative writing programs authorized ethnic writers to establish their experiences as worthy subjects of literature. While he suggests that high cultural pluralism becomes an Esperanto that allows a wide range of minority authors to arrange themselves along a legitimated continuum, he neglects how episodes of failed mutuality spark more sophisticated developments. McPherson's engagements with the Workshop demonstrate one such situation. As an MFA student, he saw the UI as a bunker where festering racial turmoil yielded to sanguine meditations on the writer's vocation. He respected the need for technical acuity in art, yet he yearned for the immediate affirmation that swirled about him in the rhetoric of the black aesthetic. Though he admired such ambitions, he sensed that fulfilling them would require less parochialism and more cosmopolitanism. He set about discovering a viable expressive style, and as he did so, his movements through Iowa City became crucial touch points for his negotiations of exile. Within his graduate school experience, these negotiations centered on the earliest days of a post–civil rights era that brought anxious wonderment about choosing writing rather than law as a profession.

McPherson's Workshop tenure did not end with him as a student. In 1981, he returned to the Workshop to teach, and by doing so, he completed an arc that he had begun thirteen years earlier. I previously argued that his fiction after his Workshop studies reflected a changed perspective on exile; here I contend that McPherson's return concludes a protracted mulling over of Iowa City. In the context of Reagan Era rifts in national unity, he finally discovers that the heartland's access to spiritual vitality hurdled whatever barriers racial reality erected. This ability to reach decisions that are decades long in the making underscores another facet of the black writer's experience in creative writing programs: the staying power to expand one's impressions. In this way, McPherson's trip from student to teacher signals not only an ideological shift but also a professional progress. The Omni-American contingent in black literature insists on scrutinizing such changes, and as scholars scrutinize their insistence, interludes like McPherson's Workshop days will fill central pieces of the tradition's puzzle.

NOTES

1. Daylanne English, *Each Hour Redeem: Time and Justice in African American Literature* (Minneapolis: U of Minnesota P, 2013), 3.

2. Mark McGurl, *The Program Era: Postwar Fiction and the Rise of Creative Writing* (Cambridge: Harvard UP, 2009), 15.

3. Eugene Garber, "Letter to Steve Wilbers" (Series XI, Box 2, Folder 2), University Archive, Department of Special Collections, University of Iowa Libraries.

4. Philip G. Hubbard's *New Dawns: A 150-Year Look at Human Rights at the University of Iowa* (Iowa City: Sesquicentennial Committee, University of Iowa, 1996) explores the university's evolving attitude toward its black students. More recently, Lena M. Hill and Michael D. Hill have probed these matters in the edited

collection *Invisible Hawkeyes: African Americans at the University of Iowa during the Long Civil Rights Era* (Iowa City: U of Iowa P, forthcoming).

5. Quoted in Loren Glass, "Middle Man: Paul Engle and the Iowa Writers' Workshop," *minnesota review* 71–72 (Winter/Spring 2009): 257.

6. McPherson's 1970 essay "The Black Law Student" carries the subtitle, "A Problem of Fidelities," and it offers a more expansive exploration of a situation that I am sketching quite briefly. See James Alan McPherson, "The Black Law Student," *The Atlantic* 225.4 (Apr. 1970): 93–95.

7. James Alan McPherson, "Ivy Day in the Empty Room," *Iowa Review* 23.3 (Fall 1993): 84.

8. James A. McPherson to Ralph Ellison, 22 Jan. 1970, Ralph Ellison Papers, Library of Congress.

9. Kenneth Warren, "You Tell Me It's the Institution: Creative Writing and Literary History," *Los Angeles Review of Books*, 13 Sept. 2015, https://lareviewofbooks.org/essay/you-tell-me-its-the-institution-creative-writing-and-literary-history.

10. Albert Murray uses the phrase "Omni-American" to describe the black citizen's role in American culture. Where others saw blacks as marginal participants, Murray believed that what he would call "Negro" experiences fundamentally informed the nation's identity. I am suggesting that McPherson attempted to fit his cross-country travels into this worldview; however, like many who experimented with integration's freedoms, he found the experiment—in this instance signified by his movements—a bit vertiginous. For an expansive treatment of the "Omni-American" concept, see Albert Murray, *The Omni-Americans: Black Experience and American Culture* (New York: Outerbridge and Dienstfrey, 1970).

11. James Alan McPherson, "Chicago's Blackstone Rangers," *The Atlantic* 223.5 (May 1969): 74.

12. Quoted in Hoyt Fuller, "Some Other Hue and Cry," *Negro Digest* (Oct. 1969): 88.

13. James Alan McPherson, "Going Up to Atlanta," *A World Unsuspected: Portraits of Southern Childhood*, ed. Alex Harris (Chapel Hill: U of North Carolina P, 1987), http://almostisland.com/monsoon_2007/prose/pdfs/going_upto_atlanta.pdf, 26.

14. *Winter in America* is the title of Scott-Heron and Jackson's third studio album (1974).

CHAPTER 10

The Program Era and the Mainly White Room

JULIANA SPAHR AND STEPHANIE YOUNG

A Brief Anecdotal History, 2010–2015

At the ReThinking Poetics conference in June 2010, we heard the literary critic Marjorie Perloff discuss Vanessa Place's *Statement of Facts*. She said that the book was a real page-turner and showed that the victims of rape are as bad as or worse than the rapists. We can't remember the gender composition of the room, but the audience that day was mostly white. Many people noticed that no one said anything in the moment. When one of us wrote about these remarks following the conference, Perloff chastised us for simplifying her position, which she qualified by referencing the "sheer evidence of the police reports and court documents" presented in Place's book.[1] Such documents, Perloff wrote, prove that "the culture of rape is largely a socio-economic problem": in Los Angeles, it occurs "mostly among Latinos . . . in 'families' that live in terribly cramped conditions."[2]

At the Associated Writing Programs (AWP) conference in 2011, Claudia Rankine presented a talk on Tony Hoagland's poem "The Change." The narrator in Hoagland's poem is watching tennis and "wanting the white girl to come out on top, / because she was one of my kind, my tribe."[3] He describes Serena Williams as "so big and so black" with "some outrageous name like Vondella Aphrodite" (20). Rankine's talk at AWP was generous. She discussed her own complicated response to Hoagland's poem and the many possible ways of reading it. She asked what it meant that Hoagland said his poem was "for white people."[4] Rankine's talk ends like this: "My alertness, my openness, my desire to engage my colleague's poem, my colleague's words, actually demands my presence, my looking back at him. So here I am looking back, talking back and, as insane as it is, saying, please." In response, Hoagland wrote a letter claiming that "The Change" is "racially complex," not racist;

that white liberal apology is "not just boring but useless";[5] that one has to get dirty if one is going to talk about race. He writes, "I don't believe in explaining my poems to other poets; they are part of my tribe, and I expect them to be resilient readers." Hoagland's recycling of the term "my tribe"—used by the racist narrator of "The Change" to describe white people—to describe his fellow poets is something that probably occurred to many of these readers.

At an AWP off-site reading in February 2014, Krystal Languell attended a reading where a male poet read a sonnet cycle at least twice as long as the other readers' sets. In her report from the field, published on the VIDA website, Languell described that the "air in the gallery was thick with 'father's cock'" and that "Male Poet proclaimed: 'I sucked her brown pussy' 'after three Molly,' and followed this up with what can only be described as a thundersnow of jizz imagery."[6] We were not there so don't know what the room looked like.

In April 2014, Junot Díaz published "MFA vs. POC," an article about his experience in the MFA program at Cornell in the 1990s. Among his mostly white peers and instructors, Díaz noted, "Race was the unfortunate condition of nonwhite people that had nothing to do with white people and as such was not a natural part of the Universal of Literature, and anyone that tried to introduce racial consciousness to the Great (White) Universal of Literature would be seen as politicizing the Pure Art and betraying the (White) Universal (no race) ideal of True Literature."[7]

In April 2014, the Brooklyn Poetry Summit was held, modeled on the East Bay Poetry Summit, with readings at Wendy's Subway, BookThugNation, the Old American Can Factory, Unnameable Books, and Molasses Books. Again, a mainly white room, a mainly male room. Judah Rubin stated after the event:

> Over the past week (since the Brooklyn Poetry Summit) there has been a lot of talk about the race/gender balance (or complete imbalance) of that event. As one of the co-curators of that event, I would like to apologize for the limitations that were on display in terms of curatorial design. While some of this limitation was due to cancellation, lack of technical capacity, money, timing, etc., much/most of it was due to a failure, on the part of the curators, at effacing privilege in favor of making sure "the show went on."[8]

In late October, Zoe Rana Mungin, an MFA student at University of Massachusetts Amherst, published an open letter about being one of two black students in her program. She described a workshop in which, despite the teacher's attempts to open a conversation about racial microaggressions on campus, her classmates still erupted in shouting and shedding of tears when Mungin raised the racial bias she had experienced in discussion of her own work. As she says, "But let's be real: this isn't the first racist thing that's happened to me in this class or in this program. Someone has told me that they don't want to be in workshop with me because even though I'm a good writer, I write about black people."[9]

In January 2015, a group calling itself Mongrel Coalition against Gringpo began to issue a series of statements about race and contemporary literature.[10] Much of their critique was focused on conceptual poetry. On March 16, 2015, Kenneth Goldsmith responded to the critiques of the Mongrel Coalition by reading one of the medical autopsy reports of Michael Brown as art, as conceptual writing at the conference Interrupt 3 at Brown University. He edited the piece so that it ended with language about Brown's penis being unremarkable. Goldsmith called this "massaging" a "dry text."[11] It was repeatedly noticed that the room was mainly white. Rin Johnson stated, "As my anger rises, I begin to count how many people of color are in the room: 3, 4, 5, 7, 8 maybe."[12] Aaron Apps commented, "How many people of color were invited to be keynote speakers at this 'experimental' conference? How many people of color are on faculty in Lit Arts? How many people of color are in the room? 2? 3? 4? 5? How many truly, economically precarious bodies? 0? 0? 0?"[13] Even John Cayley, one of the organizers of the conference, noted this and claimed "tremendous efforts to diversify the program" but also claimed that the "organizers' inability to do so reflects the issues of diversity in the arts."[14] (We might rephrase: organizers' inability reflects organizers' inability.)

By spring of 2015, Place, who had been publishing versions of *Gone with the Wind* and tweeting passages from *Gone with the Wind* (intending, she claimed, to provoke the Margaret Mitchell estate to sue to protect Mitchell's racist language) came under critique for her presentation of this project. A petition to have her removed from an Association of Writers and Writing Programs committee resulted in twenty-two hundred signatures and the AWP removing her. Place defended her tweeting of the racist language of *Gone with the Wind* as pointed in its cruelty. After saying she is "sorry for hurting people of color" but "not sorry for forcing white people to re-enact the soft comfort of individual denunciation," she ended her statement with the claim that "[t]his is a necessary cruelty, and I believe in necessary cruelties."[15] She was saying something that presumes a mainly white room, something very similar to what Hoagland said.

This is only a selective list of moments when something about race or gender has boiled over in the literary community in the last few years. During that period, we probably attended over one hundred readings. Maybe two hundred. Mostly poetry readings, but not all. The readings we attended were held in a wide variety of locations: college and university campuses, living rooms and backyards, museums, imperiled collective arts spaces founded thirty years ago, new community centers affiliated with free schools, and independent bookstores. They were organized and sponsored by English departments, student groups, autonomous individuals and collectives, curators, nonprofit arts organizations, booksellers. By our friends and friends of friends. By former students. Some had institutional funding and paid readers an honorarium. Some didn't. Some passed the hat or did a Kickstarter campaign to cover reader travel costs. Some organizers were compensated for their labor, and some did it for free. Some of the organizers identified as white. Some did not. That is, the readings we attended did not share any common relationship to institutionality, funding, public space, or even sociality. While we often saw friends, colleagues, and acquaintances at readings we attended, we never saw the same people or groups of people at every reading. They overlapped and they diverged.

But in almost every case the readings we attended took place in a mainly white room. When we say mainly white room, we do not mean to ignore people who do not identify as white who were in the room. We doubt the room was ever all white. But it wasn't in any way reflective of the diversity of American culture as documented by the US census and certainly not reflective of the diversity in the urban area—Oakland—where we most often attend readings. Among the readings we attend, there are a handful of exceptions that we can think of: those held at the college where we work (we say more about this later) and those organized in the name of specific racial- or ethnic-identity affiliations.

We are, thus, insistent on something structural: at most of the readings that we attend, the room is mainly white. This is true even when the readers do not identify as white. This is true even when the readings happen in urban areas with an other-than-white majority. We're also fairly confident the mainly white room defines most of the readings we *didn't* attend, that it defines any number of different "schools" of writing, from anything that might possibly call itself experimental to anything that might call itself lyric. From Vanessa Place to Tony Hoagland, a mainly white room. From Brown University to University of Iowa to Holy Names University, a mainly white room. From the 92nd Street Y to the St. Marks Poetry Project to the Omni Commons, a mainly white room. The reasons for this are what this chapter attempts to understand.

When we say mainly white room, we do not want to ignore possible exceptions. As we shared earlier drafts of this article with friends and presented it as a talk, someone would inevitably say, but there is a thriving literary reading scene with many mainly other-than-white rooms. When we asked which reading series they meant, they would mention a few and then add, but I never go. We would diligently go and look up the schedule of these reading series only to find that they no longer existed or barely existed. Or we would spend hours looking at their photographs on social media, only to find ourselves looking at mainly white rooms. It is not that we do not think that there are rooms out there that are other than mainly white. We know of a few. But we have had to actively search out exceptions, and after many conversations and hours of research, we do not think the presence of these exceptions negates the larger structural argument we are making. The fact that many (if not all) of these exceptions are organized in the name of specific racial- or ethnic-identity affiliations seems instead to point toward the problem of the mainly white room as a structural given. (That said, we do not feel confident including in these observations the other exception routinely presented to us by early readers of this article: the rooms of slam or spoken word. We are not convinced that these rooms as currently configured represent a significant structural exception to the mainly white room, although they did so as recently as the 1990s. And while slam and spoken-word scenes are just as embedded within not-for-profit and educational institutions, they function quite differently from the relationship to higher education this chapter attempts to understand.)

With a few exceptions, the room at these readings we attended was not noticeably male in the same way that the room was noticeably white. There is a chance this is specific to the Bay Area, which has a long history of queer and feminist writing scenes and presses, although we are somewhat hesitant to assert this without more thought, without some quantification. But we have also noticed a lot of moments when something about gender also boiled up in the last year. On March 26, 2014, for instance, at another reading hosted by Copula at Wendy's Subway (this one two women and two men), at least three women were given drinks dosed with what was probably ecstasy. In August 2014, a small group of people in the Bay Area released an anonymous online statement about "ongoing issues of misogyny and gender/sexual violence in our communities."[16] By fall, four cismen associated with Alternative Literature (Alt-Lit) were named as rapists by survivors of various gender identifications. In October, Linda Kleinbub wrote in the *Observer* about being roofied at a New School MFA reception.[17] That same month, the *Hairpin* published a piece by Emma Healey about a relationship she had with a poet-professor when she was nineteen years old. She calls this relationship abusive. She writes about telling her story at a writing residency with other women and hearing their stories about "men across the country in the same loose network—writers, editors, teachers."[18] She continues, "I heard about rapes and assaults. I heard about violations of trust and instances of gaslighting. I heard about men who had threatened women with legal action to stop them from talking about what had happened between them." In April 2015, *Quaint Magazine* published an article by Kia Grooms about finding a photocopied communiqué on the floor of a bathroom at the AWP conference written by "the Invisibles," which named seven male writers as harassers of women.[19] By summer, one of these men had a lawyer send letters threatening legal action to anyone who mentioned his name in conjunction with the allegations.

Further, because we have been trying to quantify gender representation in literary culture for some time, we knew some things about gender that shaped the room at these readings, even if these things weren't always visible. We knew the larger room of literary culture skews fairly male. In 2007, we counted the numbers of men and women and those who refuse this binary in "experimental" literary anthologies, and we noticed that, between 1960 and 1999, women make up an average of 22 percent of the writers. (None of these anthologies included anyone who refused the gender binary.)[20] A few years later, in 2010, the VIDA started "the count," an annual project in which they count gender identification in thirty-nine journals that they have subjectively determined to be important.[21] If you add up the various gender counts of all thirty-nine journals counted in 2014, there are close to four thousand women, eight thousand men, and one transgender person.[22] Recently we worked on getting some numbers on literary prizes by counting the winners announced in *Poets & Writers*. In the two years of 2010–11, more women than men won prizes: over nine hundred women to over seven hundred men (at least one prize winner identified as gender fluid, and there were three people whose gender identification we could not determine). But those nine hundred women split among themselves $10 million, and those seven hundred men split $16.5 million. Women tend to receive a prize that is on average about $10,000, while men tend to receive a prize that is on average around $22,000. Another way to put this: women are awarded more entry-level prizes (they might even possibly apply in greater numbers!) but fewer later-in-career prizes awarded on the basis of reputation. Since its inception in 1981, the MacArthur Foundation has awarded $500,000 literary fellowships to fifty-nine men and thirty-eight women. The Poetry Foundation has given the $100,000 Ruth Lilly Prize to nineteen men and ten women. The Lannan Foundation has given its $150,000 Lannan Literary Award to twenty-three men and seven women. The Academy of American Poets has awarded its $100,000 Wallace Stevens Award to seventeen men and four women.

Obviously, these two identification categories—race and gender—intersect. All the time. And they also operate independently. All the time. When we say "mainly white room," we are also trying to understand its relation to gender representation. We are trying to understand what we might now call a corrupted sociality. Why does the sociality of US contemporary literary production skew so white and so male?

These observations are a beginning. While we noticed that it is almost impossible to talk about one without talking about the other, we want to stress that they are not parallel. We sometimes thought of them as orbiting around US literary production but circling erratically on two widely different orbits. At moments these two categories brush up against each other, only to knock each other off course, although they are so resilient that they often just adopt new wobbling and different orbits.

We are not the only people who have noticed this mainly white room. It is much discussed. Those who are in the room often comment on its whiteness with a kind of bafflement. Judah Rubin seems baffled as he blames himself about the Brooklyn Poetry Summit, but even if he had done a better job as a curator, the room would probably still have been mainly white. Our observations here are about the room, and again and again we have noticed that diversifying the readers does not necessarily diversify the room. Just last week, we heard the bafflement when a colleague (who does not identify as white) who teaches at a major public university credited the whiteness of the undergraduate creative writing major in which she teaches to its being not as economically rewarding as, say, engineering. We heard the bafflement when a different colleague (who does identify as white) credited the whiteness of the MFA creative writing program in which he taught to a lack of adequate recruitment funding and said that all the "good" writers who did not identify as white went to schools with larger stipends, as if "good" writers who do not identify as white are a scarce commodity. We heard it at Small Press Traffic when a conversation about sexual violence and feminist organizing in Chicago, New York, and Vancouver turned toward the familiar exclusions, the whiteness of the women's poetry Listserv, the person who identifies as indigenous who didn't attend because she felt her concerns would never be part of this conversation.

As we talked with friends after readings and talks about the mainly white room, we often heard ourselves blame the MFA. When we did this, we used the term sloppily, as a shorthand for higher education. We were not even sure who the MFA was really. So we started there, by trying to understand the MFA. We started by going to IPEDS, the federal database of integrated postsecondary education data. We started assembling data. We ended up with thirty-six spreadsheets, one with twenty-one tabs of data sets.[23]

The Program Era and the Mainly White Room

It was not completely unreasonable for us to begin with institutions of higher education. We are both products of these institutions (one of us with an MFA and $13,000 of debt remaining from the original $27,000 borrowed who has paid, to date, over $30,000 back, and one of us with a PhD who last year, twenty years after graduation, made a final payment on the more than $70,000 required to pay back the $30,000 originally borrowed). And we got a lot of our information about how to be writers through higher education. So even though we thought of ourselves as being in opposition to the conventions of "academic verse" because we were more or less "experimental" writers, higher education had provided us with most of our information about literature and literary culture. We started thinking of ourselves as writers in the first place because we took classes in the writing of poetry at school. Higher

FIGURE 1. Degrees in creative writing awarded, 1988–2013

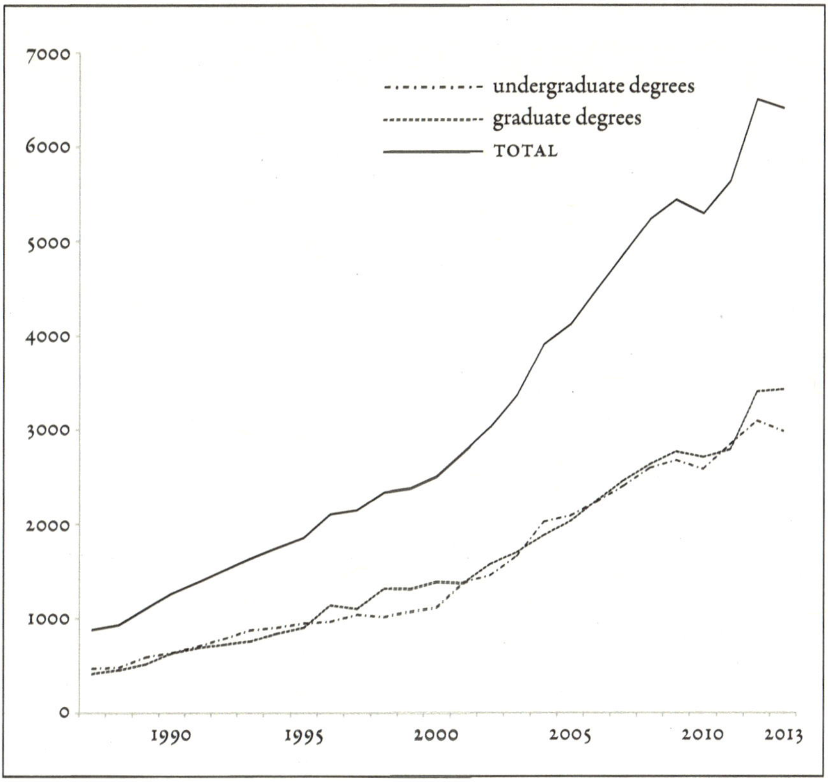

education also pointed us toward social groups and scenes we wanted to be a part of, toward writers we wanted to know, some of whom we went on to know as friends. And now we both teach at institutions of higher education.

One of the things that quickly became obvious once we had these thirty-six spreadsheets, one of them with twenty-one tabs, is that creative writing programs really started to take off in the 1990s. Prior to the 1990s, many writers taught in higher education, which shaped the aesthetics of American literature, as Mark McGurl has shown in *The Program Era*. But it is not until the 1990s that the idea that one should necessarily turn to higher education if one wants to become a writer becomes an idea that more than six thousand people have each year. At the end of the 1980s, a little more than one thousand degrees in creative writing were awarded each year. By 2013, close to six and a half thousand were awarded. Figure 1 presents a visualization of the run up as it shows up in IPEDS data from 1988 to 2013.

There are many reasons that people give for the growth in creative writing degrees. These reasons are mostly benign, if often dismissive of the pedagogical possibilities of the MFA. Some accuse the degree of being "soft." McGurl mentions its "reputation for leniency," calls it "a therapeutic educational enterprise."[24] A related explanation is that a great deal of self-exploration is tolerated in the creative writing workshop, which makes the degree attractive to many because US culture encourages narcissism. Steve Almond makes this argument in a piece titled "Why Talk Therapy Is on the Wane and Writing Workshops Are on the Rise."[25] Some discuss the rise of the MFA in relation to the decline of liberal arts at the undergraduate level. A recent *New York Times* article quotes Jean McGarry saying that MFA students are less prepared due to "undergraduate education that emphasizes specialization and pre-professionalism, with little room for the arts, reading or writing."[26] In his essay "MFA vs NYC," Chad Harbach, after noting that many MFA programs are so "lax and laissez-faire as to have a shockingly small impact on students' work," adds that they are "an ingenious partial solution to an eminent American problem: how to extend our already protracted adolescence past twenty-two and toward thirty, in order to cope with an oversupplied labor market."[27] To this we might add that, in the age of massive open online courses (MOOCs) and large lecture classes, the workshop might be one of the few remaining classrooms where there is concentrated, personal attention to student work.

The majority of these reasons have to do with student desire. It is obvious that people have to want the degree for universities to feel motivated to create programs. But there are economic pressures that induce colleges and universities to expand and aggressively advertise and recruit for programs in creative writing. We do not think it is an overstatement that, prior to the 1990s and the intensifying financial pressures that brought about the corporatization of the university, English departments tended to have a studious lack of interest that bordered on disdain about the teaching of creative writing. And top-tier schools still tend to not offer graduate degrees in creative writing. Of the top ten universities according to *US News and World Report* rankings, only Columbia has an MFA program.[28]

The story of how these financial pressures show up in the college where we work—a small liberal arts college that admits self-identified women and people assigned female at birth who do not fit into the gender binary—might provide a useful illustration. In 1990, the board of the college voted to go coed. In response, students went on strike, and the board backed down after two weeks. Despite the outpouring of support, the college still had significant enrollment issues. Administration responded by focusing on coed graduate programs. Between 1990 and 2013, graduate students increased from 25 percent of the total enrollment at the college to 40 percent. The MFA in creative writing was targeted for growth. Between 2000 and 2010, the number of MFA graduates in the creative writing program more than doubled, from an average of thirteen to thirty-four annually. This growth was not under department control. In 2005, after a long discussion, the department decided that it wanted to admit a smaller, more selective class. It was clear that "targeted for growth" meant adding more students, not more resources. But the president of the college held the acceptance letters until the department agreed to admit everyone on the wait list. This resulted in the largest class ever admitted.

The monetary stakes of this were significant. The college raised graduate tuition by 384 percent between 1990 and 2014. This again echoes national trends, although the tuition increase at the college where we work is more extreme.

Yet the college did not need to lay out much more in resources for this growth. It responded by increasing adjunct hires. In 1995, only 16 percent of English Department courses were taught by adjuncts. Even in 2000, that number had risen to only 22 percent. But as enrollment in the program grew, so did the number of course offerings. Tenure lines were the only thing that didn't grow during this time. And by 2005, 44 percent of English Department classes were taught by adjuncts. That number crept up to 68 percent by 2015. Again this growth echoes national trends; roughly 75 percent of all instructional faculty are now contingent.[29]

Here is a crude way of understanding this: the sticker price on the MFA at the college where we work is $326 per classroom hour per student (or the college would bring in $3,912 for every hour of class time if a class is fully enrolled and everyone is paying full price), but the college pays adjuncts about $22 per classroom hour per student (or around $264 per classroom hour). This might explain better than anything else why about three hundred colleges and universities added a graduate degree in creative writing between 1975 and today. Most of these programs are cheap to run (no studio space or lab space required, low technology needs, very deep adjunct pool) and tuition generating.

FIGURE 2. Graduate tuition costs, 1990–2014

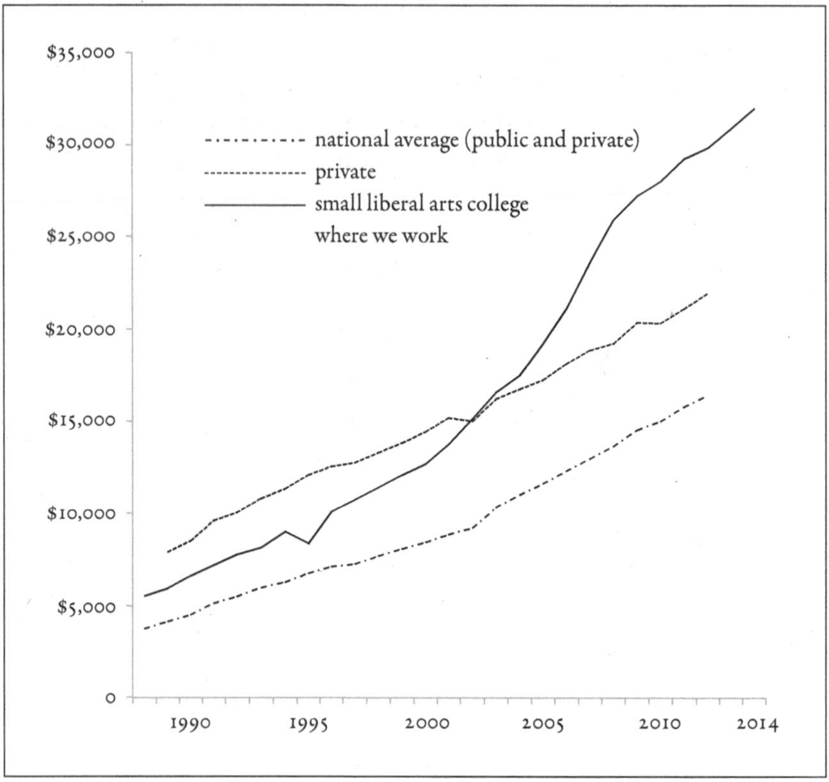

As is probably clear, this is not a story about higher education's commitment to making our nation's literatures stronger. Instead, our story is one in which it is advantageous for colleges and universities to start new degree programs because they can hire cheap contingent labor to run them.

It is not that these colleges and universities are necessarily evil. Many, like the one where we work, are filled with engaged faculty who are thoughtful about the pedagogical possibilities of the MFA. Many become lifelong mentors of their students. But an attentive and thoughtful faculty does not negate the fact that colleges and universities are caught in a series of related pressures, among them unsustainable attempts to remain competitive in terms of facilities and increases in administration costs (some of which are the fault of their administrators and some of which are imposed on them by outside forces like accrediting agencies). Public institutions, which have fewer enrollment pressures and have tended to be late to the MFA game, are also forced to increasingly act like private schools as states cut their budgets; a number have added an MFA program in recent years.

To the extent that the small-against-its-desires-not-really-thriving-but-carrying-on college where we work has been successful in generating tuition, or in carrying on, however unevenly, it has been thanks to a series of contradictory forces. What McGurl calls the Program Era began to percolate post–World War II, when over two million veterans went back to school with funding from the GI Bill. By 1950, the US government spent more money on tuition than on the Marshall Plan. Louis Menand notes that "[t]he key requirement of Title II was that the tuition assistance be used only for study in degree or certificate programs, which is why creative-writing courses grew into degree-granting creative-writing programs."[30]

This history set the stage for a moment we would argue is more crucial to this story: the 1992 Higher Education Amendments that increased student loan limits and added the possibility of unsubsidized loans, thereby dramatically expanding the number of students eligible to borrow. This allowed colleges and universities to raise tuition at staggering rates and expand the pool of potential consumers. Today, creative writing degrees are tuition generating in large part because of student loans. The federal government made $41 billion off student loans last year, and projections suggest that it will make $127 billion over the next ten years (with over three-quarters of this coming from loans to graduate students).[31]

But our question was less about these economic pressures and more about what sort of sociality these economic pressures were creating. Who was enrolling in these degree programs? What we found is that creative writing students identify mainly as female and white. Women are well represented in master's programs and even more so in the creative writing MFA. In 1988, the year IPEDS began reporting creative writing separately from other graduate study in English, women earned 52 percent of all master's degrees awarded nationally and 60 percent of all MFA creative writing degrees. In 2013, 66 percent of all MFA degrees in creative writing were awarded to women. Figure 3 presents a visual of the number of women-identified recipients of MFA degrees in creative writing nationally compared to the number of women-identified recipients of all master's degrees in the United States from 1995 to 2013. Under-

FIGURE 3. Recipients of graduate degrees who identify as female, 1995–2013

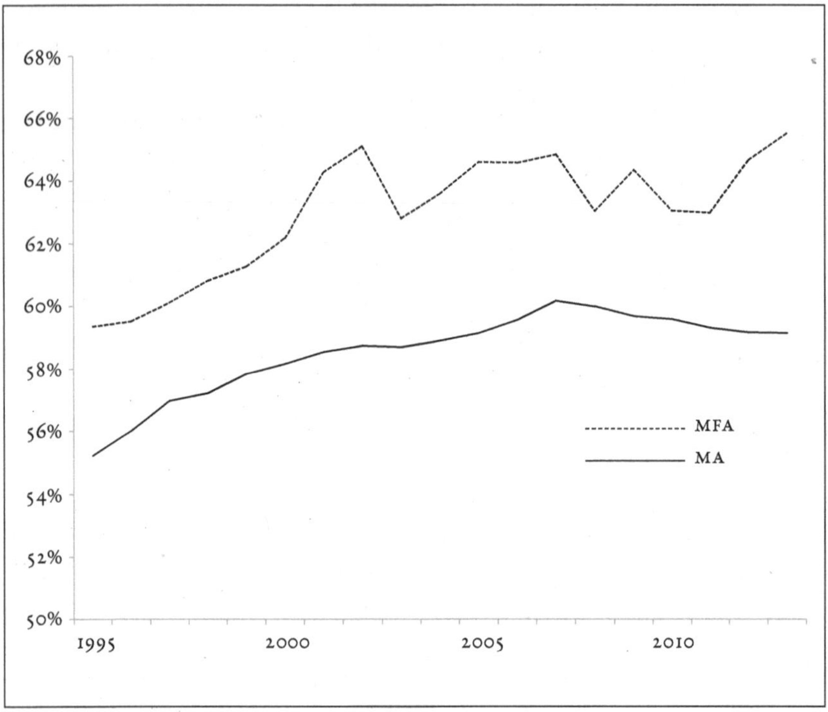

graduate degree numbers reflect this, too: 65 percent of those who earned a BA with a major in creative writing in 2013 identified as women.

The racial identification of those who earn the MFA in creative writing is a different story. We had noticed over the years that the readings for the MFA program at the small liberal arts college where we work did not take place in the mainly white room that we were used to seeing in the living rooms, museums, bookstores, not-for-profit, and collective arts spaces where we attended readings. For a long time, we thought this was true of MFA programs in general. We actually wrote about this situation, about how the MFA might provide entry to people who feel excluded from or just not that interested in the mainly white room that defines a large number of autonomously organized events. We saw the MFA as a possible alternative to the mainly white room. We thought it might provide access for those who lacked cultural connections or urban possibility to become writers on their own.

FIGURE 4. Recipients of graduate degrees who do not identify as "white only," 1995–2013

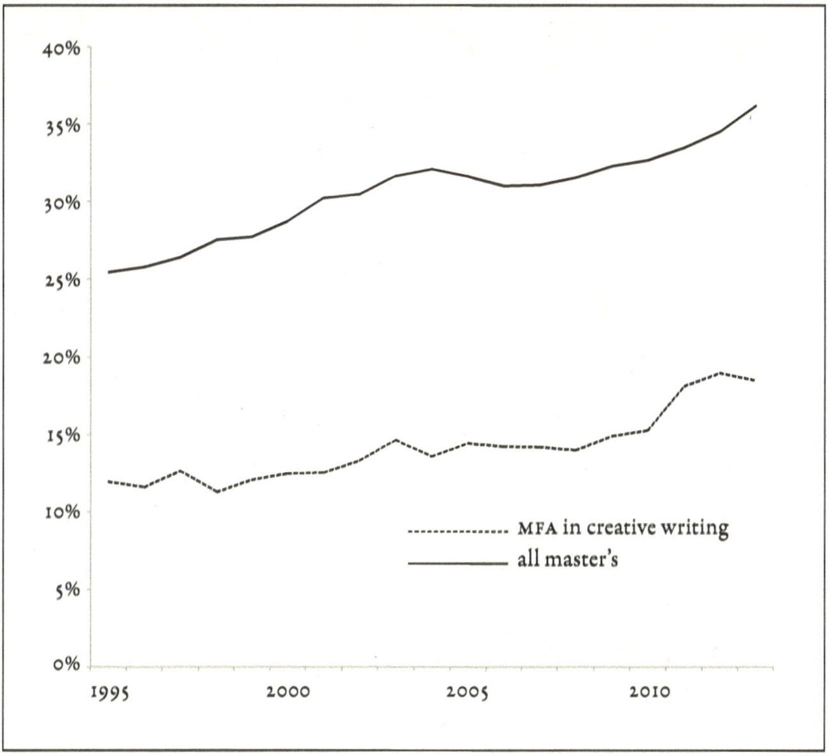

As we compiled our spreadsheets, we saw how wrong we were. The racial diversity of master's degree recipients has been on the rise over the last twenty years, if slowly, from 25 percent of graduates who identified as other than white in 1995 to 36 percent in 2013. We would need to look at more data to understand how that growth is distributed across different disciplines but can say with assurance that it's not due to the MFA in creative writing, which has stayed consistently low during the same time period: 12 percent of graduates who identified as other than white in 1995; 18 percent, in 2013. Again, these numbers hold true for undergraduates as well. Nationally, in 2013, only 21 percent of recipients of BA degrees in creative writing identified as other than white.

Our first thought was that the college where we work with its disproportionate diversity in relation to most MFA creative writing programs was unique. (In 2005, that year of very inclusive admissions, 41 percent of students identified as other than white, while the national average for MFA programs that year remained as low as ever, at 14 percent. That basic ratio has remained the same: in 2013, 48 percent of students in the program where we work identified as other than white, and in MFA programs nationally, 18 percent.) We had some guesses about factors that might make the program exceptional in this regard: its location in Oakland, its reputation for social justice concerns, certain faculty and their relation to feeder programs (one of our colleagues, for instance, cofounded VONA, "the only multi-genre workshop for writers of color in the nation").[32] It's also important to note that in 1996 the state of California passed Proposition 209, with the result that race, sex, and ethnicity were no longer allowed to be considered for admissions. This had a dramatic effect on the number of African American, Latino, and American Indian students attending the University of California (UC). The direct impact of this is felt in undergraduate admissions (UC Berkeley, for instance, admits 58 percent less of these students as a result of these changes; currently only 3 percent of UC Berkeley students identify as "Black or African American"). And it is probably not a coincidence that the undergraduate student body of the college where we work becomes increasingly diverse during these years.

But in its dependence on tuition dollars, the bulk of which take the form of federal and private financial aid, our college is not unique. So we began to wonder about the racial identification of students in programs at other tuition-dependent colleges and at colleges unlike the one where we work: top-tier programs with full funding and generous stipends. While the creative writing MFA is undeniably and overwhelmingly white, how is that whiteness distributed? And what relationship might exist between racial identification and funding? So we made some more spreadsheets.

Before we could do that, though, we had to identify programs like and unlike the one where we work. The latter was fairly straightforward; programs that offer full tuition remission tend to say so. For additional information on these schools we are particularly indebted to a recent project by Robin Tung, "Affording the MFA," which lists those programs that offer full tuition remission, at least nine thousand dollars in stipend, and health care, for all students, for the entirety of the program.[33] Over thirty programs nationally meet these criteria, and their acceptance rates hover between 0.86 percent (Vanderbilt) and 6.5 percent (University of Arkansas). The odds of getting into a fully funded program are not dissimilar from those of landing a tenured job. Johns Hopkins receives over six hundred applications annually for twelve open slots. We arbitrarily selected fourteen of these programs for our data: Arizona State University; Boise State University; Bowling Green State University; Johns Hopkins University; Louisiana State University and Agricultural & Mechanical College; Syracuse University; University of Alabama; University of California, Irvine; University of Michigan–Ann Arbor; University of Oregon; University of Texas at Austin; University of Virginia–Main Campus; University of Wisconsin–Madison; and Vanderbilt University.

Programs at tuition-driven colleges don't tend to advertise the discount rate on their declared tuition price. The discount rate is the amount of discount on tuition that schools need to offer on average to get students to enroll. Determining the actual cost of tuition (sticker price minus discount rate) at colleges and universities for any one student is nearly impossible. Each college and university has a large staff of people who, student by student, use a secret algorithm of merit, need, and what the market suggests people will pay to award what they call scholarships. College websites and other admission materials do not explain how that funding is awarded and at what rate. The complications of this system are so intense it makes airline seat pricing look transparent. (The college where we work has an average discount rate of over 50 percent for undergraduates and regularly has as few as one or two students paying the price listed on the website. The discount rate for the graduate program is often over 35 percent, but as high as 50 percent in many programs, and only a handful of students, so far as we know, have ever paid the listed price.) These schools also don't tend to advertise their acceptance rates or how many applications they receive annually. To identify this second group for our data, we relied on information gleaned over the years from colleagues, friends, and former students who have also worked in or studied at the following schools (including the one where we work): Brooklyn College, California College of the Arts, Columbia College (Chicago), Columbia University, Emerson College, Hunter College, Mills College, Naropa University, the New School, New York University, Otis College of Art and Design, Sarah Lawrence College, and School of the Art Institute of Chicago.

Because these schools are fairly expensive and offer limited funding, we started calling them "debt generators." And some of the anecdotal information we have heard includes staggering amounts of debt taken on while earning the degree: students who graduated with $55,000, $70,000, or $120,000 owed to the federal government or Sallie Mae. Information on student debt by specific programs and even by institution is particularly hard to obtain. It is collected by the Department of Education along with other data from reporting institutions but accessible only to those with an administrator password (someone who works at an institution in an administrative or staff role, most likely within offices of financial aid or admissions).

As we looked at these two groups of schools, we noticed, for example, that the large numbers of students who graduate from debt-generator schools tend to be more female and less white than graduates of fully funded programs. In 2013, 28 percent of students at the debt-generator schools identified as other than white, and 68 percent identified as female. At the fully funded programs, only 19 percent of students identified as other than white and 58 percent as female. It's worth noting that those who identify as male and white do especially well at fully funded programs. In 2013 they represented 30 percent of all graduates from fully funded programs but only 22 percent at the debt generators. Only one number remains consistent for all the schools we looked at: those who identify as male and other than white hover around 6 percent on average. So when programs do enroll more students who identify as other than white, they almost always also identify as women. In 2013, 21 percent of graduates from debt-generator schools identified as women and other than white. At the fully funded programs, that number was only 10 percent.

The debt-generator schools also produce far more graduates, over five hundred in 2013 versus around two hundred from fully funded programs. According to the AWP, there were 214 total MFA programs in 2013 (not counting an additional 153 MA creative writing programs). This means the two groups of schools each represent a little less than 7 percent of all MFA programs nationally, yet the debt generators produced 17 percent of all graduates, while the fully funded programs generated a moderate and equivalent 7 percent of total degrees. It is an open question what the consequences of this will be. There is a chance that these schools might diversify the MFA in creative writing, finally, as the debt generators are graduating not only many more students but also many more students who do not identify as other than white. The visualization in Figure 5 illustrates the number of graduates who identify as other than white between 2001 and 2013.

FIGURE 5. Recipients of graduate degrees from debt-generator and funded programs who do not identify as "white only," 2001–2013

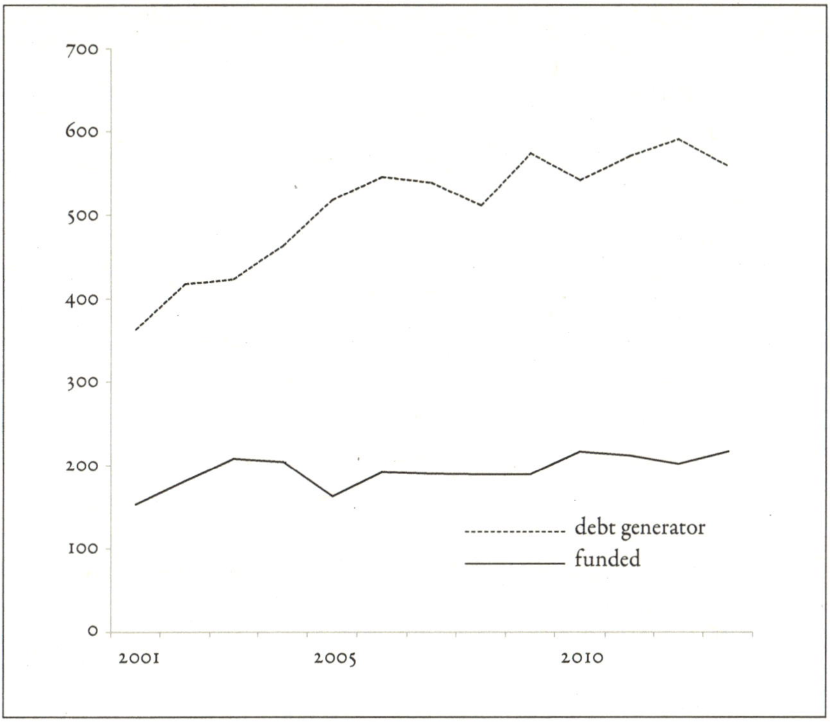

As the chart shows, fully funded programs are more or less not admitting that many more students who identify as other than white over time (from 14 to 19 percent), whereas the debt-generator programs are somewhat diversifying (from 17 to 28 percent) as they are growing. However, this is one area that could use even more spreadsheets. These data just describe differences between twenty-eight schools divided into two categories based around funding.

Yet the degree does not do much for those who pay for it. Many take on significant debt to get their MFA, and as our endless spreadsheets seem to indicate, those who do not identify as white do so more often because they tend to graduate from schools without funding. This is also debt that, because of gender and race wage gaps, they often have more trouble paying back. Not only are female MFA students at high risk of sexual harassment; they remain dramatically underrepresented in many of the aspects of literary culture that they might enter after graduation, that they might need to get tenure. They receive less prize money. They show up less often in anthologies. Their books are reviewed less often, and they are reviewers less often. While total recipients of MFA and undergraduate creative writing degrees identify as women close to 70 percent of the time, neither the writers for mainstream media nor the authors published by small presses nor the winners of major prizes are 70 percent women. Instead, they are around 70 percent men. The percentage is flipped in all those arenas where one might obtain something, from visibility to wages. The disparity is numerically intense and repetitive. We do not think it likely that other social systems that serve as feeders for these scenes, like the New York publishing scene, skew so heavily male that they would explain this disparity. And we are not buying the recent confidence-gap analysis here either.[34] Women are clearly confident enough to show up for higher education.

The MFA system does not employ that many MFA graduates itself, and those who do find teaching jobs are disproportionately contingent. While we do not have data specific to creative writing faculty, a 2011 American Association of University Professors (AAUP) report shows that full-time tenure-track faculty were 58 percent male that year, and a 2009 study by the National Center for Education Statistics shows that women make up 51 percent of all adjunct faculty.[35] A more recent, smaller survey by the Coalition on the Academic Workforce, in which adjuncts self-identified, shows the proportion of female adjunct faculty to be closer to 60 percent.[36] Again, race and gender orbit around the same planet but at different rotations and rates. A report by the American Federation of Teachers notes that "underrepresented racial and ethnic groups are even more likely to be relegated to contingent positions; only 10.4 percent of all faculty positions are held by underrepresented racial and ethnic groups, and of these, 7.6 percent—or 73 percent of the total minority faculty population—are contingent positions."[37] It's often noted that in the 1970s some 30 percent of faculty in higher education were contingent and that this percentage has since flipped, such that contingent faculty now make up 70 percent of all faculty in higher education. The faculty in the 1970s was mostly white and male. The erosion of tenure has overlapped with the entrance of women and those who do not identify as white.

The PhD data are different but not unrelated. Whenever we give a talk on this subject or discuss it with colleagues, there is always a moment when someone says something like, well, thank goodness PhD programs at least are not

FIGURE 6. PhD degrees in English awarded, 1955–2013

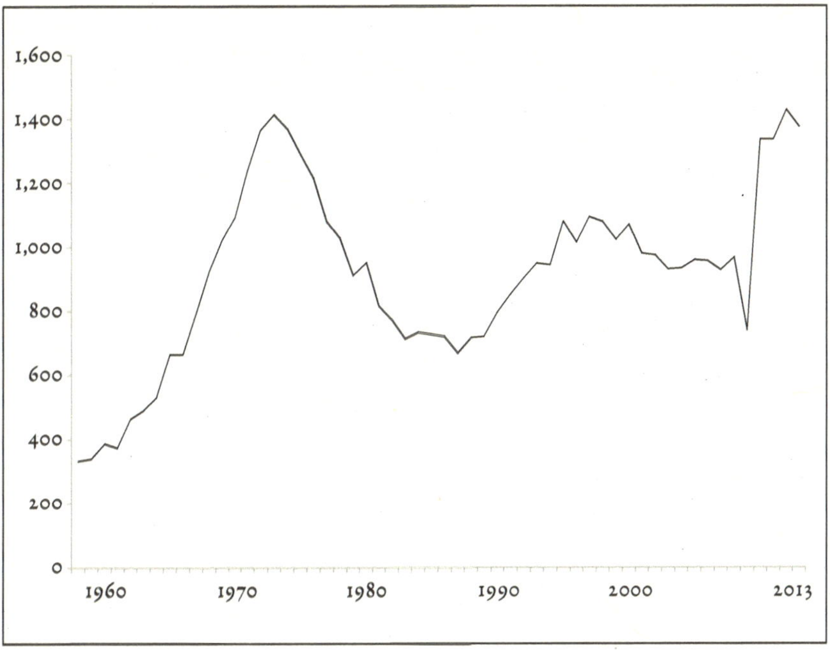

part of the problem because PhD students are funded. This is usually said by someone who teaches or studies in a PhD program. And at first we wanted to just add a note that whether someone enrolled in a program pays with labor or pays with loans, the person is still paying. Also, PhD students are often forced to supplement their stipends with loans; slightly over half of PhD students in the humanities take out student loans.[38]

But once we started compiling spreadsheets, we noticed a few things that seem worth pointing out. For context, the PhD in English is just as female as the MFA in creative writing, about 60 percent on average. And only 29 percent of its graduates identify as other than white (which is, if nothing else, higher than the 18 percent of the MFAs in creative writing programs).

But more interestingly, the PhD experienced a version of this increase-in-graduates story much earlier. The number of English and literature PhDs awarded in the United States peaks in 1973 with 1,412 awarded. From there it declines in the 1980s, hitting a low in 1987 of 669. And then it begins go back up, increasing somewhat throughout the 1990s, where it hovers from the mid-

FIGURE 7. MFA degree recipients and number of tenure track jobs, 2000–2013

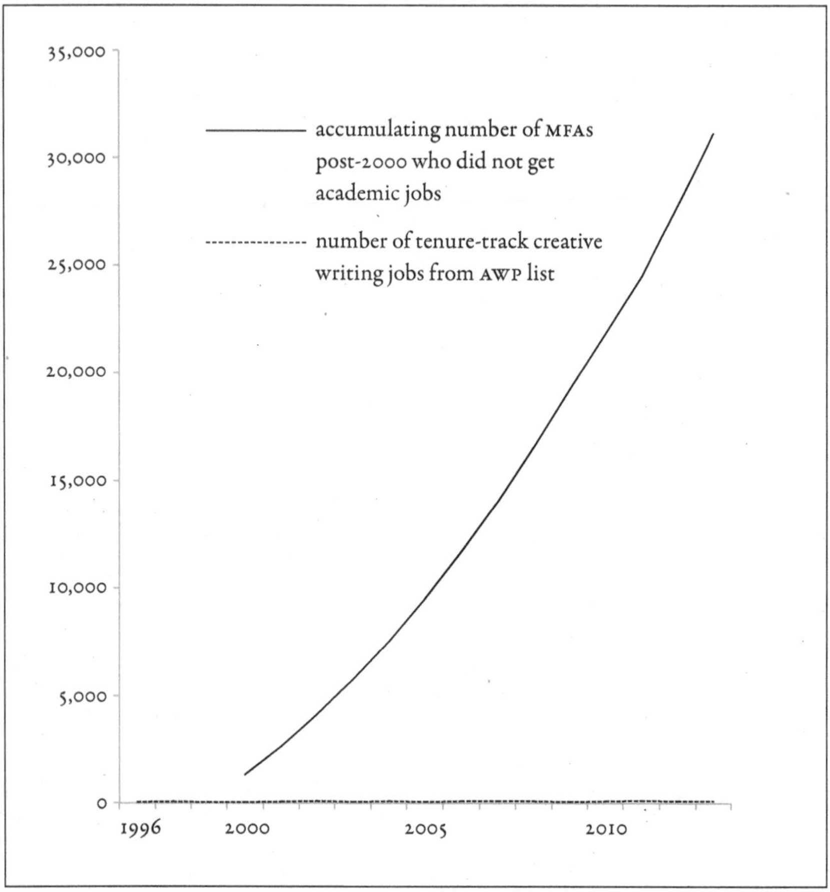

1990s onward at an average of about 1,300. Figure 6 shows the number of PhD recipients in English from 1955 to 2013.[39]

While the employment crisis for PhDs has gotten a lot of attention, there is not much evidence of an overproduction of PhDs. If you concede that the MFA's main reason for existence is as a teaching credential (and we do not, though many do), there is a lot of evidence of an overproduction of MFAs. For example, we aggregated the number of MFA graduates from 2000 forward and subtracted the small number of tenure-track jobs that were available in creative writing each year and got the visualization in Figure 7.

While the number of creative writing degrees awarded yearly increased from less than a thousand to more than six thousand from 1990 until today, the number of tenure-track creative writing jobs increased from around fifty in 1996 to a little over a hundred last year. Worth noticing here is how the MFA system resembles a Ponzi scheme. The number of graduates increases sixfold, but the number of jobs only doubles. We also suspect that there will be a decline in open tenure-track creative writing jobs in the near future, as colleges and universities realize they cannot keep adding new programs at the rate they have been without reaching market saturation (some of the large debt generators are already seeing declines in enrollment in recent years). And there does not seem to be a need for a degree in creative writing outside teaching.

The PhD crisis does not look anywhere like the employment crisis for MFAs. Since 2004, the Job Information List (JIL) has listed around nine thousand tenure-line jobs in English; during this same period twelve thousand PhDs were awarded. Presuming that the only reason one might get a PhD is to get a job, which is a fairly safe assumption, there is still an obvious surplus. Figure 8 is a bit misleading (because it shows only jobs advertised and includes open-rank hires), but what it shows is that the overproduction of PhDs is nothing like the overproduction of MFAs. During this period, over twenty-four thousand MFAs were awarded for around nine hundred possible jobs, suggesting that 74 percent of its graduates might be considered surplus. It's our guess that, if it were not for the endless numbers of MFAs and MAs who create a constantly renewable reserve army of the unemployed and thus maintain adjunct pay rates, there would probably be no job crisis for PhDs. Colleges and universities would be forced to compete for faculty. Instead, the current situation is a sweet deal for them. They get to use graduate programs to generate tuition and, at the same time, create a constantly renewable reserve labor force that they can employ at unlivable wages to teach in these same, and other, programs.

But we should also add that blaming the MFA in creative writing for the employment problem in higher education is a bit like the parable of the men in the dark feeling the elephant. It is a very small part of a much larger story of state disinvestment and administrative decisions to pursue money-losing technology partnerships and scientific research and to fund construction projects and their own salaries.

FIGURE 8. PhD degrees in English and number of entry-level tenure-track jobs, 2000–2013

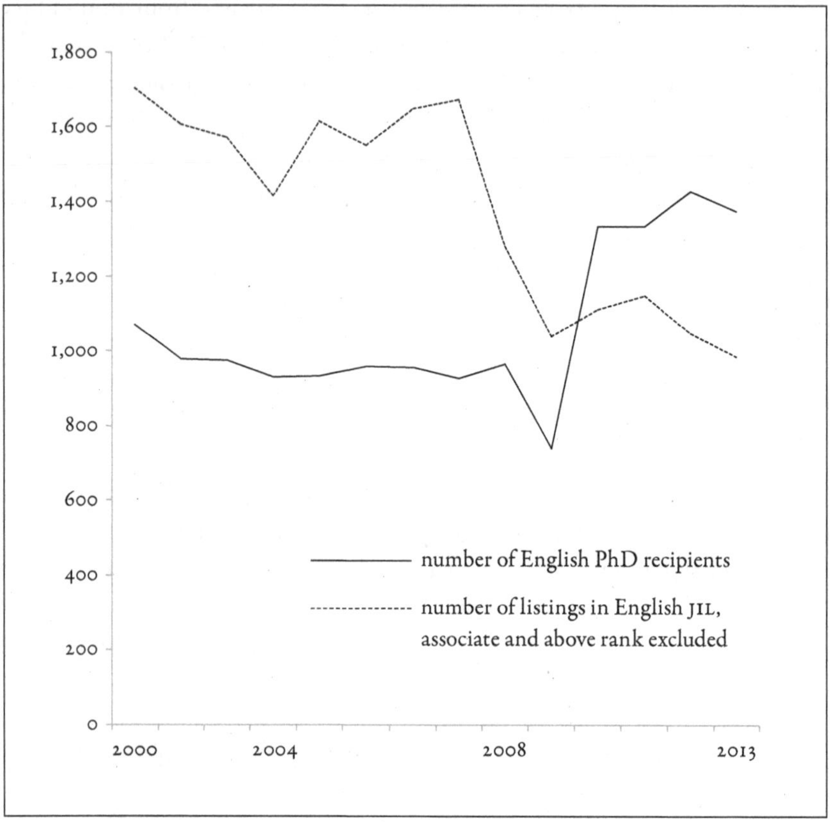

Back to That Mainly White Room

We don't know what the relationship is between this peculiar two-tiered degree structure, skewing mainly white and female at all levels, with one degree devaluing the other, and the mainly white room of US literary production, alongside the larger room of big money prizes, publications, and reviews where women and those who identify as other than white are consistently underrepresented.

We do know that the story about race is harder to tell. While we have some firm numbers about the racial identification of graduates of creative writing programs, we do not have similar data about that larger room of publication, prizes, reviews, and scholarly attention. There are some obvious reasons. Racial data are hard to obtain. People self-declare on admissions to higher education; the federal government requires those numbers; they assemble them in IPEDS. That is how we acquired data on MFA programs and how AFT and other groups acquired some of their data on contingent labor. We have been reluctant to collect our own data around race because we do not want to impose a racial identity on anyone. One cannot read bio notes and find a pronoun that easily indicates one's racial identification as one can do with gender.

But it is not impossible to tell a story about race that might begin to explain that mainly white room. In fact, there are a number of obvious things to say. And here we want to do an about-face, a zooming out and backing up, to understand and remember that in the 1970s a number of thriving literary subcultures broke ties with literature's often presumed universalism and instead wrote literatures that made clear that they were allied with and written for various specific communities. At this moment many writers grouped together under a self-declared ethnic or racial or sexual or class identification and wrote from and about that position rather than as a generic "American." Many of these literatures were created and nurtured by various cultural nationalist movements. Many of these movements had a special interest in the arts as a place that can represent and preserve cultures and their values, as a place that is ideal for political education and debate. And these various cultural nationalist movements created patronage systems such as publishing houses, journals, anthologies, and reading series to distribute and promote their work. The creation of the Black Arts Repertory Theatre/School in 1965 by Amiri Baraka is often seen as a foundational moment here. But it is just one among many, and while certainly important, it had predecessors. Umbra, a collective of mainly black poets, was founded a few years earlier in 1962. And in 1965 El Teatro Campesino was founded on the Delano Grape Strike picket lines of Cesar Chavez's United Farm Workers union. The Watts Writers Workshop was also founded in 1965 after the Watts riots; the Centro Cultural de la Raza, focused on Chicano, Mexicano, Native American, and Latino art and culture, in 1970; the Nuyorican Poets Café, with its roots in the New York Puerto Rican community, in 1973. Bamboo Ridge, the workshop and the press that publishes mainly literature written by Asian Americans in Hawaiʻi and has preserved and cultivated a literature in Pidgin, was founded in 1978; and Arte

Público, with its claim of providing a national forum for Hispanic literature, in 1979. There are many other examples.

In the late 1960s and early 1970s, it often looked as if a major national uprising might happen. There were major rebellions in Rochester, Philadelphia, and Harlem in 1964; in Watts in 1965; in Cleveland in 1966; in Newark, Detroit, and Minneapolis–St Paul in 1967; in Chicago, Baltimore, Washington, DC, and Cleveland in 1968. Politicized bombings were a regular occurrence. There were over four thousand bombings between January 1969 and April 1970 in the United States. Universities were having a similar moment of militancy in the 1960s with huge protests and shutdowns. After Kent State, as Kirkpatrick Sale notes, "students at a total of at least 350 institutions went out on strike and 536 schools were shut down completely for some period of time, 51 of them for the entire year."[40] The movements that nurtured and supported movement literatures in the 1970s played a major role in this radicalization. In short, there would be no Nuyorican literature without the Young Lords and no Young Lords without the working-class Puerto Rican communities of the Lower East Side. There would be no Black Arts movement without the various black cultural nationalist movements, and none of these would exist without the working-class black communities of New York, Chicago, Detroit, Los Angeles, San Francisco, and Oakland. There would be no Chicano/Chicana literature without El Plan de Aztlán. And there would be no Plan de Aztlán without Crusade for Justice (founded by poet and militant Rodolfo "Corky" Gonzales) and no Crusade for Justice without the working-class Chicano/Chicana communities of Denver. And so on.

And it is important not just to remember this moment but also to notice that all the radical parts were killed. Were killed in multiple ways. One way was economic. Gentrification meant that the cultural centers supporting more radical and anticapitalist literatures, most of which were located in urban working-class neighborhoods, slowly lost their demographic reason for existing and also could not afford the high rents. But state repression played an enormous role. The Watts Writers Workshop was burned down in 1973 by FBI informant Darthard Perry.[41] The story behind Perry's burning of the workshop is probably not yet fully told, might never be completely understood, but government interference in the arts is not limited to just this sort of direct action. The FBI targeted African American writers in particular during the late 1960s and 1970s for monitoring. There is not yet a lot of evidence that the FBI's relation to writers was, with the exception of the Watts Writers Workshop firebombing, much more than monitoring. But clearly the state took a much more aggressive stance with groups such as the Black Panthers, and in the case of Fred Hampton and Mark Clark, moved from monitoring to actual murder. But the goal of that monitoring, and of the murdering, was to discourage future action, discourage writers and others from making alliances with cultural national and anticapitalist state antagonists or considering themselves to be a part of these movements.

The synergy between the state and the liberal not-for-profit industrial complex was robust prior to the 1960s. Most scholars locate its development in the middle of the century, post–World War II. Greg Barnhisel in *Cold War Modernism* notices that "[t]he Ford Foundation was deeply involved and invested in cultural diplomacy, nowhere more than in Europe, where it, the Department of State, and the CIA worked along parallel or even intersecting tracks." He continues, "The Ford Foundation was eager to use culture as a weapon to prevent war and against Soviet totalitarianism."[42] And Eric Bennett in *Workshops of Empire* tells how these synergies shaped creative writing in higher education. He points out that "anxieties about totalitarianism, the containment of Communism, the repudiation of American radicalism, the newly powerful mass culture, and the nature of literature all contributed to the contours of the emerging discipline" of creative writing.[43] These alliances continue to shape the end of the century. For just as certain forms of cultural nationalism had their own literatures and support systems for these literatures, fear of militancy—a fear provoked by the riots that happened between 1965 and 1968 in the United States—guides US social policy in the years that follow and creates a counterinsurgent literature and well-funded and powerful support systems for it. This constantly mutating ecosystem of privatization and institutionalization works at moments through destruction, as in firebombing the Watts Writers Workshop, and at other moments through a sort of appropriation and occupation and neutering as foundations work with the US government to fund a mainstream artistic multiculturalism along with a number of economic development initiatives, university area studies programs, changes to school curricula, and other initiatives.

Karen Ferguson in *Top Down: The Ford Foundation, Black Power, and the Reinvention of a Radical Liberalism* tells the Ford Foundation version of this story. One of her examples is of the Ford Foundation's creation of community theaters to showcase work that encouraged assimilation into mainstream US culture rather than the revolutionary resistance and nationalism that cultural nationalist theaters were so powerfully producing. Ferguson estimates that there are around seventeen theaters directly founded or taken over by the Ford Foundation for this purpose. But the scope of these programs extended well beyond these seventeen theaters because many not-for-profits were dependent on Ford Foundation funds and the era's only other national arts funders, the Rockefeller Foundation and the National Education Association (NEA), often made their funds contingent on matching support from the Ford Foundation.[44]

The same fear of militancy led to the transformation of US universities. The Rockefeller and Ford Foundations and the State Department were there too, with funds to neutralize student resistance, often formed to be in alliance to these movements. In *Represent and Destroy*, the scholar Jodi Melamed argues that this transformation did not merely prepare certain members of marginalized groups for incorporation into "multiracial managerial classes": it also executed "a counterinsurgency against new knowledges produced by social movements," in which "English departments and discourses of literary multiculturalism did the lion's share of the work."[45] The consequence is that these synergies put US literary production largely under the control of a business elite rather than centering it in working-class cultural activist communities.

Mark McGurl does not locate the Program Era as an attack on the new knowledges produced by social movements, and he is oddly ecumenical about higher education's role in twentieth-century literary production. He concludes *The Program Era* with a series of rhetorical questions: "[D]o we not bear daily witness to a surfeit of literary excellence, an embarrassment of riches? Is there not more excellent fiction being produced now than anyone has time to read? What kind of traitor to the mission of mass higher education would you have to be think otherwise?" (410). But one of the limitations of McGurl's book is that he is so focused on higher education that he misses the moments when literary production thrived outside it. He has, for instance, some disdain for Chicano/Chicana literature because he notices only its appropriation by higher education and not its origins in the resistant moment that also produced El Plan de Aztlán. This means that he unfairly presumes that Chicano/Chicana literature is created for "the increasingly paramount value of cultural diversity in U.S. educational institutions" and is yet another "new way of accumulating symbolic capital in the fervently globalizing U.S. academy, pointing scholars toward valuable bodies of expertise they might claim as their own and offering a rationale for the inclusion of certain creative writers in an emergent canon of world literature" (333). This unwillingness to trace larger histories and see higher education as a manipulative force is one of the failures of McGurl's otherwise excellent project.

We do not intend to suggest that cultural nationalism is the right way. But we do want to remain attentive to what was unique about the late 1960s and 1970s: it was a time when some forms of literature had an unusually tight connection to thriving political movements, to cultural politics, to working-class communities, to anticapitalist and anti-nation-state nationalist imaginings. And this closeness provoked a counterinsurgency that continues to shape US literary production today.

This is where the problem with the MFA extends beyond predatory lending. It matters if those who want to become writers no longer take a workshop at the Watts Writers Workshop but instead take it at a liberal arts college. And it matters not just because those writers go into debt. It matters for what it does to literature and to the communities that produce it.

From Actual Explosions and Actual Brutality to Strategies for Professional Growth

Around the time Amiri Baraka founded the Black Arts Repertory Theatre/School, he wrote a call for revolutionary theater with "actual explosions and actual brutality."[46] While his call was never actualized, he doesn't seem to have been joking.

Here, in absurd contrast, is a handout (Figure 9) we have given students in our poetry workshops. At our most optimistic, we imagined this chart not as a guide to professionalization in communities of mainly white, mainly male back-scratching but as a demystification of the many ways that one can enter into conversation with other writers and traditions and can participate in writing scenes that at their best are places where education continues, often for life, in the autodidactic reading group, in the discussion after the reading, in the arguments and debates among those who take the stakes of literature seriously. We imagined this chart as reminding students that there are many ways to be a writer outside higher education after they graduate.

FIGURE 9. How to be a poet

POETRY
write really good poetry
send out to journals
self-publish
eventual book publication

INTERACT WITH EXISTING COMMUNITIES

find your poets
attend readings
read books
review books
support and argue
blogs
poetics list

subscribe to at least 5 journals
buy at least 10 new books a year
attend at least a reading a month
review at least 3 books a year

CREATE COMMUNITIES

reconceive the scene
what is missing?
what do you care about?
who are your heroes?

then,
edit books/journals around focus
organize reading series in home/gallery
organize a conference
blog
somewhat scholarly articles

drinks/dinner before/after readings with other poets

talking/emailing/socializing/exchanging books with poets in other locations, especially other nations

We feel far less optimistic about this chart after compiling our spreadsheets, after listing the moments when racism and misogyny boiled over in the mostly white room. Yet it remains an open question how direct the relationship might be between the growth of the MFA and the series of events we listed at the beginning, even as we are also convinced there *is* some relationship. Our analysis is limited, a mash-up of things we know and things we suspect and things we cannot really figure out. The idea that literary culture is inextricably bound to institutions such as higher education cannot help reshaping the concerns and content of literature. This is the argument that McGurl makes, and it is one that we make too, although without his optimism. But at the same time, we do not want to imply that there was a prelapsarian moment prior to this. Our guess is that literary scenes have always been as predatory as the general culture. US culture is racist; literary scenes are just as racist. US culture is sexist; literary scenes are just as sexist.

However, while higher education is probably as racist as any other US cultural institution, the MFA in creative writing seems to also have unusually small amounts of students enrolled in it who do not identify as white. Does this make it more racist? We do not know. But it does suggest that something is off. And while autonomously organized readings are probably as racist as other US cultural institutions, they too seem to have an unusually white room. And at the same time, while higher education is probably as sexist as US culture in general, this seems to not discourage women from enrolling. Why this is so is what we are trying to understand. It would probably be easy to blame this on the legacies of second-wave feminism, with its focus on workplace and educational access for middle-class white women. And we might take this as the answer if we looked only at the MFA as a privilege and did not consider how white women borrow money for a degree that is fairly useless when it comes to getting published or otherwise rewarded. That said, it would be just as reductive to say that white women are unfairly taken advantage of here.

It seems telling also that, before we spent all this time with the IPEDS data, we thought that the MFA was less white than the mainly white room of autonomously organized readings. And it very well might be. It might be that, even though the MFA skews so disproportionately white, it is still significantly less white than the mainly white room of the autonomously organized event. Why don't people move from the (relatively more) diverse classrooms of the MFA to the mainly white room of the poetry reading? It might be that the experience of the MFA for people who do not identify as white is so dispiriting that they walk away. It might be that their experience of the mainly white room is so dispiriting that they never go back. Talks with friends and students over the years have suggested as much. One told us incredulously that the gender dynamics she encountered at the few readings she attended were far worse than those in the hypermasculinist punk music scene. Another said there's no part of his social life that isn't multiracial; why would he want to be part of a writing scene that's so relentlessly white?

It might also be that those who walk away are walking away into other rooms or creating them. There is surely much we are unable to see from the vantage point of our socialities, work life, identity categories, and geography. But as far as we can tell, the only rooms that are not mainly white are, as we noted earlier, organized with an explicit mission to amplify the voices of those who have been historically underrepresented in unmarked, "universal" literary culture, those who are not in the mainly white room. Or perhaps we are left with this formulation: US culture is segregated; literary scenes are just as segregated.

In trying to figure this out, it seems naïve not to notice how little possibility there is for writing outside higher education and businessman-led foundations. It seems telling that when June Jordan decided to start Poetry for the People, an arts/activism organization, in 1991, she did it at UC Berkeley and not at a community-run center in Oakland, that its mission had an "academic focus," that it aimed to bridge the gap between the university and the community.[47] We are not arguing this is a failure on Jordan's part. Rather, it is an indication that things are structurally different in the 1990s than they were in the 1970s. One could perhaps argue that Jordan's move is a sign of a new inclusiveness on the part of higher education, but only if one ignores the IPEDS data.

Then, in the other direction, we've noticed a number of free schools and social centers that have been created recently as alternatives to higher education, which ideally would also be part of making the room less white. Yet many still have a mainly white room. A number of those readings, for instance, that we attended over the last year were at the Omni Commons, a collective space actively interested in anticapitalist and antiracist organizing. Many events we attend there at the public school, the various one-off reading groups and other sorts of events, are not mainly white, yet the poetry reading room remains mainly white.

We've also noticed that many of the social centers of today that organize themselves around racial identifications and creative writing do not claim to be resistant or hostile to the mainly white room of literary institutions, to US nationalism. Cave Canem, founded in 1996 and funded by the Ford Foundation, talks about its commitment to "the professional growth of African American poets."[48] Kundiman offers arts programming so as to "inscribe the Asian American story onto American experience, transforming and enriching the landscape of our national culture," and is proud of its graduates who are admitted to top-tier programs.[49] Kundiman and Cave Canem are regularly official Literary Partners of the AWP (which is interesting because the AWP is there to represent college and university writing programs, programs that have historically replaced these sorts of cultural projects). We do not want to take down Cave Canem or Kundiman or any of the other attempts to counter the pervasive racism of higher education. As the MFA bubble swells, and as it takes part in the appropriation and redirection of social movements, it makes sense that various writers who are underrepresented might want an advocacy group if they are going to be successful within such a setup.

At one point we asked ourselves if the answer would be a more racially representative MFA. And while we are not against it and would surely prefer it, a more representative MFA is just that, a more representative MFA. It is not free from many of these questions: even at the program where we teach, where diversity is much higher than the national average, students who identify as other than white express common frustrations about a faculty that remains far less diverse than the students, about classroom environments where neither teachers nor students are equipped to address race. Their frustrations are not just pedagogical but also structural: about their debt and about the mainly white and male room of possibility that awaits them after graduation. A more representative MFA would still be a predatory lender. It would still be a part of the privatization of literary community. It exists in its current state because of particular economic conditions. And it will go on with or without us in the face of any individual call for its abolishment.

We are not alone in our attempts to rethink this mainly white room. It is in the air, a constant question. A question that we should acknowledge probably has as much to do with the recent uprisings in places like Ferguson and Baltimore as anything else. We think it's worth noticing that something new is happening, or it feels that way to us. It might be that the scene is changing, even if slowly. Heriberto Yépez, for instance, when writing about many of the events we have recounted here, recently claimed that "North American experimental poetry is undergoing an unprecedented crisis this year and last week an historic shift occurred."[50] (The shift that Yépez refers to is the cancellation of the Berkeley Poetry Conference after many people dropped out in response to Place's work and the re-creation of a new conference called "Crosstalk, Color, Composition" that featured work by writers who do not identify as white, although it still had a mainly white room.) What we are seeing in the discussion about Goldsmith's "The Body of Michael Brown," in the discussion about Place's *Gone with the Wind* project, in the calls for more attentiveness to gender and the calling out of sexual violence in writing scenes is not burning the mainly white room down and walking away. It's the possibility of burning the room down from the inside in order to build a new one where it stood. It's not what we think of as the soft boycott, the moment when someone is fed up with being tokenized or can't deal with listening to one more example of literature that redeploys racist language to critique racism or sexist language to critique consumer culture or war and thus walks away but just as an individual, not as a call to action. This soft boycott is the moment we have heard about again and again from students.

We looked again at that handout we have given students in the past and realized we don't really have a problem with two-thirds of it; we would still feel comfortable telling people to write really good poetry and send it out for publication or to self-publish, and we think creating new communities around writing is more important than ever. But now we might include "burn it down" as one way to interact with existing communities. We might remind ourselves that burning it down is a form of making something new. How it will change remains an open question. The question of what to build next still remains unanswered. We do not have an answer. We are not sure we are the ones who should even attempt to answer this question.

We have ended this chapter many different ways, made various arguments about what is or what might be done. These arguments now seem either inadequate (reformist) or unrealistic (smash the MFA, the AWP, the private foundations, the state). At moments we struggled with our own structural positions even as these structures were created without our consent but to our advantage. We are telling this story unevenly because we are telling it through our lived experience as white women, a story inextricably caught up in our shared work life. Yet it also feels crucial that these stories be told as one story, one destruction of a form of artistic community, even if we have benefited at moments from some of the forces responsible for the destruction. Finally, we agree with McGurl when he argues that "what is needed now . . . are studies that take the rise and spread of the creative writing program not as an occasion for praise or lamentation but as an established fact in need of historical interpretation: how, why, and to what end has the writing program reorganized U.S. literary production in the postwar period?" (27). For us, for now, the best we can do is work to understand so that after the fire, what we create is not structured in a way that extinguishes the fire.

NOTES

We owe debts to Amanda Armstrong, David Buuck, Chris Chen, Joshua Clover, Amy De'Ath, Jena Osman, Jocelyn Saidenberg, Jennifer Tamayo, Truong Tran, Wendy Trevino, and Heriberto Yépez. But they should not be held responsible for any faults of this chapter. Claire Goodman was superhuman with the IPEDS numbers. Lindsay Baile also helped us. Earlier versions of this chapter were presented at the MLA Subconference in Vancouver, the UCLA Graduate Student Conference on Excess, and the Naropa Summer Writing Program.

1. Marjorie Perloff, "Too Much Work and Still to Be Poets," *Response from Marjorie Perloff*, 17 June 2010, http://could-be-otherwise.blogspot.com/2010/06/response-from-marjorie-perloff.html.

2. The scare quotes are Perloff's.

3. Tony Hoagland, *What Narcissism Means to Me: Selected Poems* (Hexham, UK: Bloodaxe Books, 2005), 20.

4. Claudia Rankine, "Open Letter: A Dialogue on Race and Poetry," Academy of American Poets, 4 Feb. 2011, http://www.poets.org/poetsorg/text/open-letter-dialogue-race-and-poetry.

5. Tony Hoagland, "Dear Claudia: A Letter in Response," Academy of American Poets, 4 Feb. 2011, http://www.poets.org/poetsorg/text/dear-claudia-letter-response.

6. Krystal Languell, "Reports from the Field: 'MISOGYNY ALERT,'" VIDA: Women in Literary Arts, 12 Apr. 2014, http://www.vidaweb.org/misogyny-alert/.

7. Junot Díaz, "MFA vs. POC," *New Yorker*, 30 Apr. 2014, http://www.newyorker.com/books/page-turner/mfa-vs-poc.

8. Judah Rubin, "Hello Friends," Facebook, 24 Apr. 2014 (site discontinued).

9. Zoe Rana Mungin, "Dear UMass MFA:," Route Nine 7 (Dec. 2014), http://route9litmag.com/post/104412514724/dear-umass-mfa.

10. The Mongrel Coalition against Gringpo, accessed 12 Aug. 2015, http://gringpo.com/.

11. Kenneth Goldsmith, "The Body of Michael Brown," Facebook, 15 Mar. 2015, https://www.facebook.com/kenneth.goldsmith (site discontinued).

12. Rin Johnson, "On Hearing a White Man Co-opt the Body of Michael

Brown," Hyperallergic, 20 Mar. 2015, http://hyperallergic.com/192628/on-hearing-a-white-man-co-opt-the-body-of-michael-brown/.

13. Aaron Apps, "The (Dis)Embodied Voice: A Response to Kenneth Goldsmith," *Bluestockings Magazine*, 19 Mar. 2015, http://bluestockingsmag.com/2015/03/19/the-disembodied-voice-a-response-to-kenneth-goldsmith/.

14. Andrew Deck, "Racial Controversy over Poem Ends Conference Event Early," *Brown Daily Herald*, 18 Mar. 2015, http://www.browndailyherald.com/2015/03/18/racial-controversy-over-poem-ends-conference-early/.

15. Vanessa Place, "Artist's Statement: Gone with the Wind," 18 May 2015, https://www.facebook.com/notes/vanessa-place/artists-statement-gone-with-the-wind-vanessaplace/10152841235969212?pnref=lhc (site discontinued).

16. "Bay Area Concerns with Misogyny and Gender/Sexual Violence," Pastebin, 19 Aug. 2014, http://pastebin.com/RtABxDzB.

17. Linda Kleinbub, "Roofied at 50: You're Never Too Old for Date-Rape Drugs," *Observer*, 30 Oct. 2014, http://observer.com/2014/10/roofied-at-50-youre-never-too-old-for-date-rape-drugs/.

18. Emma Healey, "Stories like Passwords," *The Hairpin*, 6 Oct. 2014, http://thehairpin.com/2014/10/stories-like-passwords/.

19. Kia Groom, "A Call to Arms: Bite the Hand That Feeds You," *Quaint Magazine*, 24 Apr. 2015, http://quaintmagazine.com/a-call-to-arms-bite-the-hand-that-feeds-you/.

20. Juliana Spahr and Stephanie Young, eds., *A Megaphone: Some Enactments, Some Numbers, and Some Essays about the Continued Usefulness of Crotchless-Pants-and-a-Machine-Gun Feminism* (Oakland: ChainLinks, 2011).

21. "About the VIDA Count," VIDA: Women in Literary Arts, 21 Feb. 2012, http://www.vidaweb.org/the-count/.

22. A note on gender assignation: In all the work we have done around counting gender, we have relied on pronouns in author bio notes. If someone has transitioned and uses female or male pronouns, we have counted the individual as female or male. We have counted someone as gender fluid only if the person used gender-neutral pronouns in the bio note. "Transgender" is VIDA's designation.

23. Unless noted otherwise, all information on undergraduate and graduate creative writing degree programs and students presented in this chapter was drawn from the IPEDS Data Center (National Center for Education Statistics, accessed 22 June 2015, https://nces.ed.gov/ipeds/datacenter/Default.aspx). We used only final-release data. The bulk of our research was conducted within the "Compare Institutions" option, working with variables available through the data center. We looked primarily at completions by year: total number of degrees conferred by program, award level, race/ethnicity, and gender. Program designation is tracked

in IPEDS using the Department of Education's Classification of Instructional Programs (CIP) codes, first developed in 1980. CIP is a taxonomic system that uses two-digit codes for around fifty broad instructional areas and five-digit codes for subcategories within those areas. Creative writing was not included as a five-digit subcategory of English Language and Literatures until sometime after the 1985 CIP revision. The first year for which we were able to select the five-digit creative writing CIP code as a variable along with total number of degrees conferred by award level and gender was 1988; the first year for which we could also select race/ethnicity alongside these other variables was 1995. The last year for which we were able to extract data was 2013. When looking at racial identification, we first selected variables for total white students by gender, then the total by gender of those whose racial identification was unknown (that is, who chose not to identify their race). We then subtracted these numbers from the total number of graduates in a given year to obtain the total number of students who identify as other than white that same year (rather than select all specific racial/ethnic categories used by IPEDS and reporting institutions). At least one study suggests that those students who choose not to identify their race predominantly identify as white at other moments (see Doug Lederman, "Identifying the Racial 'Unknowns,'" *InsideHigherEd*, 5 Jan. 2006, https://www.insidehighered.com/news/2006/01/05/unknown), and we suspect that the total number of white students in all areas we looked at is higher than represented. For the purposes of this chapter, we decided to look only at the percentages of students who chose to self-identify their race. A note on missing data: All institutions that participate in or are applicants for any federal financial assistance program authorized by Title IV of the Higher Education Act of 1965 must complete IPEDS surveys every year, but we encountered inconsistently reported data, particularly when looking at a specific set of institutions (such as those in section 7). In these cases, we have indicated those years and institutions where data are missing.

24. Mark McGurl, *The Program Era: Postwar Fiction and the Rise of Creative Writing* (Cambridge: Harvard UP, 2009), 16.

25. Steve Almond, "Why Talk Therapy Is on the Wane and Writing Workshops Are on the Rise," *New York Times Magazine*, 23 Mar. 2012, http://www.nytimes.com/2012/03/25/magazine/why-talk-therapy-is-on-the-wane-and-writing-workshops-are-on-the-rise.html.

26. Cecilia Capuzzi Simon, "Why Writers Love to Hate the M.F.A.," *New York Times*, 9 Apr. 2015, http://www.nytimes.com/2015/04/12/education/edlife/12edl-12mfa.html.

27. Chad Harbach, *MFA vs NYC: The Two Cultures of American Fiction* (New York: n+1, 2014), 11.

28. "National Universities Rankings," *US News and World Report*, accessed 31 Mar. 2016, http://colleges.usnews.rankingsandreviews.com/best-colleges/rankings/national-universities?int=9ff208.

29. "Background Facts on Contingent Faculty," AAUP, accessed 17 July 2015, http://www.aaup.org/issues/contingency/background-facts.

30. Louis Menand, "Show or Tell: Should Creative Writing Be Taught?," *New Yorker*, 8 June 2009, http://www.newyorker.com/magazine/2009/06/08/show-or-tell.

31. Jordan Weissmann, "The Big Secret about Washington's Student Loan Profits," *Slate*, 16 Apr. 2014, http://www.slate.com/articles/business/moneybox/2014/04/student_loan_profits_the_government_makes_its_money_off_grad_students.html.

32. VONA Voices, accessed 20 May 2015, http://www.voicesatvona.org/.

33. "About," Affording the MFA, accessed 10 May 2015, https://affordingthemfa.wordpress.com/about/.

34. Katty Kay and Claire Shipman, "The Confidence Gap," *The Atlantic*, May 2014, http://www.theatlantic.com/features/archive/2014/04/the-confidence-gap/359815/.

35. John W. Curtis, "Persistent Inequity: Gender and Academic Employment," prepared for "New Voices in Pay Equity," an event for Equal Pay Day, 11 Apr. 2011, http://www.aaup.org/NR/rdonlyres/08E023AB-E6D8-4DBD-99A0-24E5EB73A760/0/persistent_inequity.pdf.

36. Coalition on the Academic Workforce, "A Portrait of Part-Time Faculty Members," June 2012, http://www.academicworkforce.org/CAW_portrait_2012.pdf.

37. AFT Higher Education, "Promoting Racial and Ethnic Diversity: What Higher Education Unions Can Do," Mar. 2010, files.eric.ed.gov/fulltext/ED511576.pdf.

38. Jordan Weissmann, "Ph.D. Programs Have a Dirty Secret: Student Debt," *The Atlantic*, 16 Jan. 2014, http://www.theatlantic.com/business/archive/2014/01/phd-programs-have-a-dirty-secret-student-debt/283126/.

39. MLA Office of Research, "Midyear Report on the 2009–2010 MLA Job List," Mar. 2010, https://apps.mla.org/pdf/jil_midyear_update2009_lg.pdf.

40. Kirkpatrick Sale, *SDS* (New York: Vintage Books, 1974), 635.

41. Roger Rapoport, "Meet America's Meanest Dirty Trickster," *Mother Jones*, Apr. 1977, 18–23, 59–61.

42. Greg Barnhisel, *Cold War Modernists: Art, Literature, and American Cultural Diplomacy* (New York: Columbia UP, 2015), 185.

43. Eric Bennett, *Workshops of Empire: Stegner, Engle, and American Creative Writing during the Cold War* (Iowa City: U of Iowa P, 2015), 8.

44. Karen Ferguson, *Top Down: The Ford Foundation, Black Power, and the Reinvention of Racial Liberalism* (Philadelphia: U of Pennsylvania P, 2013).

45. Jodi Melamed, *Represent and Destroy: Rationalizing Violence in the New Racial Capitalism* (Minneapolis: U of Minnesota P, 2011), 95, 96, 95.

46. Amiri Baraka, "The Revolutionary Theatre," *The Liberator* 5 (1965): 6.

47. "Poetry for the People," UC Berkeley, African American Studies & African Diaspora Studies, accessed 27 June 2015, http://africam.berkeley.edu/content/poetry-for-the-people.

48. Cave Canem: A Home for Black Poetry, accessed 1 Apr. 2016, http://www.cavecanempoets.org/mission.

49. Kundiman, accessed 1 Apr. 2016, http://kundiman.org/what-is-kundiman/.

50. Heriberto Yépez, "La conferencia de poesía en Berkeley," *Milenio*, 27 June 2015, http://www.milenio.com/cultura/milenio_laberinto-columna_heriberto_yepez-conferencia_poesia_berkeley-archivo_hache_0_542946056.html. Trans. Guillermo Para, 28 June 2015, http://venepoetics.blogspot.com/2015/06/la-conferencia-de-poesia-en-berkeley.html.

CHAPTER 11

Humanities Fiction

A Genre

SIMON DURING

In the first few paragraphs of *The Program Era*, Mark McGurl stakes the claim on which his important book rests. "The rise of the creative writing program," he tell us, "stands as the most important event in postwar American literary history."[1] And it does so by inserting "modernist principles of writing"—in particular, techniques for organizing point of view—inside the academic/pedagogic system so as to entrench them as a standard for American literary fiction more widely (x).

McGurl's case persuades me. But it has its limits. After all, during the period that he is concerned with, literary fiction and the university also came together in quite a different way, and one that has been insufficiently recognized. Many of the period's writers did indeed work in universities (at least for periods of their career) but *not* in creative writing programs. They were humanities academics, often English professors. These academic novelists, too, have shaped contemporary literary history in America, and, significantly, not just in America.

Are they authors of a distinct genre—*humanities fiction*?

WHEN I RECENTLY ASKED Facebook friends to list humanities professors who also wrote novels, names came pouring in. This profusion was distracting, however, since it became clear that professors write all kinds of novels for all kinds of reasons, many of which have little to do with their disciplinary attachments. Thus, to consider just one example, between about 1920 and 1950 it was fashionable for English professors (at least in the British Commonwealth) to write detective novels. But this kind of writing was peripheral to their academic work. In the genre I am investigating here, however, the academic and the literary are continuous: that is what makes it relevant to McGurl's argument. Academic novelists work at a different intersection of the university and the literary than those employed in creative writing programs, but one that also enables flows from the professional to the imaginative.

Who are academic novelists? Iris Murdoch, Saul Bellow, A. S. Byatt, W. G. Sebald, J. M. Coetzee, Javier Marías, along with many others. These are, of course, among the most admired writers of our era, at least as much as fiction writers who work in creative writing programs, maybe more so.[2] And I would suggest that these novelists have been acclaimed not *despite* being academics but *because* they were academics, which means because they command knowledge produced in the academic humanities and have done so in a period when the humanities have been massively extended. After the Second World War, the old (classically based) "liberal arts" were transformed into the current transdiscipline of the "humanities," which educated a sufficiently large minority of the population to form its own extramural public sphere.[3] In this situation, education rather than (or in addition to) class filiation came to organize the reproduction of taste. It is in this quite large minority—the "humanities public," as we may call it—that writers of humanities fiction find their readership and recognition.

This claim carries difficulties, not all of which can be addressed here. But let me gesture to some. Given that the humanities public, although a minority formation, extends so far into society, it is artificial to separate writers who actually teach in academic humanities departments from novelists (some of whom have advanced degrees in the humanities) who write primarily for humanities graduates but who have never been academics. For instance, Jean-Paul Sartre, whose fictions were informed by work in philosophy (including his own), was not, by my definition, an academic fiction writer, since he never held a university position. This seems weird.

Let me concede the point by admitting that the category of "academic novelist" has a broader reach than simply someone who has been a professional scholar. Nonetheless, my argument holds: there exist novelists whose fictions depend on advanced work in the academic humanities and are stronger for that reason.

Similarly, it is not as though academic knowledge was never called on by novelists before the twentieth century. The research-informed novelist first appeared in the middle of the nineteenth century, for example, with George

Eliot, whose narrative voice drew on the physiological psychology of her time. She also wrote in the interests of a philosophy that had been developed by young Hegelians like Ludwig Feuerbach whose work was a product of German research universities. There certainly exists a continuity between intellectual novelists like Eliot (or James Joyce or Samuel Beckett) and the contemporary academic novelist.

This leads to a third, more searching difficulty with the attempt to mark the academic novelist as a distinct kind. How, specifically, do the academic humanities find themselves expressed by the academic novelist? It would be easy to say that this depends on the novelist and, indeed, on the particular novel, and when I later concentrate on one novelist—J. M. Coetzee—and one novel—*The Childhood of Jesus*—that will become clear. However, let me speculatively suggest a more general, structural relation between the humanities and the academic novelist. It is not a matter of theme, not even of one of the genre's most favored themes—the tensions between the humanities student or academic and everyday life in the world outside the university. While this is a powerful *topoi*—one that orders novels like Saul Bellow's *Herzog* and Coetzee's *Disgrace*, for instance—it represents rather than enacts the humanities and therefore does not best illuminate the structures connecting the academic to the fictional.

The transfer from the humanities to the novel form has two, albeit fused, aspects: one at the level of form, the other at the level of content. Formally, humanities fiction is narrated from a position that assumes the limited authority conventionally granted to academic knowledge in contemporary society. This authority cannot, however, legitimate the "omniscience" that George Eliot's narrators commanded. In part, that omniscience relied on external social hierarchies: Eliot's narrator controls a cultural range by virtue of his (implicit) class position. His omniscience was also *moral*, compelling to the degree his moral judgments won assent. Against this, academic knowledge grants narratorial authority on the basis of its erudition, autonomy, and neutrality, however much it practically may be engaged in particular political (rarely just moral) projects. In fact, advanced novelists themselves stopped being able to perform moral authority from about the 1880s—this was one of modernism's preconditions—and the "neutral" academic novelist inherits this ban.

The academic novelist's authority is, then, like the modernists', subterranean. It is as if the novelist's personal confidence that he or she has good access to (a sector of) the most advanced, most thoroughly researched forms of cultural analysis and interpretation, and is institutionally entitled to engage a particular (necessarily partisan) line within such analysis and interpretation, is expressed as, and displaced onto, a narratorial style and tone able to connect abstract concepts, experiences, affects, and judgments to one another at various discursive levels—sentences, paragraphs, chapters, and so on.

This is to say that the academic novelist's authority is enacted when a professionally endorsed conceptual order is fleshed out or tested *imaginatively*—in plot, allegory, character, descriptions of mood, perceptions, corporeality, and so on. In this framework, that imagining may take the form of an argument or at least invite readers to suppose that an argument is in question. Or it may take the form of a problematization, inviting its readers to question and worry about relations between, for instance, freedom and necessity, absolute and relative value, newness and heritage, topics that ground academic debates and research programs.

Let me demonstrate this by citing a long passage from Iris Murdoch's *The Bell* (1958), a humanities fiction that makes an argument. It is a passage that is characteristic of the genre in other ways, too:

> Dora had been in the National Gallery a thousand times and the pictures were almost as familiar to her as her own face. Passing between them now, as through a well-loved grove, she felt a calm descending on her. She wandered a little, watching with compassion the poor visitors armed with guide books who were peering anxiously at the masterpieces. Dora did not need to peer. She could look, as one can at last when one knows a great thing very well, confronting it with a dignity which it has itself conferred. She felt that the pictures belonged to her, and reflected ruefully that they were about the only thing that did. Vaguely, consoled by the presence of something welcoming and responding in the place, her footsteps took her to various shrines at which she had worshipped so often before: the great light spaces of Italian pictures, more vast and southern than any South, the angels of Botticelli, radiant as birds, delighted as gods and curling as tendrils of a vine. . . .
>
> Dora was always moved by the pictures. Today she was moved, but in a new way. She marvelled, with a kind of gratitude, that they were all still here, and her heart was filled with love for the pictures, their authority, their marvellous generosity, their splendour. It occurred to her that here at

> last was something real and something perfect. Who had said that, about perfection and reality being in the same place?[4]

Dora is a humanities (art-school) graduate, and she is married to a professional art historian. So her knowledge of and authority over the National Gallery's works of art, which allow her to condescend to the guidebook-clutching tourists, is not based on class (in fact, she comes from the lower middle class) but on her education. She has come to the gallery for spiritual solace that she finds in paintings: for instance, in Botticelli's angels. The passage also has philosophical implications that serve as an argument. Imaginative works, we are being instructed, are as real as—more real than—reality; and reality is not other to perfection but its home. And the citation ends with a question as if in a tutorial: Who was it that said that perfection and reality coincide? Spinoza of course! We good humanities graduates know that, even if we have not read Murdoch's own philosophical works that make the same case.

So here an action—visiting an art gallery—is embedded in character and plot to make a conceptual or philosophic argument in the academic manner. The passage's energy, however, also relies on a distance between the character and the narrator, a distance that is not based on the narrator's moral authority or in irony but in the narrator's ability (which is shared by the implied reader) to conceptualize more complexly and intelligently than the character. For instance, the Botticelli angels that Dora sees are described, remarkably, as part gods, part birds, part vines in a voice that is more narratorial than indirectly free. And for all its literary virtuosity, it belongs to the neutrality of the academy, too. That virtuosity is also connected to erudition: it is the reader and narrator who recognize Spinoza, not Dora.

This is also to suggest that narratorial authority relies on a particular implied reader: one who shares the humanities ethos, which, in its most basic form, consists of a belief that the life of the mind and its conditions of possibility are all but essential both to individuals and to society and, more specifically, that it is immeasurably valuable for individuals to have at least some command over the disciplined information and intellectual practices that allow one best to understand the situation in which we find ourselves.

I HAVE SUGGESTED THAT humanities fiction characteristically draws on the disciplinary *topoi* of its time to make arguments or problematize relations between concepts. I have further suggested that the genre's narrational authority is indirectly based on the academy's putative, and routinely transgressed, autonomy and neutrality. I want now to solidify this case by offering a brief intellectual history of Coetzee's *The Childhood of Jesus*, a humanities fiction that does not wage an argument but sets up a problem. Why appeal to intellectual history? Just because the novel draws on already somewhat dated academic knowledge to which the *history* of that discipline now gives us access. Humanities fictions, as containers of academic knowledge, contribute to intellectual history as they do to literary history. And I have chosen *The Childhood of Jesus* in particular because it problematizes the concept of neutrality itself, although it does so via a related but nonetheless different concept—"the neutral"—which was important to the discipline of literary criticism in the years that Coetzee practiced academic criticism.

In sum, my argument is that Coetzee's novel may be read as a contribution to the theory of the neutral in imaginatively realizing it. In that way it invites us into the history of literary theory. Our sense of what Coetzee is up to is adequate to the degree that we are familiar with that history.

IN FRANCE AFTER the Second World War, "the neutral" was a central term for two major French critics—Roland Barthes and Maurice Blanchot—whence it came to inform anglophone poststructuralism more widely and thus was widely dispersed through academic literary studies at the period when Coetzee was professionally engaged with them. While Barthes and Blanchot developed their theories of the neutral in relation to each other, their interests and arguments differed, so literary theory's category of the neutral has, in fact, two separate inflections.

Barthes's theory of the neutral was first sketched out in essays published in book form as *Le degré zéro de l'écriture* in 1953. These essays read modern literature—indeed, "literature" as such since Barthes argues that literature is a modern concept that emerges out of the history that he describes—as an (ultimately political) struggle, with the realization that bourgeois literary writing is now impossible for any writers fully engaged by their times. Bourgeois realism has become merely "classical"; it has lost its claim to universality. Language is breaking up into different idiolects so that writers must now find new strategies for dealing with this "plurality of modes of writing."[5]

One such mode—the neutral—is "a colourless writing, freed from all bondage to a pre-ordained state of language" (76). Barthes goes on to argue that the neutral's aim is "to go beyond Literature by entrusting one's fate to a sort of basic speech, equally far from living languages and literary language proper" (77). This basic speech is a vernacular stripped of collective experience. It is merely instrumental although in the service of avoiding all received cultural modes and, most of all, of avoiding the literary itself. But Barthes is quick to point out that this avoidance is always compromised: the neutral will be quickly pulled back into literature as "society demotes [such] writing to a mere manner," and then the writer is returned to the prison that literature is for Barthes (78).

Barthes's neutral, then, is a simultaneously linguistic and political concept. It is a predicament (the structure of contemporary discourse delivers it to us) but at the same time a tool to be used against bourgeois society, not in the spirit of bohemia but of a certain activism in which writers can join the struggle against hegemony. That activism is limited to a form of literary entryism: literary writing uses the neutral language of a technologized, post-revolutionary, democratic society to renew itself by erasing itself. It is, among other things, a language of technique, a language of neutralized, practical knowledges and pedagogies.

Blanchot's concept of the neutral is philosophically more ambitious than Barthes's. He presents it most carefully in a 1964 review essay of Réné Char's poetry, collected in the volume *L'entretien infin* (1969). The neutral, Blanchot tells us, has nothing to do with objectivity or indifference.[6] It instead names a stance toward the "unknown," which is that metaphysical concept designating what cannot be signified or experienced. The neutral is a literary relation to the outside. The neutral is neither an affirmation nor a negation of the unknown; indeed, it is "foreign to every exigency of identity, or unity, even of presence" (300). In it, even death/finitude is not "marked as a lack" (311). So it cannot be thought. Thus, it shelters in literary texts where it poses itself as something like a question that hollows out writing's propositional force and substantive categories. In particular the neutral dissolves genres, most of all the genre of "fiction." It also follows from Blanchot's analysis that, as their encounter with otherness and death hollows out the substance of their writing, writers turn to the *style* of neutrality as Barthes had defined it.

Arguably at least, Blanchot's idea of the neutral, like Barthes's, contains political resonances. On the one hand, as is spelled out in Blanchot's later speculations on community, it points to, or imagines, abstruse, barely figurable, forms of collectivity quite different from those we actually have, in which individuals associate not to form a unity or "to make up the substance of integrity" (to use Blanchot's paraphrase of Georges Bataille) but rather endlessly to make and unmake society by being true to the hollowness of authenticity, interiority, the common.[7] On the other hand, the neutral, for all its metaphysical elaboration, points to the Nietzschean "last man"/Kojèvean "end of history" complexion of postwar social democracy as seen from a radical perspective.

Blanchot himself thinks primarily of Kafka when he thinks of the neutral in literary terms. Here plot is more important than style: it is Kafka, he notes, who shows us that it is "storytelling that brings the neutral into play" (*Infinite Conversation* 384). And it is in thinking about Kafka that Blanchot offers a summary history of literary narration to set against the one that Barthes outlined in *Writing Degree Zero*. Remarkably, unexpectedly, Kafka set story free, abandoning realism. Narrative voice and characters became pawns of plot, and plot was unconstrained by the difference between subjectivity and objectivity as well as by the principle of sufficient reason. Anything might happen. Under this regime, characters lost their interiority, and the narrator, all aesthetic affectations.

If, in Kafka, story is no longer presented as transmitted experience, where does it come from; what utters it? It is uttered by "a voice that has no place in the work, but neither does it hang over it," and that does not fall "out of some sky under the guarantee of a superior Transcendence" (*Infinite Conversation* 385). The neutral narrative voice "says nothing, not only because it adds nothing to what there is to say (it knows nothing), but because the narrative voice subtends this nothing" (385). Indeed, Kafka's/the neutral's narrative voice is

> always different from what utters it. . . . Let us (on a whim) call it spectral, ghostlike. Not that it comes from beyond the grave, or even because it would once and for all represent some essential absence, but because it always tends to absent itself in its bearer and also efface him as the center. (386)

It is, we might say, an institutional voice, not a personal or subjective one.

BARTHES AND BLANCHOT'S concept of the neutral—especially Blanchot's —haunts and shapes *The Childhood of Jesus*, marking it as a humanities fiction. Certainly it is not difficult to see the novel as instantiating their theories of the neutral. After all, like much of Coetzee's fiction, it is written in that neutral style to which Barthes drew attention. Further, it is written in a third-person present tense that hovers between signifying time now and the "historic present" as it is used to locate a past event in the present, mainly in academic-humanities prose itself. This ambiguous tense structure allows the narrative all the more easily to elide those causal chains that make coherent the flow of events from past to future. By the same stroke, judgments about exactly when events occurred/are occurring are difficult: the narrative tense prepares the way for a shift of narrative temporality implied on the novel's last page. And the tense does not express any specifiable narratorial persona. The narration is "not recorded by anybody," as Blanchot put it: it is institutional (*Infinite Conversation* 385). And just for that reason too, as in Blanchot's Kafka, story rules in the sense that anything at all might happen next. The narration belongs to the neutral in all this and, more particularly, to a neutrality with academic overtones: the neutral first of "theory" and, by implication, of the academy in general.

The Childhood of Jesus's story is not just *in* the neutral but also *about* the neutral. Its flat narration presents a plot that can itself be seen as an allegory of Blanchot's theo-literary-metaphysics. *The Childhood of Jesus* tells a tale about a man (Simon) and a young boy (David) who arrive by boat in a society where everyone else has come from somewhere else too. It turns out, however, that they have arrived in a country unlike our own, although one that is not wholly unfamiliar to us: a reassemblage of elements we recognize from our society, at least as it once was or maybe as some would like it to be.

In this new land, civil society and the public sphere are thin: theaters, cafés, newspapers, parks, public squares seem to be absent. The local vernacular is beginner's Spanish. The market barely plays a role: no one seems to own private property, few commodities are available, and there is no consumerism. Workers appear to manage production without thinking about profit. There is a state and legal system but no politics or nationalism. The institutions that count are workplaces, housing associations, and welfare agencies that help unexpected newcomers when they arrive. Apart from that there is no integral community: institutions have taken over from community. There is little apparent suffering. In sum, this new place appears to harbor a perfected laborist society under the reign of neutrality. It exists, we may venture, at an end of history.

This society functions smoothly mainly because people possess an unwavering benevolence toward each other. Theirs is a passionless benevolence, however: the often frictional and ambivalent feelings and tones that drive relations between people in the world we actually inhabit have been erased. Irony, love, competitiveness, eros, resentment, disagreement, expressions of interiority are rare and mild if not completely absent. The society also works because passive obedience prevails: rebelliousness has vanished too. Everyone accepts the prevailing social order, the hollow collectivity, except Simon—and David, too, by the novel's end.

When David falls into difficulties in the classroom and is sent to a special-needs boarding school, he rebels. He organizes another flight, this time away from his and Simon's new migrant life. This allows the story to end pretty much where it began, with David prophesizing that when they leave their new land,

> "we are going to say, *Good morning, we are new arrivals, and we are looking for somewhere to stay.*"
>
> "And?"
>
> "That's all. *Looking for somewhere to stay, to start our new life.*"[8]

The country in which Simon and David have arrived, then, is finely balanced between utopia and dystopia. A new Erewhon in which security and welfare triumph over freedom and enterprise. A society from which the only exit seems to be a return to the beginning. But it is not quite secular. Indeed, it quickly becomes apparent that although the migrant society is a version of our own society, it is also an afterlife.

That concept is evoked principally because the characters have little or no memory of their past existence. In this, their nature is not ours. They have, at best, a memory of memory; they live in what Blanchot, defining neutrality, called the "ruin" of memory (*Infinite Conversation* 385). They are disjunct from the past in ways that no culturalism or even any naturalism bound to sufficient reason could endorse.

Once we accept that Simon and David's new life is not just being lived in alternative secular society but beyond the grave, they—and the neutral society they now find themselves inhabiting—demand to be considered spiritually as well as politically. All the more so because their posthumous world is obviously not Heaven or Hell or Purgatory, which is structured around penance and expectation, neither of which exist here. It is rather a Limbo—a reminiscence of that province of Dante's Inferno in which those who have had no chance to encounter Christ's word in this world, and who, accordingly, escape the machinery of eschatological judgment, live out eternity.

What is at stake becomes clear in passages like this, in which Simon thinks about the people he is meeting, especially his foreman Álvaro, and Elena, the mother of a friend of David's who lives in his housing block and who has also become his casual lover:

> Álvaro does not trade in irony. Nor does Elena. Elena is an intelligent woman but she does not see any doubleness in the world, any difference between the way things seem and the way things are. An intelligent woman and an admirable woman too, who out of the most exiguous materials—seamstressing, music lessons, household chores—has put together a new life, a life from which she claims—with justice?—that nothing is missing. It is the same with Álvaro and the stevedores: they have no secret yearnings he can detect, no hankerings after another kind of life. Only he is the exception, the dissatisfied one, the misfit. What is wrong with him? Is it, as Elena says, just the old way of thinking and feeling that has not yet died in him, but kicks and shudders in its last throes.
>
> Things do not have their due weight here: that is what he would like, in the end, to say to Elena. Our lovemaking lacks weight. The food we eat, our dreary diet of bread, lacks substance—lacks the substantiality of animal flesh, with all the gravity of bloodletting and sacrifice behind it. Our very words lack weight, these Spanish words that do not come from our heart. (Coetzee 80)

That its inhabitants feel that nothing is missing in their world itself points to its posthumousness. The afterlife does not offer a better future: that is one more thing it shares with the end of history. It lacks an "other." So Elena does not grasp an opposition between the ideal and the real, between romance and the real, between what is present and what is absent. Once nothing is missing, once there are no irony and doubleness, once sacrifices are never required, once there is no fit acknowledgment of difference, life becomes "weightless." This quality of insubstantiality also locates the story in the (neutral) afterlife, this time as if to challenge us to reexamine the conditions of our actual worldly condition and, most of all, our modes of living together.

This complex presentation of the afterlife as a version of the welfare state under the rule of a neutrality, which also signifies an institutionalized society and perhaps one institution in particular (the English department), belongs to the history of an academic discipline. But at the novel's heart something more still is at work, because it also references the story of Christ's childhood. This, then, is also a postsecular story about the limits of immanence.

Parallels between David and Christ organize the plot. *The Childhood of Jesus* tells a version of the story of the virgin birth. David preaches nonaggression and turns the other cheek. He has miraculous powers that he uses casually enough: for instance, rejuvenating Simon at one point (170), causing him to walk at another (284). He expresses an interest in "saving" people and animals too (234–35). He possesses unaccounted-for talents—winning chess games, knowing how to read and write, all without lessons. He writes "I am the truth" on a blackboard at school (263). He meets a kind of devil. He thinks that he has walked through a barbed-wire fence unscathed and persuades others that this miracle has occurred. He has an extraordinary capacity to command other's admiration and allegiance. At the story's end, he sets out with a few disciples for another new life—in the teasingly named Estrellita—picking up whoever comes their way, no questions asked.[9]

David's spiritual presence is, however, granted to him by virtue of a singularity, defined across three registers, each of which, once again, may be understood in academic and intellectual-historical terms.

First, David does not take to math: he will not accept the concept of number. For him, the world cannot—and should not—be organized into discrete abstract counters in an endless sequence. That is to open up a kind of infinity that is opposed to his own, which is that of the unknowable, recursive, mysterious. His refusal of number seems to refer back eruditely to the way that the seventeenth-century Cartesian/Leibnizian mathematicalization of the natural world undid the old Platonic/Aristotelian metaphysics on which Latin Christian orthodoxy was based. It places David outside a modernity whose culmination the neutral society to which he has immigrated may perhaps be.

Second, as we have begun to see, David is also unwilling or unable to make the distinction between the real and the fiction, the real and the ideal. For him, practical reason and the life of the imagination are not disjunct. This would appear to refer to, and repudiate, the notion, put forward by new historicists in the 1990s, that the category of fiction was invented in the early Enlightenment and that it was corrosive of religious faith.[10] In resisting *Don Quixote*'s separation of the imagined from the real, David is resisting a form of *secular* magic, as academic scholarship knows it, that indirectly helps remove God from the world.

Third, David is not at home in the vernacular—the simple Spanish spoken in his new homeland. He wants to speak his own private language, which Ludwig Wittgenstein and Stanley Cavell assure us is impossible. Here his singularity takes a specifically literary form as we discover when Simon, attempting to persuade David from using his private vocabulary, tries to figure him out:

> He looks into the boy's eyes. For the briefest of moments he sees something there. He has no name for it. It is *like a fish*—that is what occurs to him in the moment. Like a fish that wiggles loose as you try to grasp it. But not like a fish—no, like *like a fish*. Or like *like like a fish*. On and on. Then the moment is over, and he is simply standing in silence, staring.
>
> "Did you see?" says the boy.
>
> "I don't know. Stop for a minute, I am feeling dizzy."
>
> "I can see what you are thinking!" says the boy with a triumphant smile.
>
> "No you can't."
>
> "You think I can do magic."
>
> "Not at all. You have no idea what I am thinking. Now pay attention. I am going to say something about language, something serious, something I want you to take to heart.
>
> "Everyone comes to this country as a stranger. I came as a stranger. You came as a stranger. . . . We come from various places and various pasts, seeking a new life. But now we are all in the same boat together. So we have to get along with each other. One of the ways in which we get along is by speaking the same language. That is the rule. It is a good rule, and we should obey it. Not only obey it but obey it with a good heart. . . . With a good heart and goodwill. If you refuse, if you go on being rude about Spanish and insist on speaking your own language, then you are going to find yourself living in a private world. You will have no friends. You will be shunned." (Coetzee 220)

Simon believes that he has fleetingly caught sight of something like David's soul, his mysterious, elusive inner self. It is only expressible in metaphor, a

Christological metaphor. It is like a fish. But putting it like that is too constative: the figure of speech requires a typographical diacritical mark (italics), and then a recursive leap, for David's full evasiveness and mystery to be articulated. *Like like a fish.* Whatever that might be. Whatever it is, behind David's loss of substance as Simon's language turns self-conscious, one feels the breath of academic literary theory and specifically the poststructuralist (i.e., Paul de Man's) critique of metaphor's capacity to embody transcendence.

THIS BRIEF AND INCOMPLETE reading of the novel has two purposes. It is designed to show how embedded in institutionality and disciplinary erudition the novel is. And it also helps us see that in allegorizing Blanchot's neutral as an end of history, within a narrative mode that owes much to Barthes's (and Kafka's) different concept of neutrality, it exposes a space in which the reader can problematize the concept of neutrality, perhaps even to join David's (and Dora's) affirmation of perfection, transcendence, mystery. Thus, it hints at a critique of a certain poststructuralism, perhaps even begins an argument in that direction. But it asks us further: How neutral is the academy? More specifically, how neutral are the humanities? Is the novel's bloodless, end-of-history, last man, institutionalized world *ours*?

Nevertheless, this reading of the novel offers evidence for there being a different way of writing literary fiction than that prescribed by McGurl's creative writing programs, if no less connected to the university. Where exactly this leads us, only more investigation into humanities fiction will show. But it seems no accident that Coetzee (like Saul Bellow, say) is a Nobel Prize winner. The global humanities public has canonizing powers that are unavailable to sections of the literary field more distant from the advanced, academically legitimated, knowledges of our time. And, importantly, those powers may be harnessed on behalf of humanities fiction for which the academic humanities know themselves as a kind of death.

NOTES

1. Mark McGurl, *The Program Era: Postwar Fiction and the Rise of Creative Writing* (Cambridge: Harvard UP, 2009), ix.

2. Clearly the category of "humanities fiction" is not confined to what Nicholas Dames has called the "theory generation" in an article that, however, to some de-

gree anticipates the argument I am making here. See Nicholas Dames, "The Theory Generation," *n+1* 14 (Summer 2012): 157–69.

3. In calling the humanities a "transdiscipline," I am gesturing to the ways in which, from the outside, they—not the disciplines they shelter—are regarded as unified and distinct. For more on this, see Simon During, "Postdisciplinarity," Academia, accessed 1 Mar. 2015, https://www.academia.edu/764233/Postdisciplinarity.

4. Iris Murdoch, *The Bell* (London: Chatto and Windus, 1958), 191.

5. Roland Barthes, *Writing Degree Zero*, trans. Annette Lavers and Colin Smith (New York: Hill and Wang, 1968), 61.

6. Maurice Blanchot, *The Infinite Conversation*, trans. Susan Hanson (Minneapolis: U of Minnesota P, 1992), 303.

7. Maurice Blanchot, *The Unavowable Community*, trans. Pierre Joris (Barrytown, NY: Station Hill, 1988), 5.

8. J. M. Coetzee, *The Childhood of Jesus* (Melbourne: Text Publishing, 2013), 324.

9. *Looking for Estrellita* is the name of a book of essays by Coetzee's Adelaide colleague Brian Castro, whose publisher advertises it like this: "Castro explores foreignness, the multiplicity of the self, the business of writing and language, and celebrates the novel as a way of understanding the world."

10. See Catherine Gallagher, "The Rise of Fictionality," *The Novel, Volume 1*, ed. Franco Moretti (Princeton: Princeton UP, 2007), 336–63.

PART III

Prospects

CHAPTER 12

"My Ghost Life"

Russell Banks and the Limits of Aesthetic Democracy

SEAN MCCANN

The owl of Minerva flies at dusk. Mark McGurl's *The Program Era* is surely the most comprehensive and illuminating account of postwar literary fiction in the United States we can expect to receive—of the artistic problems that motivated that fiction and of the institutional structures that sustained it. Yet it may be that, like the model to which the book's title alludes—Hugh Kenner's monument *The Pound Era* (1971)—McGurl's book will turn out to be a valedictory for a cultural movement whose greatest days have passed. Kenner's book celebrated the achievements of literary modernism at a moment when, as McGurl's study emphasizes, the once avant-garde techniques and principles championed by Pound had been assimilated into the institutions of higher education. McGurl's work analogously celebrates the "literary excellence" of the creative writing program and its reflexive relation to "the mission of mass higher education" at a moment when the coherence of those institutions appears to be rapidly crumbling.[1]

This hypothesis can be put more precisely by following out the implications of the intertwined histories McGurl traces. At the core of *The Program Era*'s account of postwar literary fiction lies an argument about the "dynamic oppositions of value" that structure the pedagogy, and the products, of the creative writing program and their homologous relation to the larger tensions of mass higher education (18). As McGurl explains, the postwar writing program's reiterated emphasis on the internal feedback between creativity and criticism, between personal expression and public form, between the individual writer and the workshop that critiques her, turns out, both genealogically and structurally, to mirror at a smaller scale the dynamic oppositions that organized the postwar academy, and it implicitly reflects the pluralist models of social organization and the progressive theories of education that justified the rapid expansion of the era's "multiversity."

As Clark Kerr memorably defined that "new type of institution," the postwar multiversity was "not really private and . . . not really public" but a mediating fabric stretched between apparently opposed poles of value.[2] The university, Kerr explained, was neither a research facility nor an undergraduate college but a hybrid structure that combined a highly diversified graduate research institution, tracing its lineage to Humboldt and Berlin, with a new mass undergraduate teaching program indebted to the "British" or "humanist" model of liberal education (13). The multiversity, Kerr thus pointed out, was committed to producing "new knowledge" in ramifying fields and, through that research, to supporting "economic and social growth." At the same time, it was dedicated to providing the liberal education that would allow a mass public to aspire to "trained intellect" (xii, 95). As both the research and educational arms of the university expanded dramatically, these competing missions grew ever more complex and diverse. On a day-to-day basis, the multiversity thus struggled to negotiate among the distinct interests of faculty, students, and the public and to sort out the fractious demands of metastasizing schools and departments. Seen from a higher remove, it maintained a constantly shifting "dynamics of balance"—between "teaching and research, . . . between the humanities and science," between the goal of nurturing "intellectual creativity" and the responsibility of developing useful "skills," between its natural tendency to elevate "an elite of merit" and the broader "egalitarian philosophy" of a "populist society" (85, 91).

The multiversity, in Kerr's account, was thus less a single "organism" defined by a unitary "soul" than a "series of processes," which nevertheless somehow managed to produce "out of all these fragments, and conflicts a kind of unlikely consensus" (15, 13). By Kerr's reasoning, however, that apparent weakness was in truth a great strength. For its manifold internal differences made the multiversity a gleaming example of what Kerr, following the then-prevailing theories in the social sciences, praised as the pluralistic features of "middle-class democracy" (94). "Pluralism in higher education matches the pluralistic American society," Kerr averred (88). Indeed, its constantly renegotiated "dynamics of balance" made the postwar university a compelling contrast to what Kerr called the "Communist City of Intellect"—a "planned community" that "grows only in certain directions and in certain ways"(93). Precisely because it served diverse communities and constituents, and because it grew in various and unpredictable ways, the multiversity seemed to Kerr a counter to the monolith of state socialism. At its best, Kerr suggested, the pluralist multiversity promised a "demonstration of how excellence makes democracy more vital and its survival more assured" (viii, 91). "Will it be," he wondered in his closing pages, "the salvation of our society?" (92).

CERTAINLY, THE ACADEMIC entrepreneurs crucial to the growth of the creative writing program expected the multiversity to play a vital role in the salvation and propagation of literature, and they thought of the mission of literary education and its place in the larger institution in ways quite consistent with Kerr's reasoning. As D. G. Myers has shown in his history of creative writing, the roots of the discipline lay in the theories of progressive and humanist education that viewed schooling as a means to enable the process that McGurl calls "autonomous self-creation" (3). In the pivotal postwar decades when the creative writing program became the predominant institution of professional literary training, writers and literary critics justified its growth by casting this vision of creative self-realization as a crucial component in the larger dynamic balance of the multiversity. Along with its ideological helpmate, New Criticism, creative writing would rescue the study of literature from the deadening academicism of philology and thus make the revivifying experience of art a therapeutic counter to the broader dangers of academicism and scientific reductionism. Literature, and the arts and humanities more broadly, would thus be academic disciplines like any other, but at the same time they would be antidisciplines, opposing the research university's inherent tendency to bureaucratic functionalism with a counterinstitutional care of the self. In their responsibility for "defin[ing] the good as well as the true," Kerr remarked in this spirit, and in their task of "add[ing] wisdom to truth," the arts and humanities would thus provide a counterbalance to the rapid growth of the sciences and to the increasing bureaucratic routinization of the university (93). In doing so, they would preserve the therapeutic vision of both liberal and progressive education, and they would counter and transcend the pathologies of fragmentation, coercion, regimentation, and narrow self-interest to which Kerr feared the multiversity was prey.

Such attitudes are evident throughout the writings of the academic entrepreneurs most responsible for the growth of the creative writing program in its golden era. Wallace Stegner, for example—who received an MA and a PhD from Iowa and who taught at Wisconsin and Harvard before founding Stanford's legendary creative writing program—defended the literary artist's place in the university in 1958 by invoking the premium that Kerr's multiversity placed on producing new knowledge. But he simultaneously made sure to preserve a supplemental role for the traditionally literary quality of unrationalizable intuition. "Science and art both represent original questionings," Stegner claimed. Both were "pure research," and "both rely upon an originating intuition," even as they depended on the research university to advance. At the same time Stegner, like Kerr, was not willing to abandon the visions of cultural training and personal self-realization that had been passed down by the traditions of liberal and progressive education alike. "Any writer had better be concerned with the development of his personality and his character," Stegner warned, and thus want to grow in "sensibility or humanity or compassion or the largeness of mind."[3]

Stegner's colleague Paul Engle, who directed the Iowa Writers' Workshop for the crucial quarter century of its rise to preeminence, made virtually the same points. "All art is intuitive," Engle remarked, but "the great and structured works of writing" required the critical insight that came only with scrupulous training. They were "done with the intelligence playing over against the intuition, each bracing the other, the mind giving form and sense, the intuition giving immediacy of impression." Like Stegner, too, Engle aligned this dialectical vision with a tacitly ethical description of the trained artist as the fully realized person. "The writer must . . . have a more than ordinary capacity for life" and "an astonishing degree of self-knowledge."[4] To this account of artistic self-realization, however, Engle also added a complementary defense of the institution that echoed Kerr's "dynamics of balance." The "Program in Creative Writing at the University of Iowa," Engle declared, had shown that the creative artist need not suffer "alienation . . . from his times and his country." Its history revealed not only that "writing talent can be found" and trained but that, "in an open society such as ours, writer, businessman, and university can join to make an environment which is useful to the writer, friendly for the businessman, and healthy for the university." In doing so, they enabled a kind of artistic life that depended on and legitimized the structures of the multiversity even as it transcended its limits—a "community of the imagination" that included "young writers from all regions of the USA and many areas of the earth" (vii).

Similar invocations of transcendent literary community were commonplace among the founding generation of the Program Era. In her stints teaching at the University of Kansas, Princeton, Columbia, and the New School, Caroline Gordon, for example, played an important role in making the Jamesian aesthetics of point of view the prevailing concern of the era's focus on craft, and she copublished with her husband, Allen Tate, the textbook and anthology *The House of Fiction* (1960) to enable students at "institutions of learning" to grapple with "the techniques" of artful writing. "The struggles which used to go on in lonely garrets or basements, by the light of a taper or oil lamp," Gordon noted, "are now enacted in the classroom or lecture hall by the light of day." But when she spoke about the goals of the "technical training" she advocated, Gordon understandably downplayed talk of institutional design or pedagogical method and focused instead on the ethical rewards of literary community. Writers who undertook the demands of a proper literary education were prepared, she suggested, to "join hands across time and space" in a "mighty dance" made up of "dancers . . . of all races, all ages, all conditions of servitude."[5]

Lionel Trilling, who despite his long tenure at Columbia never ceased warning his contemporaries about the dangers of bureaucratic organizations and the people who staffed them, spoke similarly about the allure "of a multitudinous democracy of letters" that arose among those "who lov[e] civilization and culture in and for themselves."[6] So, too, did Trilling's colleague John Crowe Ransom invoke "the community of letters" as both complement and alternative to the institutional demands of the school.[7] When he referred to the community of letters, Ransom had only recently collaborated with Trilling and F. O. Matthiessen in founding the Kenyon School of Letters, an institution established in 1947 with funding from the Rockefeller Foundation, to offer summer-session graduate training in literary criticism with the aim of challenging the still lingering dominance of old-school philology. The Kenyon School of Letters was a great success and, when the Rockefeller money ran out in 1951, Indiana University stepped in to absorb the institution, keeping on Ransom and Trilling, along with Philip Rahv and Allen Tate as senior fellows, and later inviting such eminent guests as R. P. Blackmur, William Empson, Frank Kermode, Randall Jarrell, René Wellek, and Northrop Frye.[8]

For Ransom, however, the "community of letters" both depended on and transcended the School of Letters, much as Engle's community of imagination depended on and transcended the enabling structures of the university. As Ransom explained, the intangible world that sprung among readers of literature was "an alternative way of living." It amounted to "a community of a sort which could scarcely have been contemplated in the formal organization of society, a community . . . based on a common sympathy."[9]

The founding thinkers of both the creative writing program and of postwar literary study, in short, thought of literature as both a component of and supplement to the multiversity. The democracy of letters was at once dependent on the university's patronage and institutional structures and at the same time outside and alternative to those structures, and in this manner it promised to realize the high aspirations that the university pursued but that were inevitably compromised by the pathologies built into its institutional structures.

It is the distinctiveness and the enduring force of that aesthetic ideology that *The Program Era* shows us most clearly. McGurl's study offers a deeply illuminating conceptual map of the landscape of postwar literary fiction, and the map is illustrated with a stunning range of virtuoso critical readings. But in its overarching argument, *The Program Era* does more than remind us that postwar literary writers depended on the patronage of the university or adapted their careers and expectations for art to the demands of the institution. More fundamentally, McGurl reveals how deeply the assumptions shared by writer-teachers like Ransom, Trilling, Gordon, and Engle were institutionalized in the pedagogy of the creative writing program and echoed in the self-reflective, "systematic creativity" of literary fiction itself (69). As McGurl shows, writers trained in the aesthetic and ethos of the program obsessively staged and restaged, with often dizzying inventiveness, a coherent set of artistic problems. The true revelation of his study, however, is that those problems gained resonance by dramatizing the tensions of social mediation and personal development to which advocates of the program like Stegner and Engle compulsively returned. Perhaps not surprisingly, then, the achievements of the Program Era demonstrate for McGurl something quite similar to the pluralist models of American democracy invoked by Kerr and the imaginative counterparts invoked by Gordon, Ransom, and Trilling. Seen as an "aesthetic-institutional totality," McGurl remarks, the fiction of the Program

Era displays an admirable effort "to realize a diverse aesthetic democracy." It is a "model of the modern pluralistic society as an assemblage of different and conflicting, but always aesthetically redeemable, points of view" (74, 50).

But does that model still retain force? Does the multiversity still occupy the central place in American society, and does literary fiction still enjoy the cultural prestige, that Kerr, Stegner, and Engle all took for granted? *The Program Era* opens and closes with the reasonable suggestion that in at least some important senses they do. More than ever, we live in an "information" or "experience" economy, McGurl suggests, and in such an economy, intellectual training and educational accreditation remain crucial to middle-class success. Furthermore, the creative self-fashioning modeled by program writing appears to be touted more widely than ever as an invaluable resource in the pursuit of prosperity and personal happiness (13–21). So, too, McGurl adds, do we live in an age of "literary excellence" in which the writers nurtured by creative writing pedagogy produce "an embarrassment of riches" for our appreciation (410). It is still the Program Era.

Yet there is surely another way to see this picture. As Kerr himself came to acknowledge, the grand visions he had invoked in 1963 were a product of the wealth and power, and the ideological prestige, American higher education enjoyed at the height of the Cold War. This was also the era of détente among the "countervailing powers" of Big Business, Big Labor, and Big Capital—or, if one prefers, of Fordism. And it was near the high-water mark of the renowned great compression in American incomes and of the ideological influence of postcapitalist theories of social organization. In such an environment, visions of the middle-class democracy that could be sustained by pluralist institutions may (or must?) have seemed especially compelling. In addition, however, as Evan Brier points out, the founders of the Program Era worked at a moment when a tacit alliance of literary publishing and monopoly mass media gave ambitious writers a more plausible claim to vast public influence than they enjoyed any time before or since.[10]

None of those conditions still obtain. Kerr responded to their rapid decline by worrying that the multiversity would lose its coherence and integrity and that its increasing assimilation into industry and the employment market would hasten "fractionalization of the academic guild" (216). *The Program Era* shows us the power and resilience of the aesthetic ideology of a literary-academic guild in the years of its greatest prestige. Have not the guild and its ideology become as fractionalized as the multiversity that once sustained them?

IF THAT PICTURE is accurate, the transition may be illuminated in a compelling way by the work and career of Russell Banks. For Banks, who is in many ways an exemplary representative of the vocational training and aesthetic ideology of the Program Era, produced over the latter fifteen years or so of the twentieth century a remarkable string of brilliant novels that exemplified the ethos of the program while simultaneously tracing its limits and dramatizing its declining authority.

As Banks himself repeatedly notes, it would be difficult to conceive his life story apart from the postwar transformation of American higher education. Born in 1939 into the family of an alcoholic, itinerant plumber, Banks distinguished himself early by his educational aptitude and artistic interests. As a young man, he was recruited to attend Colgate University as part of a special scholarship program for children of the working class. He later went on to complete undergraduate and graduate degrees at the University of North Carolina before going on to teach writing at Emerson College, the University of New Hampshire, New England College, Columbia University, Sarah Lawrence College, New York University, and Princeton. In these experiences, Banks remarks, adopting the pluralist university's language of diversity, he was "sort of an early affirmative-action kid," and he describes his own experience as emblematic of the broader meritocratic transformation of higher education. When he arrived, the culture of the university was still "run by upper-class white men." By the time he became a professor of creative writing, he was a member of a community in which "the contributors come from everywhere—white men, women, African-Americans, Asian-Americans, [and] Native Americans."[11]

In addition to the language of pluralist democracy, the disciplinary ethos of the creative writing program is evident throughout Banks's work. Its hallmarks appear in the way Banks refers to fiction writing as a craft and a profession characterized by "the rigorous disciplines of art" and in the manner in which he places that non-alienated work in contrast both to the vocational rivals of journalism and sociology and, more seriously, to the penurious labor and anomie suffered by the working-class protagonists of his major novels.

"Because I was able to write these novels and stories," Banks remarks, "I have managed to live a different story than the one I was given by my childhood" (68, 67).[12] Its influence is equally evident in Banks's nearly obsessive preoccupation with the technical and ethical problems of point of view. But the ethos of creative writing appears most significantly in the novelist's repeated invocations of fiction as a technology of sympathy at odds with both the commercial market and the bureaucratic structures of government—in, that is, his own version of Ransom's community of letters or McGurl's aesthetic democracy. He is, in fact, remarkably direct in viewing literary creativity as a distinctive means to realize the potential of a pluralist American democracy otherwise damaged or neglected by American institutions:

> The language that we have available to us as American writers is a chorus of voices; it's not officially classified as upper and lower or middle, it moves in and out, it invades itself. It converts and alters itself on an ongoing basis. It's this big, crabby, wonderful, loving family of voices—the English American Language: southern and northern, upper class and lower class, black and white, Hispanic.... That's the beauty of the American language for writers—access to speakers comes through language, comes through voice. If you can hear the voice, you can speak in that voice, and then you can imagine the speaker. (Interview by Benedict)

The import of this perspective appears most clearly in Banks's remarks on his novel *Affliction* (1989), whose resonant title was drawn, Banks explains, from his reading in Simone Weil. Banks's novel tells of the self-destruction of Wade Whitehouse, a middle-aged well digger and part-time police officer in rural New Hampshire who is driven to fury by the straitened circumstances of his life and by a legacy of parental abuse that he is surprised to find himself continuing. In the final, maddened days of his life, Whitehouse descends into paranoid delusion and ends by beating his father to death and then shooting and killing a coworker before disappearing from view. In relating these events, the novel is concerned, Banks acknowledged to the *Paris Review*, with "domestic violence or male violence... or child abuse." Yet those terms, he explained, seemed "too reductive and simplistic" to identify the subject of his work. "They didn't describe the condition" that Wade Whitehouse's life represents "the way the word *affliction* did which implies something greater than a disease but still a disease.... I couldn't get at the condition without a metaphor that was large enough and suggestive enough to handle it. I needed a religious term almost" ("Art of Fiction" 64, italics in original).

In making these remarks, Banks places his work squarely in the disciplinary and intellectual tradition of creative writing. Indeed, the foundational textbook of the Program Era, Cleanth Brooks and Robert Penn Warren's *Understanding Fiction*, emphasizes a contrast remarkably similar to the one central to *Affliction*. Fiction can achieve a "tragic quality" or "even pathos," as opposed to "sentimentality," Brooks and Warren stress, only if it avoids taking a "morbid interest" in its characters and instead allows readers to engage in "imaginative sympathy."[13] So, too, does Banks present his protagonists as figures of tragic grandeur whose lives refuse the patronizingly clinical or sentimental views.

For Banks, such imaginative sympathy brings literature near the orbit of religious consolation. But Banks emphasizes the significance of that consolation by implicitly placing it in contrast to both the stories he tells and the generic conventions he calls on in telling them. Indeed, the most evident feature of Banks's fiction is the way it appears to depart from the dominant styles and attitudes of Program Era fiction. According to Banks, his novels are modeled in part on a tradition of naturalist fiction—exemplified for him by Theodor Dreiser, Richard Wright, and Nelson Algren—to which he had turned as an alternative to the "formalism" he distrusted in the enduring influence of the high modernists, such as Hemingway, celebrated by the founding generation of Program Era writers ("Art of Fiction" 55). Accordingly, in the most obvious respects, as a number of critics have pointed out, Banks's novels strongly resemble—in subject matter, in narrative design, in diction and tone—naturalist fiction's narratives of fatal constraint. The similarity is apparent not just in the way that *Affliction* invokes the naturalist terminology of "native environment" and "social forces" to describe the factors that shape Wade Whitehouse's life but in the fact that Banks, like his predecessors among the naturalist writers, calls on these terms to narrate and explain a widening gulf in the life chances and cultural environments of manual and mental laborers.[14] If, as June Howard among others has observed, naturalist fiction appeared in the United States in the first decades of the twentieth century to address the growth of an industrial proletariat and the challenges and opportunities it presented to an emerging managerial middle class, Banks returns to an illuminating variant of this issue at the other end of the century.[15] The people he consistently makes his material are those that the earlier novel *Continental Drift* describes as "men and women without money, with trades instead of professions, [who] go on breaking their lives trying to bend them around the wheel of commerce."[16]

Affliction emphasizes this context by placing Wade Whitehouse in a larger pattern of class mobility. Lawford, New Hampshire, we are told, is a town "abandoned by several generations of the most talented and attractive of its children," a development illustrated by the departure of Wade's former wife, a woman who has married an insurance agent and who moves first to Concord and then to Seattle, where she prepares herself for a career as a realtor. Set in counterpoint to the downward mobility of her ex-husband, who, having lost his career as a skilled worker, is imagined in the final pages of the novel to be hiding out in the lower depths of the service economy—"one of those faceless fellows we see working behind the counter at our local video . . . store"—her fate highlights what looks to be Banks's prescient subject: the economic gulf that began to open in the American middle class in the late twentieth century and the seething affective currents surrounding it (354).

Yet what is at issue in Banks's novels turns out to be more complex than a depiction of cruel opposition or an indictment of injustice alone. And the knot of that complexity is evident, among other places, in a subtle pattern of generic disharmony that runs through *Affliction* and is alluded to in the novel's title. For, having mentioned the apparently fatal power of "environment" and "social forces," Banks's novel goes on to suggest that those facts are useful but not finally sufficient explanations for understanding the tragedy of Wade Whitehouse. His fate, we are told, "makes no sense" by those terms (202).

In fact, despite the novel's apparent indebtedness to Dreiser, Algren, and Wright for theme and style, and despite Banks's avowed distrust of high modernists, we might plausibly call *Affliction* a modernist artwork masquerading as a naturalist novel. Or, perhaps better, we might describe *Affliction* as a novel in which naturalist and modernist impulses compete for control over the same narrative. In this battle, if the subject matter suggests its naturalist inheritance, the novel's title would mark its modernist bona fides.

Here, too, the title *Affliction* clues us into Banks's indebtedness to principles that remain at the core of literary education. For the novel's title is introduced in the book's epigraph, a quote from Weil that asserts that "the great enigma of human life is not suffering but affliction." "Enigma" is a particularly appropriate term here. For, as Banks acknowledges in his colloquy with the *Paris Review*, the plots of most of his novels hinge on an epistemological question that the characters pursue with great zeal and little success. This "quest for knowledge . . . for information" alludes to and echoes the larger project—to "decod[e] the universe"—in which Banks sees himself engaged as a novelist. "The mystery *in* the book, the literal mystery that might exist *in the plot* of the book, is really a metaphor for the other, deeper quest that the author is engaged in" ("Art of Fiction" 68). Banks's allusion to Weil, in short, marks not only the difference between sociology and spirituality, or between suffering and affliction, but between information and enigma, the shallow puzzles that bedevil characters and the deeper quests of authors.

In *Affliction*, we can see this contrast quite clearly. Wade Whitehouse's path to self-destruction develops in his obsession with an ostensible criminal conspiracy. (He believes that his boss and the coworker he eventually murders are entangled in a secret plan to use embezzled union dues to buy up his townsmen's property for the development of a ski resort and that they conspire to kill off a corrupt official who becomes aware of their scheme.) But his suspicions, we ultimately learn, are entirely mistaken. (The development scheme exists, but there is nothing criminal about it, and the alleged murder is nothing more than a chance hunting accident.) What motivates Wade on this misguided pursuit, we might say in light of Banks's Weilian terminology, is "suffering." What Banks himself reveals in the very collapse of his protagonist's delusion is the more obscure enigma of "affliction."

Despite Banks's avowed distrust of modernist formalism, in short, his book makes use of and thematizes the very artistic principles that were brought to the novel by the modernists and became the guiding framework of postwar literary culture. Another way to put the implication of his title and epigraph, after all, would be to say that they mark the difference between what T. S. Eliot, the presiding genius hovering over New Criticism, called "the man who suffers" and "the mind that creates."[17] That distinction, of course, was as crucial to Hemingway, to Banks's avowed antagonist, and to the curriculum of the creative writing program that canonized Hemingway's methods as it was to Eliot and the New Critics.

Yet as Banks's invocation of an alternative naturalist tradition suggests, this modernist inheritance remains a tradition toward which Banks is ambivalent. That ambivalence, moreover, is just as evident in the construction of Banks's novel as are its modernist affinities. For *Affliction* is narrated by Rolfe Whitehouse, Wade's younger brother, who as a young man escaped the town of Lawford by attending university and grad school and who is now a high school teacher in an "affluent suburban town" outside Boston (201). Rolfe, who lives a life of austere isolation, has escaped the legacy of parental abuse that destroys Wade by devoting himself to scholarship, "that place where no one lives" (203). To continue the Eliotic allusions, he is this novel's Gerontion—the desiccated intellectual, preoccupied with his estrangement from a decadent world. And indeed he repeatedly discourses about the subject of his narrative like a latter-day Spengler, describing the world from which he has come as a community devastated by cultural decline. The out-migration of Lawford's talented youth, Rolfe laments, means that "those who refused or were unable to leave no longer exist as a family, a tribe, a community. They are no longer a people—if they ever were one. . . . I teach history; I think about these things" (6).

Narrating a story through a center of consciousness who is both witness and character is, of course, perhaps the most fundamental innovation of modernist fiction—its key inheritance from James and Conrad and the most evident technical manifestation of the creative writing program's preoccupation with point of view. But in *Affliction*, as elsewhere in his writing, Banks gives an additional turn of the screw to this common feature of literary fiction. For, importantly, Rolfe Whitehouse is not only our witness to Wade Whitehouse's tragedy; he is complicit in its creation. As it turns out, Rolfe has nurtured and, to a significant degree fabricated, the very delusions that drive his older brother to violence. Wade "followed my advice to the letter," he remarks, "which is why I feel today less than innocent" (290). And his narrative is suitably marked by inconsistencies and incoherence. At issue is not merely the fact that our narrator is distant from and unlike, yet nevertheless bound to his brother. Still more important is the fact that he appears to need his brother's self-destruction as a complement to his own alienation.

His literary vantage, in short, is not only one of epistemological privilege but also one of dependency and bad faith. Describing his isolation, Rolfe refers to "my ghost life" (2), and the remark provides a counterpart to the quasi-religious perspective implicit in the book's title and to the more general spiritual consolation of literature that title invokes. Banks titled his collection of short stories *The Angel on the Roof*, using the phrase to refer to the benevolent work of literature in providing a secular equivalent to grace.[18] Rolfe's "ghost life" inverts that perspective. Whereas one phrase refers to literary expression as a vehicle of charity, the other describes it as a vile kind of parasitism.

Banks returns to the problem of literary parasitism often. His fiction is full of narrators like Rolfe whose literary abilities are described with wariness and distaste and whose personas demonstrate what we might call the ethical disappointments of the liberal subject. They are, that is, isolated individuals who, though shallow, vain, and narcissistic, remain tormented by shame and anxiety and by their awareness of their dependence on others. This is not a conjunction, it's worth noting, that is distinctive to Banks or unusual in the aesthetics of Program fiction. Consider the unexplained narrator of Toni Morrison's *Jazz* (1992), who, having related the tragic history of Violet and Joe Trace in classic third-person omniscient mode, in the last chapter suddenly steps into the narrative to announce that she is a Peeping Tom with a "sweettooth" for the pain of others.[19] Or consider the eponymous narrator and protagonist of Tim O'Brien's lionized *The Things They Carried*, who struggles mightily over the course of that story cycle with survivor's guilt and the problem of "tell[ing] a true war story."[20] Or Nathan Zuckerman, who prefaces his narration in *American Pastoral* of the tragic fall of Swede Levov by first detailing the condescension with which he once scoffed at the great man's triviality. Or Henry Park, the self-preoccupied narrator and protagonist of Chang-Rae Lee's *Native Speaker*, who plays a similar role in relation to that novel's tragic John Kwang.

Like Rolfe Whitehouse, all these narrator figures, at least at first glance, appear to traduce the literary ambitions for which their novels speak. With the exception of *Jazz*, all do so in novels that fairly directly cast themselves as post–Cold War narratives. Banks is a particularly useful figure in this context not only because he treats these matters in especially rigorous and complex ways but also because he's unusually explicit in laying out the problems that he wants his work to address. By his own account, he has a distinctive way of framing the historical issues that faced the United States in the last decade of the twentieth century. "I am interested," Banks comments, "in the whole question of the possibility of heroism, especially in a secular age and especially in a democratic society. There are two things that are ongoing perplexities for me: First, is there such a thing as wisdom? And second, is there such a thing as heroism?" ("Art of Fiction" 77). Heroism and wisdom—although they may seem at first glance strange preoccupations and surprising ways to address the issues apparently at the core of Banks's fiction—are ideological counterparts to the roles played by Wade and Rolfe Whitehouse in *Affliction*. Wade explicitly wishes to be a hero to his community and fails terribly in the effort. He expects his townspeople to finally understand his pursuit of justice and to "make me into a goddamned hero," only to realize that the world perceives him as a "stupid, unimaginative man" (294, 315). Rolfe meanwhile presents himself as a voice of wisdom and, though less evidently, is likewise unsuccessful.

But to see the broader resonance of what Banks is getting at here, it's worth recalling that the alleged decline of the heroic was a commonplace of public commentary in the United States in the 1990s when opinion leaders concurred that the close of the Cold War had left the country a society of petty pleasure seekers—bobos in paradise, in David Brooks's bestselling formulation. The ideological contrast between heroic vigor and personal complacency had been, after all, a central element of Cold War ideology. Key figures in its creation, like George Kennan and Arthur Schlesinger Jr., had agreed that the global struggle between democracy and communism should be a moral cause that rescued the American people from effeminacy and aimless individualism. Though with a significantly different valence, the contrast between the authenticity of political struggle and the pallid alienation of consumer society was equally important to left intellectuals like C. Wright Mills and Norman Mailer, and, as historians like Van Gosse and Douglas Rossinow remind us, to the New Left for which they helped lay the groundwork.[21] (Banks points often, it is worth noting, to the influence of the New Left on his own life.)

In the years following the end of the Cold War, all of these assumptions began to seem doubtful. When Francis Fukuyama famously declared the global victory of liberal democracy, he drew on Tocqueville, Nietzsche, and C. S. Lewis to warn that "the end of history" might result in a world of "men without chests"—trivial figures "clever at finding new ways to satisfy a host of petty wants" but dehumanized by their indifference to "excellence and achievement."[22] David Brooks thought similarly that the prevailing ideological current of our "new age of complacency" would be "disenchant[ment]" with the "glorious heights" of "national politics." "America will decline," Brooks worried, "not because it overstretches" but "because it enervates as its leading citizens decide that the pleasures of an over-sized kitchen are more satisfying than the conflicts and challenges of patriotic service."[23]

If Banks's fiction is full of would-be heroes and parasitic intellectuals, it is not hard to see how, in this context, their complementary balance—the shallow narcissist poised against the grandly self-destructive protagonist—echoes, even as it shifts, this central axis of Cold War ideology. But we need not rely only on echo and implication to see how directly the framework organizing Banks's fiction was shaped by the larger ideological context of the Cold War. Banks's breakthrough novel, *Continental Drift*—which was published in 1985 and composed partly with support from the National Endowment for the Arts—points directly to the significance of that long-running conflict in framing our understanding of the story. *Continental Drift* tells a tale revealingly similar to and yet different from that of *Affliction*. The novel's protagonist is Bob Dubois, a thirty-one-year-old oil-furnace repairman who abandons his life in New Hampshire and moves his young family to Florida, where he pursues a series of failed career moves (liquor-store clerk, fishing-boat captain, smuggler of Haitian refugees) that lead ultimately to his death. Unlike in *Affliction*, however, Bob DuBois's story is set in point-by-point comparison to a second narrative, which follows an impoverished Haitian woman, Vanise Dorsinville, and her nephew as they attempt to immigrate illegally to the United States. The differences between these two narratives and two sets of characters are conceived, moreover, not only as differences of wealth or privilege, or even primarily as differences in culture, but in the terms that, as we have been seeing, are central to Banks's work. Bob DuBois's desperate wandering represents a kind of narcissistic drift that Banks describes as typical of commercial society. Vanise's quest to find America, in contrast, is depicted as an epic journey, comparable to the travels of Columbus.

Furthermore, the contrast between these two characters is enabled by the larger context of the Cold War. When Bob DuBois confronts the "entropy" that defines his life, he imagines himself a prisoner of the gulag. He envisions himself "somewhere in Siberia, as if he were being carted late at night from one prison to another . . . a passive man, inert and shackled" (20). Vanise, however, is described as typical of various third-world peoples (Pashtun, Khmer, Somalis, Iraqis, and Iranians) who have been displaced by the proxy wars of the world powers and are compelled to rise to heroic efforts to remake their lives. Such people, Banks's narrator remarks, "[fill] us with wonder and admiration" (39) and, in their global sojourns, point to the need for a universal transformation of humanity. "We are the planet," Banks writes after describing the transnational migrations of several displaced populations and their "old-fashioned, Biblical kind of heroism" (40, 39). "If the planet survives it will only be through heroism. Not occasional heroism . . . but constant heroism, systematic heroism, heroism as a governing principle" (40). Like other left-leaning intellectuals of his generation, Banks gives prevailing Cold War ideology a significant spin, but at the core of his narrative remains an implicit contrast between a soulless, bureaucratic social prison—the gulag of American life—and the heroic people who rise to challenge and transform it.

More important is that the Cold War not only provides the terms of Banks's narrative but also by extension enables him to conceive the work of his novel itself in distinctly elevated terms—as a means to reproduce the very heroism and wisdom the novel describes in the lives of displaced third-world migrants. In the closing pages of the book, Banks's narrator makes this aim explicit and describes fiction as a unique mode of communication that, in enabling us to sympathize with the lives of others, counters the rampant self-interest encouraged by capitalist society and, remarkably, as in this way a kind of cultural sabotage. "Go, my book," the novel ends, "and help destroy the world as it is" (366).

But this heroic stance can be maintained, it turns out, only because in the preface of the book—or its "invocation"—the narrator has established his ability to speak authoritatively about the life of Bob DuBois and because, making use of the novel's Haitian associations, he has done so by calling on the *vodou loa* Legba as a muse enabling him to present the life of the character before the reader. "Give body and entitledness and boldness to this white mouth-man's [that is, the narrator] pity and anger," Banks addresses the *vodou* muse. "Let this man speak that man [Bob DuBois] to life" (2). Were it not for the proxy conflicts and puppet regimes of the Cold War, in other words, we would have no heroic third-world people to see in contrast to Bob DuBois. But, still more important, we would not have the spiritual warrant that such people can be imagined to provide—resources that, in this particular example, enable Banks to solve the problem of point of view. The narrator of *Continental Drift* can speak authoritatively about the misery of Bob DuBois's life because the Cold War gives him the ideological resources and the epistemological warrant to do so. To put it another way, what saves the significantly unnamed narrator of *Continental Drift* from becoming like Rolfe Whitehouse—the parasitic narrator of *Affliction*—is voodoo.

In Banks's subsequent novels, all of those ideological resources are gone or are severely compromised. In *Affliction*, in particular, we remain confined within the circuit of Wade and Rolfe Whitehouse's life. (Their last name is no coincidence; that their world is entirely white is implicitly viewed by Banks not as a historical accident or a reflection of privilege but as a kind of cultural and ethical impoverishment.) No alternative is provided to the different privations they represent, and although Simone Weil is called on to play something like the role that voodoo plays in *Continental Drift*, there are good reasons for doubting her utility in this context. The narrator of *Continental Drift* is able to send his book into the world, ostensibly to destroy it. The last line of *Affliction*, in contrast, acknowledges that Wade's "story will be over" but "that I continue." The personal narrator of the first novel is displaced by the impersonal authority of the inspired narrative he fashions. Unable to fashion such an impersonal structure, Rolfe Whitehouse will extend his shallow personal life after his story has died. Thus, what we may see in *Affliction*—as in a somewhat less intense manner, in the work of Banks's contemporaries—is a literary ideology running up against its limits and responding to the declining influence of the political and institutional framework that sustained it.

All of the fiction that Banks has published since *Continental Drift* wrestles with this problem and, as is perhaps typical of ideological formations in crisis, oscillates dramatically between works that can be taken to fervently reassert the core principles of the faith from which they emerge and texts that bitterly lament their failure. *The Sweet Hereafter*, the novel Banks published immediately after *Affliction* is, at one level, the story of how an isolated and impoverished town responds to the tragic death of a large number of its children—significantly, in a school bus accident. But, as a series of first-person monologues that culminate in a vision of the town's collective renewal, it is also a model of literary community equal to anything in John Crowe Ransom. ("They do not behave heroically as individuals," Banks remarks to the *Paris Review*. They "locate heroism in a community" ["Art of Fiction" 78].) The subsequent *Cloudsplitter*, on the other hand, a novel nominally about John Brown, is also about the fateful failure of liberal pluralism to overcome racial injustice and of the way such failure leads both to terrible violence and to narratives of insular self-laceration. The novel's narrator, John Brown's son Owen, is, like Rolfe Whitehouse, a narcissistic would-be intellectual who laments that "an Age of Heroism ha[s] acceded to an Age of Cowardice" and who refers to himself as "a ghost bawling into the empty night."[24]

So, too, may *Affliction* undermine what appears to be its own core agenda. Like *Continental Drift*, *Affliction* casts itself as a means of creating a community of sympathy denied by political and economic institutions. The novel opens with Wade Whitehouse's rage building as, in his role as town traffic cop, he directs the school bus that fails to contain his child. The novel ends with the narrator directly addressing the reader and charging that although you have "read the same kind of story numerous times in your own newspaper," you "move quickly on to news about the Middle East . . . or a huge drug bust in Miami. . . . You cannot understand how a man, . . . a man like you and me, could do such a terrible thing" (354). The novel by implication is to be our alternative and complement to the school bus and the newspaper—a means of understanding a man drawn into our world by the bureaucratic agencies of the state and the communicative reach of the mass media but who can nevertheless not otherwise be understood.

Yet *Affliction* also reveals this project to be incoherent. In one important respect, the novel suggests that the project of literary inclusion cannot really apply to people like Wade Whitehouse. Their identity is simply to be unsympathetic. Throughout the novel but especially in one key passage, Banks adopts what might be called an extreme culture-of-poverty account of the fate of the working class: "It was a question of what had happened to him. . . . How was it that he, . . . a man who had once been as intelligent and complexly aware as . . . [his upwardly mobile ex-wife, had become] a man wearing cheap mismatched clothes . . . , a man without a proper home to call his own, without a job, without any respect in the community. . . , kept outside the family of man." In this view, Wade is "like his father before him and like that man's father, too." They are all "solitary, dumb, angry men" who pass on a culture of violence to their children and who are therefore alien to "men and women and children full of good intentions and competence" (321–22). Wade's cultural identity, in other words, is one of working-class violence, which thus appears not merely an accident of social injustice that can be redressed by tolerant inclusion but in effect a racial identity that differs from other racial identities only in that, by definition, it is inconsistent with tolerance itself. "We wear a face," Rolfe remarks of himself and his brother, "shaped by thousands of years of peering into firelight . . . evolved over tens of thousands of years of holding the reins of another man's horse . . . , of drawing sticks on a cart from someone else's woods to someone else's fire" (56–57).

But in more direct ways as well, the novel casts doubt on the virtue of empathy itself. Rolfe Whitehouse, who is importantly inconsistent on key details of the story he recounts, also tells us explicitly that he relates Wade's story not to include him in a community of literary understanding but "only to be rid of him" (2). Less evidently, the story he tells reveals sympathy to be, at least in some guises, not a redemptive but a pathological and destructive sentiment. Notably, it is Wade's avowed fellow feeling for his coworker that sets him on the path to murdering the young man, and, more subtly, it is only when Rolfe renews his interest in his older brother that this writer-figure plants the seeds of the conspiracy theory that will lead Wade to his self-destruction. Sentimental identification with others in this novel turns out to be literally murderous.

The point I'm trying to suggest here is not precisely that *Affliction* makes use of an implied author who ironizes and undermines its explicit narrator. Nor am I mainly concerned to say that in this way the novel amounts to a critique of educationally privileged people like Rolfe or ourselves. I'm not even trying to claim that in this fashion the novel draws attention—as, say, Chris Hayes or Nicholas Lemann have done—to an underlying structural conflict between the postwar visions of educational democracy and the meritocratic and, by definition, exclusionary institutions that sustained them.[25] All those arguments seem to me partly right. But I think they also do not go far enough in accounting for the tensions that split Banks's fiction. My idea, rather, is that *Affliction* simply does not have a coherent agenda—that Banks is equally committed both to the vision of literature as a means to an "alternative community" of the sort valorized by Ransom and his contemporaries and aware not only of the increasing unlikelihood of such ambitions but of the fact that they were never fully plausible in the first place. To put it another way, Banks's attempt to integrate the methods of literary modernism, with its emphasis on literature as a model of cultural inclusion, and literary naturalism, with its emphasis on the irrevocability of class conflict, like the visions of literary community that flourished in the world of postwar higher education cannot finally be maintained.

There are a number of ways that Banks's novel hints at this incoherence in the inconsistencies of its narrator. But one particularly telling example comes in a passing moment when the novel briefly raises the suggestion of an alternative narrator who might have told a different story from the one that preoccupies Wade Whitehouse and his brother. As I've mentioned, Banks is obsessive about point of view, so Rolfe Whitehouse's ability to know things he was not on hand to witness must be explained. The novel provides for him a source of key information in the minor character Alma Pittman, the treasurer of Lawford and keeper of the town's tax records. Alma is notably not a sympathetic person and not warmly beloved by her townsfolk. She is, we are told, "a woman who kept herself aloof from the town but seemed to love it nevertheless" and is in this way a comparable figure to the novel's narrator—who, though now apart from the community of his birth, knows it intimately (279).

It is Alma who informs Wade about the property transactions that lead to his conspiracy theory and Alma who in turn warns him not to become carried away by his fantasies—that "sometimes things are simpler than you think" and that "there always has been" unsavory "business going on in town." Her view is that the conspiracy Wade believes he has discovered shows simply that a wealthy and powerful man in town is going to abuse his public role to make himself still wealthier—he "was going to become a very rich man by using his position as selectman to exploit his neighbors" (285). Wade does "not hear her," and he replies to Alma's warning about the danger of self-confirming theories by saying: "This is different than a little public drunkenness or vandalism or maybe someone beating on his wife or a couple of the boys pounding on each other down at" the local bar (281). He is, as I mentioned previously, wrong in this impression. And it may be that in subtly foreshadowing his error in this scene, Banks is pointing toward a larger mistake that shadows his novel. Wade Whitehouse wants there to be a criminal conspiracy destroying his town; his younger brother wants to view his community as culturally bereft in a manner dramatized by the self-destruction of his brother; but neither of them can take account of the ordinary privation that characterizes their community. It may be, in other words, that despite Banks's own comments to the contrary, stories about the grandeur and passion of men like Wade can easily be told by alienated intellectuals like their brothers. The hard thing to see is not affliction, from this point of view, but suffering.

To put this point more, well, programmatically, Alma Pittman appears in Banks's novel as an alternative to the angel on the roof and as a counter to the vision of "systematic heroism" that runs through Banks's reflections on the art of fiction. By the same token, she presents an alternative to the promises of pluralist democracy that provided the ideological core of postwar American liberalism and the aesthetic ideology of the Program Era. Her unattended voice suggests that that vision is not merely troubled by uncertainty but is an enticing and misleading means of conceiving the problems of personal misery and social injustice. The greatest achievement of Banks's fiction in this light may not be that its internal divisions dramatize the tensions of aesthetic democracy crucial to the Program Era but the fact that its structural incoherence reveals the deep allure and profound limitations of what the program had to offer.

NOTES

1. Mark McGurl, *The Program Era* (Cambridge: Harvard UP, 2009), 410.

2. Clark Kerr, *The Uses of the University*, 5th ed. (Cambridge: Harvard UP, 2001), 1.

3. Wallace Stegner, *One Way to Spell Man* (New York: Doubleday, 1982), 8; Wallace Stegner, *Teaching and Writing Fiction*, ed. Lynn Stegner (New York: Penguin, 2002), 48.

4. Paul Engle, "The Writer Writing," *On Creative Writing*, ed. Paul Engle (New York: E. P. Dutton, 1964), 7, 8.

5. Caroline Gordon, *How to Read a Novel* (New York: Viking Press, 1957), 8, 12, 228, 24, 25.

6. Lionel Trilling, "Edmund Wilson: A Backward Glance" (1952), *A Gathering of Fugitives* (Boston: Beacon Press, 1956), 55.

7. John Crowe Ransom, "The Communities of Letters" (1952), *Poems and Essays* (New York: Vintage, 1955), 116–17.

8. See Marisa Hudspeth, "Indiana University School of Letters Director's Records, 1947–1979: A Guide to the Records at the Indiana University Archive," accessed 18 Apr. 2016, http://purl.dlib.indiana.edu/iudl/findingaids/archives/InU-Ar-VAA2672; Lawrence Schwartz, *Creating Faulkner's Reputation: The Politics of Modern Literary Criticism* (Knoxville: U of Tennessee P, 1988), chap. 3; Evan Kindley, "Poet-Critics and Bureaucratic Administration," *The Cambridge Companion to Modern American Poetry*, ed. Walter Kaladjian (New York: Cambridge UP, 2015), 248–57.

9. John Crowe Ransom, *The New Criticism* (Norford, CT: New Directions, 1941), 42.

10. Evan Brier, *A Novel Marketplace: Mass Culture, the Book Trade, and Postwar American Fiction* (Philadelphia: U of Pennsylvania P, 2010).

11. Russell Banks, "The Art of Fiction: CLII," interview by Robert Faggen, *Paris Review* 40 (Summer 1998): 56.

12. For his dismissive remarks on journalism and sociology in comparison, see Banks's interview in *Bomb*. Pinckney Benedict, "Russell Banks," *Bomb* 52 (Summer 1995), http://bombsite.com/issues/52/articles/1879.

13. Cleanth Brooks Jr. and Robert Penn Warren, *Understanding Fiction* (New York: Appleton-Century-Crofts, 1943), 204, 250, 205.

14. Russell Banks, *Affliction* (New York: Harper Perennial, 1990), 201.

15. June Howard, *Form and History in American Literary Naturalism* (Chapel Hill: U of North Carolina P, 1985), 127–41.

16. Russell Banks, *Continental Drift* (New York: Harper and Row, 1985), 366.

17. T. S. Eliot, "Tradition and the Individual Talent," *Selected Prose of T. S. Eliot*, ed. Frank Kermode (New York: Harcourt Brace, 1975), 41.

18. The title is occasioned by Banks's memory of his father's unsuccessful effort to fabricate a story of origins in an effort to win his son's approval. "His story was a prayer, like all good stories, but it went unanswered. The one to whom he prayed—not me, but an angel on the roof—was not listening." Banks, *The Angel on the Roof: The Stories of Russell Banks* (New York: HarperCollins, 2001), xiv.

19. Toni Morrison, *Jazz* (New York: Knopf, 1992), 219.

20. Tim O' Brien, *The Things They Carried* (New York: Mariner Books, 1990), 65–66.

21. Van Gosse, *Where the Boys Are: Cuba, Cold War America, and the Making of a New Left* (New York: Verso, 1993); Doug Rossinow, *The Politics of Authenticity: Liberalism, Christianity, and the New Left* (New York: Columbia UP, 1998); see also Kevin Mattson, *Intellectuals in Action: The Origins of the New Left and Radical Liberalism, 1945–1970* (University Park: Pennsylvania State UP, 2002).

22. Francis Fukuyama, *The End of History and the Last Man* (New York: Free Press, 1992), xxii.

23. David Brooks, *Bobos in Paradise: The New Upper Class and How They Got There* (New York: Simon and Schuster, 2000), 270, 265, 271.

24. Russell Banks, *Cloudsplitter* (New York: Harper, 1998), 24.

25. Nicholas Lemann, *The Big Test: The Secret History of the American Meritocracy* (New York: Farrar, Straus and Giroux, 1999); Chris Hayes, *Twilight of the Elites: America after Meritocracy* (New York: Crown, 2012).

CHAPTER 13

Getting Real

From Mass Modernism to Peripheral Realism

DONAL HARRIS

One of the most basic, but also most instructive, claims in Mark McGurl's *The Program Era* is that the various strands of postwar American literature that critics loosely call postmodernism might better be thought of as *institutionalized* modernism. Rather than read the novels of Vladimir Nabokov, John Barthes, Robert Coover, Toni Morrison, Shelley Jackson, and others as "radically 'deconstructive,' as they sometimes are," McGurl writes, one might think of them as "radically conventional"; that is, as examples of an attitude toward systematic formal experimentation that began with the modernists, on the edges of literary culture in the early years of the twentieth century, and after several decades of cultural steeping moved to the center of literary production, systematized in their own right.[1] The "institutionalization of modernism" takes "the product of urban coteries, circulating in the tiny sphere of little magazines" and relocates them "helpfully on the syllabus as objects of study" (50, 51). Modernism had its own institutions, of course, but according to McGurl postwar university-based creative writing programs and English department syllabi made the literary experiments of "the Pound Era" part and parcel with mass higher education and hence the ambivalent beneficiaries of a very different kind of institutional affiliation. Without giving up fine-grained attention to the plurality of postwar literary output, McGurl lets us see how the aesthetic principles and literary cultural assumptions of early twentieth-century European and American artists become integrated as another kind of research in the university. And adopting an analogous methodological standard to that of the hard sciences, modernist experimentation and the hermeneutic practice of close reading succeed in part because they are replicable. Modernism is brought indoors, so to speak: for students, coterie works enter the literary lab to be scrutinized under the microscope of close reading to better understand the craft of writing; for faculty members, literary outsiders become the subject of graded writing assignments and, later, colleagues.

This summary of *The Program Era*'s opening gambit accentuates the book's attention to the sociological "normalization" of early twentieth-century artistic practices via the "culture of the school."[2] It brings into view the integral connection between the rise of writing programs, the ascension of New Criticism, and the midcentury popularization of modernism in the United States. At the same time, it produces a vision of what one could call, with a slight tweak, postwar *mass modernism*, where the attitudes and styles of artistic exiles come home to roost at the vital center of US culture: first gathered in the classroom, then dispersed into the cultural firmament via the newly elevated literary taste of ever-larger cohorts of alumni. Thus, in the sweeping demographic inclusiveness of postwar mass higher education, modernism-as-genre undergoes what Loren Glass refers to as "the signature career arc" of the American modernist writer, "from the restricted elite audience of urban bohemia and 'little magazines' to the mass audience of the U.S. Middlebrow," landing in midcult institutions like the general-interest magazine by way of the college classroom.[3]

The Program Era does not end with the "resounding conclusion of a post-program era." Instead it "trail[s] off into an uncertain future" (McGurl 28), a future made all the more uncertain by the global economic shake-up that arrived almost simultaneously with McGurl's book. If one were to posit a hypothetical "Volume 2" of *The Program Era*, it might begin by taking stock of the Great Recession's effect on the English department, particularly on the recent widespread investment in realism, in both artistic and scholarly circles, as evidence of a certain discomfort with the success of institutionalized, that is, massified, modernism for which McGurl gives such a compelling account. One particularly rich strand of this interest is "peripheral realism," a formation recently coined in a special issue of *Modern Language Quarterly*. The essays therein resuscitate realism as a site of critical attention by showing how, at the present moment, the genre is peripheral both in terms of literary practice (that is, it is currently a "minor" form) and in that it finds its richest current manifestations on the geopolitical periphery of the world-literary system (that is, not in New York, London, or Paris).[4] Though realism is undeniably central to the development of the novel, this inauguration of a "new realist turn," as coeditors Jed Esty and Colleen Lye call it (276), would seem to be a conscious move to bring realism out of a *pejorative* peripherality—realism as naïvely mimetic, as politically suspect, as formally old-fashioned—and into a forward-leaning periphery: to make realism avant-garde, speculative, daring, of our times; to make realism "edgy." As a literary practice this is "realism after modernism," in Joe Cleary's words, and as a critical practice the return seems to be, more accurately, realism after institutionalized modernism.[5] This is not to criticize the reemergence of realism in contemporary literature or the renewed interest in two of its great theorists, György Lukács and Erich Auerbach, but only to attempt to see the rise of studies of realism as at least partially a reaction to the felt overpresence, and perhaps exhaustion, of the literary-institutional formation that *The Program Era* so compellingly systematizes. That is, the new realist turn takes stock of the decreasing novelty of both modernist aesthetic practice and "new modernist studies," a field that was institutionalized in 1998 with the founding of the Modernist Studies Association and for some no longer seems very new. In various ways new modernist studies operated by pluralizing its object of study—not modernism but modernisms: bad modernism, late modernism, depression modernism, exo-modernism, metamodernism, para-modernism, and, finally, institutionalized modernism. These categories have broadened our understanding of an extraordinarily far-reaching and complex moment in literary history, and they show us that the insides and outsides of modernist practice in terms of time frame, artistic practice, and national and geographical location are more difficult to ascertain than they might initially appear. Yet, once again following McGurl's sociological perspective, it's hard not to see this proliferation of modernisms as the functional differentiation of a field that has been fully institutionalized. That is, despite Lukács's hundred-year-old claim that modernism is a dead end, we can see that it has moved from the periphery to the center at the same time that realism has become peripheral.

But maybe we should question just how "peripheral" realism really is. Without contradicting the genre's importance for self-identified Third World and postcolonial writers, for whom realism offers an escape hatch from the felt tyranny of a Euro-centric version of modernist formalism, we can also point out that a certain brand of quietist realism has dominated the *New York Times* Best Seller Lists and Book Club selections in the United States since such lists came into existence. In the last fifteen years Jonathan Franzen, Chad Harbach, Michael Chabon, Dana Spiotta, Jeffrey Eugenides, and others have made strident claims for a return to nineteenth-century realism, though they have a quite different relationship to the literary world system and its attendant identity and geopolitics than those writers clustered on the periphery. In fact, if one were to undertake a statistical analysis of the postwar novel, the vast majority of entries would fall into the category of "realistic fiction" that Gordon Hutner calls "good but not great, interesting without being indispensable, accomplished without being profound," which makes them resistant to productive close reading but, at the same time, a much safer financial bet for publishers than a "late modernist" experiment in point of view.[6] So realism energizes a politically marginalized group of writers, but it also becomes the calling card of mainstream American writers, Franzen and Harbach among the most successful and vocal.[7]

Fredric Jameson convincingly argues that the category of realism is so pervasive, yet also slippery, because it exists only in its binary relationship to other genres or narrative modes—realism versus romance, or idealism, or modernism, for example. For Jameson it is a genre without a center; therefore, studies of it always fall off either to its formation (the rise of the novel) or its dissolution (the end of the novel's representation of totality), not what it actually *is*.[8] In this way realism's peripherality in the literary world system is mirrored in the literary critical tendency to treat only its rise or fall. Nevertheless, we can also acknowledge its continuing and contemporaneous centrality to the present-day literary world, especially from the point of view of the publishing corporations for whom the genre "literary fiction," and what the sociologist John Thompson calls the "big book," are more or less synonymous with contemporary anglophone realism.[9] To wit: Realism can exist as a peripheral category for those trying to theorize something after or outside modernism, and it can also occupy the very center of the literary world system for the increasingly centralized institutions that purchase, edit, print, translate, and distribute those novels. But within this periphery/center formulation, we can also see how those at the center look out, survey the field, and romanticize a kind of peripherality. What I mean is that those writers of literary fiction who sell hundreds of thousands of copies of their novels and whose reputations cross over into the popular, nonliterary media—that is, the Jonathan Franzens of the world—often present their own brand of realism as a peripheral enterprise, both as a way to assert their own place within the field of cultural pluralism and as a response to the felt anachronism and overfamiliarity of modernist aesthetics.

That the Franzen School of realism mourns the felt obsolescence of white, midwestern, middle-class life as a subject of novelistic interest is fairly well documented, but that his preoccupation grows out of the discomfort with normalized, mass modernism is less so. Yet this seems to be the situation that Chad Harbach has in mind in his recent campus novel *The Art of Fielding*, when the character Guert Affenlight offers an impromptu cultural history of postwar anomie. Affenlight, a Melville scholar–cum–college president, is watching the Westish College Harpooners baseball team, particularly Henry Skrimshander, the shortstop. Skrimshander, whose athletic prowess looks like the same disciplined genius one finds in the creative writing seminar, is on the verge of setting a record for most games without an error when he contracts what baseball players call "the yips," an affliction in which a player can no longer complete mindless, routine tasks like throwing the ball to first base. As Affenlight surveys the baseball diamond, pondering Henry's problem, he offers a capsule genealogy of modernism's slow creep to the center of American culture, which seems to reach its apex at a specific moment in the 1970s. Wondering where exactly it all went wrong, he thinks:

> Nineteen seventy-three. In the public imagination it was as fraught a year as you could name: Watergate, *Roe v. Wade*, withdrawal from Vietnam. *Gravity's Rainbow*. Was it also the year that Prufrockian paralysis went mainstream—the year it entered baseball? It made sense that a psychic condition sensed by artists of one generation—the Modernists of the First World War—would take a while to reveal itself through the population. And if that psychic condition happened to be a profound failure of confidence in the significance of individual human action, then the condition became an epidemic when it entered the realm of utmost confidence in the same: the realm of professional sports. In fact, that might make for a workable definition of the postmodernist era: an era when even the athletes were anguished Modernists, in which case the American postmodern began in spring 1973, when a pitcher named Steve Blass lost his arm.
>
> *Do I dare, and do I dare?*[10]

According to baseball lore, Steve Blass is patient zero for the much-dreaded "epidemic" that Henry Skrimshander contracts. Though theories abound for its cause, the novel depicts "the yips" as the result of an overburdening self-consciousness: Henry starts thinking too much and acting too little. And ever the Melvillean, Affenlight looks for a cosmic connection between T. S. Eliot's poetry, *Gravity's Rainbow*, the cultural revolutions of the 1970s, and the unlucky fate of his college's shortstop, who falls into self-reflexivity when he accidentally throws a ball into his team's dugout and knocks his roommate—who, incidentally, is also Affenlight's undergraduate lover—unconscious.

In many ways *The Art of Fielding* can look like the "program novel" par excellence: It takes place on a midwestern college campus; it is highly self-reflexive (or in McGurl's neologism, autopoetic), incorporating a baseball self-help manual also called *The Art of Fielding* into its plot; Harbach began it in a writing workshop while receiving his MFA at the University of Virginia, then subsequently went on to edit a collection of essays, *MFA vs NYC*, that name-checks *The Program Era* in its introduction. With this vulgarly biographical ammunition, we might read *The Art of Fielding*'s none-too-subtle analogy between the disciplined arts of athletics and writing, and the deleterious effects of overthinking one's decisions in both realms, as a trace of the author's own highly publicized difficulty with finishing the book. Here, Henry's pathological self-consciousness stands in for Harbach's, who spent ten years writing and rewriting the manuscript, sending it to agents and publishers, and receiving a substantial stack of rejection notices.

Yet *Fielding*'s utterly uncool subject matter, its focus on families, and its character-driven story line also point in another direction. Those years of revision, according to Keith Gesson's *Vanity Fair* article on the novel's painfully slow path to publication (which was subsequently expanded into its own eBook), entailed shedding the influence of postmodernist reflexivity and narrative involution, particularly the work of David Foster Wallace.[11] Henry, the baseball player who becomes too self-conscious of his movements, becomes the cautionary example that Harbach must overcome. Self-consciousness becomes a self-conscious realism in the novel. And along with the ridiculous bit of armchair cultural history that Affenlight lays out (presented by Harbach with the straightest of faces), it can make *The Art of Fielding* look like McGurl's institutionalized modernism held up to a dark mirror, where a generation inherits all the pathologies of modernism—here given the shorthand formulation of "Prufrockian paralysis"—without any of the elevated taste or cultural prestige. And whether or not one actually buys Affenlight's slipshod logic is less important than accepting Harbach's invitation to mull over the counterintuitive vision of the contemporary United States as a land of uncritical modernists, a place where Eliot's self-conscious formal innovations have mutated into a widespread compulsion to degenerative reflexivity. Harbach's thematic doubling of baseball and writing is not very innovative as a conceit, even if it makes literal the gamelike quality of writing and publishing.[12] It is more interesting, though, as a contemporary attempt to historicize a version of a pathological self-consciousness that begins in modernism and spreads via modernism's popularization in America.

Here, it opens up a way to understand the literary historical pressures, along with sociocultural ones, that lie behind the new realism. The list of examples that Affenlight reels off would seem to be the repetition of Eliot's ennui in the general population—"Do I dare, and do I dare?" Not just *Gravity's Rainbow* but also Watergate, *Roe v. Wade*, and Vietnam become benchmarks of just how widespread and pervasive the "anguish" of modernism has become. All cultural upheaval is read as modernist. "Even the athletes," he thinks. With this in mind, the allegorized discipline of baseball as writing reads a little differently, and, fittingly, Jonathan Franzen argues as much in his review of *The Art of Fielding*. Franzen sees the novel as transcending the very authorial self-consciousness that artistically crippled Harbach for ten years, the felt need to be "Mr. Difficult" that Franzen spent most of the late 1990s and early 2000s writing against. In reviewing Harbach's book, he writes that "reading *The Art of Fielding* is like watching a hugely gifted young shortstop: you keep waiting for the errors, but there are no errors."[13] *The Art of Fielding*'s success in the marketplace, its status as a Big Book, its association with Michael Pietsch, who was also David Foster Wallace's editor, and the staggering $650,000 advance that Harbach received from the publisher Little, Brown all suggest that while self-awareness and reflexivity might make for excellent thematic content in the contemporary novel, they are crippling when taken up at the level of form or style. In this way, *Fielding* strangely resembles a Horatio Alger story, where getting schooled in modernist difficulty is the limiting background that Harbach and Henry both must overcome. The novel succeeds by elevating itself above the too-common pathologized self-reflexivity of contemporary culture; thereby, its insistence on its own realist mode inverts the distinction between an elitist modernism and a populist, or at least popularly accessible, realism. But it's more than a simple inversion of terms, and for Harbach and others, the contemporary reevaluation of realism as a worthwhile literary enterprise becomes a further complication of modernism's formal difficulty and epistemological uncertainty, because, according to the previous passage, modernism is no longer difficult, no longer uncertain; in fact, "Prufrockian paralysis" is what makes people "common." Harbach's realism, then, attempts to turn the dial of literary distinction once more, to close off a coterie of realist readers and realist writers who want to distinguish themselves from the modernists, who are now, also, all too common.

This attempt to turn inside out realism's literary cultural significance should sound familiar to those aware of Franzen's seemingly contradictory attitudes about the "contract novel." In fact, the hypothetical modernist saturation seems to be especially dense in the Midwest. It takes up residence in the "slightly decrepit liberal arts school on the western shore of Lake Michigan" of Westish College (51), but it can also be reimagined, literally, as the background noise of suburban boredom in the opening passage of Jonathan Franzen's *The Corrections*. The long tail of Eliot's modernism doesn't have far to go, as Franzen's novel begins in what he calls, alluding to Eliot's "Gerontion," the "gerontocratic suburbs" of St. Jude, a fictionalized version of St. Louis, where Eliot and Franzen grew up. In *The Corrections*, Eliot's revolt from the village has come full circle, boomeranging back into the late twentieth-century suburbs as a foreboding sense of alienation. The book opens with Alfred Lambert, the family patriarch who by novel's end will be leveled by dementia, sleeping in a blue chair to the sound of "the alarm bell of anxiety." The complex sound of this anxiety, but also its utter ordinariness, gives rise to one of the novel's most lyrical disquisitions on the emotional burden of what might be called suburban modernism.

> It was like one of those big cast-iron dishes with an electric clapper that send schoolchildren into the street in fire drills. By now it had been ringing for so many hours that the Lamberts no longer heard the message of "bell ringing" but, as with any sound that continues for so long that you have the leisure to learn its component sounds (as with any word you stare at until it resolves itself into a string of dead letters), instead hears a clapper rapidly striking a metallic resonator, not a pure tone but a granular sequence of percussions with a keening overlay of overtones; ringing for so many days that it simply blended into the background except at certain early-morning hours when one or the other of them awoke in a sweat and

> realized that a bell had been ringing in their heads for as long as they could remember; ringing for so many months that the sound had given way to a kind of metasound whose rise and fall was not the beating of compression waves but the much, much slower waxing and waning of the *consciousness* of sound.[14]

Note how the alarm, because of its perennial persistence, has become both more and less than itself; it devolves into its components like a "string of dead letters," and it becomes a "metasound" that corresponds to Alfred's consciousness of hearing the sound rather than the thing itself. The sound emerges for Alfred simultaneously with his wife Enid's realization that her coupons are expired, that the expiration dates "lay months and even years in the past," and that "they had all gone bad. . . . The dates were not even *close*. The dates were *historical*. The alarm bell was ringing for *years*" (4).

The complex single-sentence treatment of the "alarm bell of anxiety" that Alfred feels pervading these blandly sad suburbs gives way to Enid's histrionic fear of anachronism. The description of the sound unfolds in dependent clauses that run over and under the "sound," much like the waves of overtones and particularizations that make up the sound itself. And then, in pushy italics—*close, historical, years*—Franzen stamps the scene with the dull pain of belatedness. Getting with the program, for Franzen, has less to do with creative writing and more to do with shedding the burden of historicity that he calls "the postmodern program," which entails "the notion of formal experimentation as a heroic act of resistance" that begins with Eliot and the modernists and reaches its apogee in the 1970s with the midcareer novels of William Gaddis, the titular "Mr. Difficult" of Franzen's infamous denunciation of his former father figure.[15] Not that the Difficult Program is free from the university. It is certainly related, particularly to the curriculum in the English Department at Swarthmore College where Franzen studied. This is where he learned that literary and artistic merit could be earned only with experimentation, complexity, the posture of total knowledge, and the tone of cool, unaffected irony. Indeed, the cultural capital that accompanies artistic difficulty, as it filters through the school, holds special purchase for literary culture, he claims. "You can walk past a painting fifty times before you begin to appreciate it. You can drift in and out of a Bartók sonata until its structures dawn on you. But a difficult novel just sits there on your shelf unread—unless you happen to be a student, in which case you're forced to turn the pages of Woolf and Beckett" (108). It's telling here that the examples harken back to modernism rather than the writers of the 1960s and 1970s, as their exaggerated distance only exacerbates the uncomfortable sense of anachronism he feels when trying to write a systems novel in the twenty-first century. It is historical, it has been commonplace for years, and Franzen articulates the experience of finding an expiration date on modernism. Yes, his novel is about numerous corrections—economic, familial, personal. But it also intends to ring the bell for those who still think modernist ennui is avant-garde rather than the bread-and-butter affect of "the squarest people in America," as Alfred and Enid's son Chip, a failed English professor, will later call his parents (23). When college presidents, suburban retirees, and baseball players alike are familiar with Prufrockian paralysis, Franzen and Harbach seem to be suggesting, even the bestselling version of realism can be seen as a powerfully peripheral undertaking.

That this mainstream version of "realism after modernism" finds a prefabricated home in gerontocractic suburbs and crumbling college residence halls only accentuates how genre stands in for a certain kind of identity politics. Rather than read it as the refusal of cultural pluralism and the increased visibility of minor literatures, one could more generously see this mainstream version of realism as an attempt to reinsert a slightly rusted version of midwestern white masculinity into the pantheon of socially acceptable hyphenated American identities. So while Franzen's tone-deaf lamentations about the rise of the "Interesting Childhood" novel are clearly reactionary—and despite the many political and aesthetic faults we can find in Franzen's often ludicrous commentary—at the same time his despair at the obsolescence of modernist distinction and ensuing foray into "tragic realism" can look almost communitarian. "Once I stepped outside my bubble of despair," he writes in reference to his depression over being a novelist in a culture that doesn't care about novelists, "I found that almost everyone I met shared many of my fears, and that other writers shared *all* of them."[16] For all its grandiose gestures, then, the Franzen School's allocation of modernist ennui to "almost everyone" can look like a humbling. It figuratively scales down the system-oriented, postmodern literary project so as to speak from *a* place and *a* time, and, intensely, *a* point of view. Thus, the peripheralization of mainstream realism, which initially looks politically and aesthetically conservative, becomes an experiment in its own right. In the face of the "present-day enfeeblement of historical consciousness," to quote Jameson's basic tenet of postmodern culture (259), it insists that the institutionalization of modernist experimentation has its own historicity and hence mutability. And the fact that these novels narrate the decay of the institutions that provided modernism with its market shelter is especially telling for figuring out the real heart of contemporary realism. We might see the return to literary realism, as well as the new realist turn, as "a very earnest description of middle-class mortal desperation," to quote a character in Dana Spiotta's novel *Stone Arabia*.[17]

That mortal desperation feels especially pressing in departments of English, where realist novels are read and written about by literary scholars, as well as composed by creative writing students and teachers. *The Program Era* arrived on the cusp of the Great Recession to explain the ambivalent codependence of these two factions in the postwar university, and six years after its publication, creative writing is still by all accounts the growth industry in the department, even if the institutions that house them are under sustained threat of reduced funding. If anything, the economic contraction of the Great Recession only exacerbated a trend in the redistribution of capital (cultural and otherwise) within the trifurcated English department, which is home to creative writing and literary studies as well as composition. One way to read the new realism alongside *The Program Era* (if not "the Program Era" in general) would be to follow the fault lines of the post-2008 crash from the bank statements in the bursar's office, across the quad, and into the English department, where the declared "crises in the humanities" have different effects on each of its three disciplinary outposts. From this perspective literary realism, as well as renewed critical attention to it, might be read not just as an allegory of modernism's cultural saturation but also as a response to the reorganization of the institutions that brought modernism indoors in the first place. Creative writing's close proximity to artistic genius—along with the more mundane ability to attract majors and tuition-paying graduate students—has helped buffer MFA programs from departmental downsizing. Likewise, composition's long association with unglamorous, high-enrollment gen-ed "service" courses like "freshman English"—where its practitioners teach nuts-and-bolts communication *skills* that serve as something like a déclassé corollary to creative *craft*—has more or less secured its hiring lines in the utilitarian eyes of deans and provosts. These changes are not new, but the disciplinary downward mobility of literary scholars within English studies occurs in tandem with a general disinvestment in the humanities. And reading the new realism now, peripheral and otherwise, can offer a response—symbolic, to be sure—against the flood tide of collegiate reorganization. In any event, this is the institutional situation in which *The Program Era Volume 2* would appear: one that has little real interest in supporting the kind of research that it undertakes.[18]

NOTES

1. Mark McGurl, *The Program Era: Postwar Fiction and the Rise of Creative Writing* (Cambridge: Harvard UP, 2009), 48.

2. See Langdon Hammer, "Plath's Lives," *Representations* 75.1 (2001): 61–88.

3. Loren Glass, *Authors Inc.: Literary Celebrity in the Modern United States, 1880–1980* (New York: New York UP, 2004), 6.

4. Joe Cleary's foreword and Jed Esty and Colleen Lye's introduction are especially explicit about this double periphery. See Joe Cleary, "Realism after Modernism," *MLQ* 73.3 (2012): 255–68; Jed Esty and Colleen Lye, "Peripheral Realisms Now," *MLQ* 73.3 (2012): 269–88.

5. The phrase also provides the title to Devin Fore's study of twentieth-century literature and visual culture, *Realism after Modernism: The Rehumanization of Art and Literature* (Cambridge: MIT Press, 2012).

6. Gordon Hutner, *What America Read: Taste, Class, and the Novel, 1920–1960* (Chapel Hill: U of North Carolina P, 2009), 2. For two recent attempts to do this kind of counting, see Matthew Wilkins, "Contemporary Fiction by the Numbers," *Post45 Contemporaries* 1 (2011), post45.research.yale.edu/2011/03/contemporary-fiction-by-the-numbers/; and Mark Algee-Hewitt and Mark McGurl, "Between Canon and Corpus: Six Perspectives on 20th Century Novels," *Stanford Literary Lab Pamphlet* 8 (Jan. 2015), http://litlab.stanford.edu/LiteraryLabPamphlet8.pdf.

7. While realism as a genre is primarily associated with novels, contemporary experimental poets are also staking a claim to the moniker. This is most visible in Kenneth Goldsmith's "uncreative writing," which he also calls "hyperrealism," which for Goldsmith has its origin in Whitman's catalogues. While primarily positioned as a response to the information anxiety of digital culture, it is also a response to identity politics: "Uncreative writing is a postidentity literature," he claims, and hyperrealism is its poetic mode. See Goldsmith, *Uncreative Writing: Managing Language in the Digital Age* (New York: Columbia UP, 2011), 85–86.

8. Jameson's afterword to Esty's and Lye's *Modern Language Quarterly* special issue was subsequently expanded into a monograph. See Fredric Jameson, *The Antinomies of Realism* (London: Verso, 2013).

9. John B. Thompson, *Merchants of Culture: The Publishing Business in the Twenty-First Century* (Cambridge: Polity, 2010), especially chap. 5, 187–222.

10. Chad Harbach, *The Art of Fielding* (New York: Little, Brown, 2011), 328.

11. Keith Gesson, *Vanity Fair's "How a Book Is Born": The Making of "The Art of Fielding"* (New York: Vanity Fair, 2011). On Wallace as paragon of the Program Era, see Mark McGurl, "The Institution of Nothing: David Foster Wallace in the Program," *boundary2* 41.3 (2014): 27–54. For evidence of Harbach's indebtedness to David Foster Wallace, see his enthusiastically titled essay, "David Foster Wallace!," *n+1* 1 (2004), nplusonemag.com/issue-1/reviews/david-foster-wallace/. In it, Harbach draws a direct line between Wallace's exhaustion of modernist experimentation and Franzen's realism, claiming that "Wallace has already written his next big novel—its called *The Corrections*."

12. Robert Coover's *The Universal Baseball Association, Inc., J. Henry Waugh, Prop* (New York: Random House, 1968) is the ur-text of this subgenre.

13. Quoted in B. R. Myers, "A Swing and a Miss," *The Atlantic*, 2 Apr. 2012, theatlantic.com/magazine/archive/2012/05/a-swing-and-a-miss/308943/.

14. Jonathan Franzen, *The Corrections* (New York: Farrar, Straus and Giroux, 2001), 3–4.

15. Jonathan Franzen, "Mr. Difficult: William Gaddis and the Problem of Hard-to-Read Books," *New Yorker*, 30 Sept. 2002, 100–111.

16. Jonathan Franzen, *How to Be Alone: Essays* (New York: Picador, 2002), 88.

17. Dana Spiotta, *Stone Arabia* (New York: Scribner, 2011), 65.

18. McGurl's post–*Program Era* scholarship turns in exactly this direction. See especially "The Posthuman Comedy," *Critical Inquiry* 38.3 (2012): 533–53, which opens with a lament of the dishearteningly brief life afforded to even the most long-standing human institutions from the point of view of geologic time.

CHAPTER 14

From Modernism to Metamodernism

Quantifying and Theorizing the Stages of the Program Era

SETH ABRAMSON

The dramatic expansion of the American network of graduate creative writing programs over the last half century belies the limited consideration still given to how these programs differ from one another pedagogically and how these pedagogies influence young writers' poetics. Even as robust a study as Mark McGurl's *The Program Era* seeks to consider hundreds of creative writing institutions and their tens of thousands of graduates through a single critical lens: the presumptively causal relationship between the "workshop" pedagogy and the writing its current and former subjects produce. While McGurl offers several case studies in support of his approach, *The Program Era* is nevertheless an "institutional" analysis of a phenomenon whose heterogeneities resist such an intervention. Indeed, the Program Era is not novel for its aggregation of writers into institutional spaces, as writers have been aligning themselves with nonacademic institutions for centuries. The era is notable, instead, for its idiosyncratic uses of a writing pedagogy that, particularly in poetry, has never been formally standardized. Understanding how workshops help shape authors' philosophies of language requires considering the origin of the workshop, the historical circumstances of its evolution and popularization, and the complex ways its practices interact with the cultural paradigms in which they have been and continue to be situated. While some academic research into these topics has been conducted, most of it, including McGurl's study, has focused on fiction. Yet these questions are particularly intriguing, and their answers particularly idiosyncratic, with respect to poetry—as in recent years it is in the American poetry community that the question of the workshop's value and its abiding influence has been most contentious.

To speak of the Program Era is to speak of several discrete periods within a single span of American history that begins in the late nineteenth century and continues to the present day. Creative writing was born at Harvard in the early 1880s, when a cadre of professors began permitting advanced composition students to write imaginative responses to civics prompts.[1] The pedagogical premise was a simple if then-revolutionary one: by permitting students to respond to academic queries using forms and concepts of students' own devising, Ivy League pedagogues encouraged their strongest writers to not just write but also to think idiosyncratically. In this respect, professors such as A. S. Hill, Barrett Wendell, LaBaron Briggs, and George Pierce Baker were advancing a cause proposed by Ralph Waldo Emerson in coining the term "creative writing" at Harvard in 1832. Addressing a gathering of Phi Beta Kappas in Cambridge, Emerson observed that

> [t]here are creative manners, there are creative actions and creative words: manners, actions, words, that is, indicative of no custom or authority, but springing spontaneous from the mind's own sense of good and fair.... [T]here is, then, creative reading as well as creative writing.[2]

Emerson's "creative writing" was entwined with a pedagogical principle—that students deserve the opportunity to respond creatively to the canon—as well as a political one: that such work produces language and behavior "indicative of no custom or authority" (230).

Harvard's multigeneric, reading-intensive, civics-oriented, composition studies–housed iteration of the writing workshop is not what would famously emerge at the University of Iowa a half century later. Although a number of Harvard's late nineteenth-century writing faculty were half-secretly avid creative writers themselves, their pedagogies imagined writers as civic and interdisciplinary creatures; they presumed that writing students' intuition, imagination, and intellectual ingenuity could add heft to not just their own but also entire classrooms' considerations of literary and nonliterary material. While, as at Harvard, the students who matriculated at the Iowa Writers' Workshop during its inaugural years would read their work aloud to classmates for the purposes of receiving critique, they did so in an environment substantially more cloistered than that of the men of the generation preceding. As the nation's first-ever graduate creative writing program—Harvard had offered writing workshops to graduate students, but not programmatically

—the Writers' Workshop was conceived of and entirely populated by creative writers. Moreover, whereas the writing instructors of the nineteenth century had been, particularly with regard to poetry, rebelling against an American literary canon whose themes and compositional gestures had long since become worn—a small cadre of so-called Fireside Poets had anthologized themselves and one another into an exclusive place in American letters—the workshopping poets of the late 1930s and 1940s were confronted by a national and international literary sphere that was more diverse. In fact, whereas the men of Harvard had sought to resist convention through creative writing, the early years of the Iowa Writers' Workshop were peopled by new humanists hoping to return American poetry and America itself to its pastoral roots.[3] While the American canon had broadened between the 1880s and the 1930s, the Workshop was nevertheless a self-conscious response to the continued domination of American letters by East Coast elites. In so responding, the Workshop's emphasis was on the individual rather than the rhetorical. If the literary works workshopped in Cambridge in the 1880s were acts of persuasion, the breed of creative writing that flourished in the Midwest in the prewar years was self-expressive.[4]

What has been lost in the debate over the Program Era's legacy is that, while the Writers' Workshop was indeed the first "program-as-such" of the era, its bohemian, studio-oriented model was not pursued by many of the graduate creative writing programs that would follow. Whereas the Workshop would secede from the English department in order to permit its self-governance as an enclave exclusively of literary artists, no other graduate creative writing program in the last half century has so distanced itself from literary studies' scholarship, administrative frameworks, subcultures, or subcommunities.[5] Whereas the Workshop would prohibit cross-genre study, the programs that followed it would encourage and in many instances require it; whereas the Workshop would eschew grades, attendance records, homework, and academic prerequisites in favor of a "salon" model, the programs we associate with the "second" stage of the Program Era—properly deemed the third, given the centrality of Harvard's nineteenth-century role in promulgating creative writing in the academy—would juxtapose critical and creative modes of intellectual inquiry, compel their matriculants to engage with university subcultures sometimes hostile to the arts, and return the writing workshop to its Emersonian roots as a reading- as well as writing-oriented pedagogy.

More than a quarter century after the Workshop's founding, not one institution in the United States had adopted Iowa's "Master of Fine Arts" model. Other models were attempted and abandoned during the period, however. Between 1933 and 1957, Black Mountain College offered a nondegreed, ungraded, communelike approach to creative writing with nearly none of the administrative niceties present on university campuses; meanwhile, Iowa alum Wallace Stegner developed an undergraduate creative writing program at Stanford that was inextricably tied to that university's undergraduate curriculum. And a host of universities—among them Johns Hopkins, Indiana, and Florida—founded MA programs in creative writing in the 1950s as much intended to prepare matriculants for doctoral scholarship in literary studies as the life of a working writer. In the fall of 1964, at a time when the Workshop was still the only MFA program to graduate a class of creative writers, the English Department of the State University of New York at Buffalo revised its internal policies to permit the creation of an English program in which working poets would be hired as "academic professionals"—teaching primarily literature, rather than writing, to undergraduates.[6] The revision included the following language: "[W]e do not at present plan to follow the Iowa and Johns Hopkins plans of formal graduate degrees in Creative Writing... [though] we will henceforth accept some course work in creative writing... as a part of training for an advanced degree" (253). Anxious to distinguish itself from Iowa's salonlike congregation of artists, Buffalo's English Department's statement of first principles noted that "professional poets with little or no academic experience... are best utilized, transitionally or permanently, only as visitors" (253). Meanwhile, outside the academy, "workshops" were being founded whose operations were at once reminiscent of salons yet devoid of academic-institutional markers or administrative coherence; perhaps the best known of these was the Black Arts movement's Umbra Workshop, first conceived in 1962.

In 1964, what may properly be termed the third stage of the Program Era began with the founding of new MFA programs in creative writing at the University of Massachusetts Amherst, University of North Carolina at Greensboro, and University of Oregon—the second, third, and fourth universities in the world ever to develop a terminal-degree program in creative writing.[7] Of course, to speak here of "stages" in the Program Era, let alone of discrete "booms" in the rate of MFA program creation, necessitates additional hard data. For instance, we know that between the first creative writing workshop at Harvard in the 1880s and 1932, there were no graduate programs in creative writing, a fact remedied only by the University of Iowa's development of a creative writing MA and PhD in 1932 (effectively supplanted, as to the former, by the awarding of MFA degrees beginning in 1942). Between 1942 and 1966, only one MFA program graduated even a single class of poets or writers: the Iowa Writers' Workshop. While at least six universities developed creative writing MA programs during this period, most would not transmute their academics-oriented MA programs into studio-intensive arts programs for many decades: Johns Hopkins, for instance, founded its creative writing MA in 1947 and its creative writing MFA almost sixty years later in 2004. From 1964 to 1969, eleven MFA programs were founded in North America; from 1970 to 1979, the pace of program creation slowed, with only eleven programs founded over a span of time twice as long.[8] The 1980s saw the creation of the first-ever MFA outside North America—at De La Salle University in the Philippines in 1985—and twenty-seven programs in North America. The first half century of what we now denominate the Program Era thus saw only a glacial pace of program creation: on average, not even a single sustainable full-residency MFA program in creative writing was founded in North America each year during the period, and it wasn't until the 1980s that the per-year program creation rate inched appreciably above one. While the per-year program creation rate for full-residency MFA programs in the 1990s was much higher (about 3.5), by 2000 there were still fewer than eighty such programs in the United States. However, there were more than twice this number of law schools in the United States by 1977.[9]

This comparison between the disciplinary history of legal study and of creative writing is useful, given that in 2014 there were only 205 law schools in America approved by the American Bar Association (ABA), but 265 terminal-degree creative writing programs—with another 66 in other countries, all founded after 1977.[10] What this underscores is that the first discernible boom in creative writing occurred in the 2000s, when nearly 10 new terminal-degree programs were founded each year. This 272 percent increase over the previous decade suggests that it was not until the twenty-first century that creative writing experienced its first statistically significant spike in popularity. Despite these figures, the 2000s did not see the largest program-creation rate of the era; in the 2010s, the per-year program creation rate has thus far been an astonishing 40 percent above even the historic expansion of the discipline in the 2000s. Interestingly, nearly half of the discipline's expansion in the twenty-first century is attributable to "low-residency" programs whose habitual use of idiosyncratic distance-learning pedagogies, virtual communal spaces, and social media suggests that presumptions or generalizations about the era dependent on critiques of conventional workshop pedagogy will have to be reconsidered.

With such a dramatic increase in the number of terminal-degree creative writing curricula, the pedagogical diversity has commensurately expanded. While none of the 180 full-residency MFA programs now operating worldwide advertise themselves as having abandoned the fundamental structure of the creative writing workshop—one student workshopped at a time, sworn to silence as his or her peers discuss how best to "improve" the work under review—beyond this central point there is little agreement as to how best to build a community of artists or encourage those artists in their art.[11] Some programs encourage or even mandate cross-genre study and writing, while others disallow matriculants from taking workshops outside the genre in which they applied; some programs feature workshops with enrollments of as few as six, and others with as many as fourteen; some programs require students to take electives in other academic disciplines, while others permit enrollees to take only workshops, independent studies, and nonacademic seminars; some programs feature study-abroad options or public-service requirements, while others so encumber their students with nonwriting academic credit requirements that even holding part-time employment outside the program seems unthinkable. Some programs emphasize their roster of contest-winning alumni, while others have developed homegrown publishing networks that offer alumni the opportunity of publication without the frustration of competing nationally.

The demographics of individual programs also vary widely. The best available data suggest that, nationally, many more women than men apply to and matriculate at graduate creative writing programs, though the gender demographics of individual institutions are highly variable.[12] There is anecdotal evidence that programs in populous urban zones enjoy a higher degree of racial, ethnic, sexual-orientation, and gender-identity diversity than their peer institutions in suburban and rural settings. Age-wise, low- and full-residency programs are readily distinguishable by the median matriculating age of their first-year students: at full-residency programs, this figure is 26.5, while at low-residency programs the figure is 36.5. These figures underscore the implausibility of accusations that the workshop pedagogy is in practice rigidly doctrinal; when full-residency programs are matriculating, on average, students who have been out of college for more than half a decade, and low-residency programs, thirty-somethings who have been in the workforce for more than fifteen years, it is unreasonable to credit the sort of submissive reading, learning, and writing practices routinely assigned to American graduate creative writing students.

There are nearly as many administrative and curricular structures at academic-institutional creative writing programs as there are such programs. Program sizes range from as small as 12 students in total (University of Wisconsin–Madison) to more than 250 (Columbia University). The shortest graduate creative writing program is one year (Boston University), while the longest is four years (University of Alabama and University of Arkansas). There are programs that offer only one genre concentration (e.g., Goucher College, offering a single thesis track in creative nonfiction) and those that offer as many as ten (University of Southern Maine, offering thesis tracks in creative nonfiction, fiction, poetry, popular fiction, scriptwriting, translation, cross-genre literature, nature writing, young-adult fiction, and "performance"). While the most commonly offered genres of study at full-residency programs remain creative nonfiction, fiction, poetry, and scriptwriting, the disciplinary diversity at individual programs varies depending not only on how many of these academic tracks a program offers but also how many students it admits in each genre. The total number of genres available for study at terminal-degree creative writing programs in the United States is many more than even the ten noted here as being available at the University of Southern Maine: for instance, Brown University students study electronic writing; at Bard, interdisciplinary writing; at Seattle Pacific, Christian writing. Other programs offer themed courses of study in conventional or emerging literary genres, for instance, the California Institute of Integral Studies offers tracks in art and social justice, writing and consciousness, and interdisciplinary art and creative inquiry. Meanwhile, Pratt Institute offers a hybrid of common literary genres while foregrounding "collaboration, radical pedagogy, administrative transparency, and non-hierarchical learning."[13] In short, to speak of the Program Era as the institutionalization of a single pedagogy rather than the acculturation, via academic settings, of numberless approaches to writing instruction is inapt. Even in classrooms in which the most common features of the workshop pedagogy are employed—classwide critiques; an author sworn to silence; and a greater emphasis on technical craft than on poetics—the amount of nonstudent reading assigned, the duration and range of conversations on student work, and the diversity of writing approaches taken by both the students and their professor will vary.

Founded as a new humanist endeavor, the Writers' Workshop has today become, at least in poetry, an equally archetypal refuge for writers of a more experimentalist bent. With no formal curriculum, no grades, no attendance taken, no regular interface with its host university, and a professorial class known for frequenting the same bohemian subcultures as its students, the Workshop's poetry track has in recent years become capable of producing notable authors of verse informed by poststructuralism's first principles rather than modernist doctrine.[14]

In contrast, the first three decades of the second stage of the Program Era—from the founding of the Writers' Workshop in 1936 to the 1966 graduation of the first creative writing graduate students not to attend the Workshop—were arguably defined by the Workshop's doubling down on a much older dialectic: the long-standing tension between critical and creative classes. The Workshop, in seceding from the English Department and divesting itself of all conventional academic prerequisites, codified Matthew Arnold's belief that critics and creatives occupy separate (if mutually influential) spheres. If some of the seminal figures of theory-driven Language Poetry of the 1970s, such as Bob Perelman, would later recount having been driven to their experimentalist bent by prior affiliation with the Writers' Workshop, it is therefore no surprise that many of these young authors felt the Workshop had erred in segregating critical consideration of poetics from the more conventional study of verse aesthetics.[15] The resulting Language Poetry was a rebuke of the Iowa model.

What could be accurately said of the early decades of the Iowa Writers' Workshop could not be said of those graduate creative writing programs founded during the third and subsequent stages of the Program Era. These programs eschewed the Workshop's single-minded emphasis on aesthetics and the Language Poets' correspondingly militant emphasis on poetics. What these latter stages of the Program Era have helped codify in contemporary poetry is a cultural paradigm quite apart from either the modernist impulses of Iowa's early years or the poststructuralist inclinations of its 1960s and 1970s alumni. Broadly, we can term this Internet Age paradigm "metamodernism" and theorize the direction the Program Era is likely to take in the near term by considering the origins and implications of this paradigm.

In the early 1970s, at the dawn of the third stage of the Program Era, a University of Oregon literary studies professor named Mas'ud Zavarzadeh coined the term "metamodernism" to describe what he saw as a burgeoning tendency in American fiction. Zavarzadeh circumscribed metamodernism as a deviation from the three cultural paradigms he believed had informed the first six decades of twentieth-century American literature. Delineating discrete literary responses to the modernism of the prewar years, Zavarzadeh remarked on the emergence of both "anti-Modernism" (a "reaction against" Modernism) and "para-Modernism" (a "modified and sometimes radicalized continuation of the Modernist aesthetics").[16] He distinguished metamodernism from these two postmodernist paradigms by terming it "an historical phase" in which "a crisis in the perception of reality has taken place" (74–75). This crisis, for Zavarzadeh, was primarily identifiable in a "blur[ring of] the dichotomy between 'life' and 'art' . . . combining such allegedly antithetical elements as the 'fictional' and 'factual,' 'critical' and the 'creative.'" Students in contemporary writing workshops will need little additional introduction to the phenomenon outlined by Zavarzadeh, as nowhere is the dialectic of thesis and antithesis more dramatically collapsed than in the programmatic creativity endemic to the Program Era. Indeed, the contemporary writing workshop is typified by the juxtaposition of polar spectra contemplated by metamodernism. This juxtaposition is conducive to the paradoxical "surreal reality" and "empirical fiction" envisioned by metamodern theory (72).

In enumerating contemporary creative writing pedagogy's metamodern qualities, we might first consider the workshop's spatial dynamics, which are rigidly hierarchical (one workshop leader sits before six to fourteen students) even as all voices are given equal time and, increasingly, equal weight—as in a period of such frenetic publication that students often publish work alongside their professors, it has often been noted that the scourge of the workshop is not top-down indoctrination but a decidedly bottom-up antiauthoritarian malaise and arrogance. With terminal-degree graduate creative writing programs producing more than six thousand arguably competent and certainly pedigreed poets and novelists each year, one would expect workshop students to be humbled by their own obsolescence; instead, as Steve Almond notes, "a significant number of the students . . . in creative writing programs display a curious arrogance toward published authors, as well as an inflated sense of their own talents and importance."[17]

The paradoxes of the workshop do not end with students' conflicted sense of centrality. The workshop juxtaposes three spaces conventionally kept distinct by working authors: the compositional space, the performative space, and the critical-reflective space. The workshop student is literally caught publicly in the act of composing and in the midst of such an intricate and elongated process is asked to perform her work for classmates as though it were complete. Then, having given a whiff of finality to work assuredly half-formed, she is forced to silently endure public censure and approbation from an eclectic mix of largely untrained critics whose commentary is in no way animated by knowledge of her artistic aims. Indeed, by compelling its most heavily scrutinized subjects to absolute silence—an element of the workshop model introduced not at Harvard but Iowa—the workshop seeks to normalize a paradox of procedure: students are asked to aid classmates with processes of authorial growth that have never yet been vocalized to them. While this practice may have seemed sustainable when workshop students remained unacquainted, during the course of their undergraduate studies, with the basic tenets of poststructuralism, in the Internet Age the irony of sincerely diagnosing a possibly nonextant and certainly not complained of malady is lost on no one. The credulous workshop student may continue to offer technical suggestions that adhere to current aesthetic conventions, but we live in a time of incredulity, and to posit the workshop as a routinized space for such groupthink is unrealistic. Moreover, the very monotony of workshop pedagogy operates against such a perpetuation; bored workshoppers in their third year of study with the same peers, and inundated with drearily competent MFA-produced work by literary magazines, are as likely to advise radical deviance as sheepish conformity—or, more probably, a juxtaposition of the two.

As Zavarzadeh's term gained more purchase in the academic community, its contours continued to seem well suited to the evolving discipline of creative writing. In the 1980s and 1990s, metamodernism was intermittently used by scholars to describe a compositional mode distinguishable by its juxtapositions of modernist and postmodernist principles. In 1996, Justo González proposed "metamodernity" as a means of simultaneously challenging and foregrounding metanarratives. Metamodernity, wrote González, "would insist on the authority of certain texts that serve to pry open the structures of power created by modernity and are allowed to continue standing unchallenged by postmodernity."[18] González's model for metamodernity mirrors the positioning of texts in the most progressive writing workshops: the work under review is at once a central through line in the discussion it produces and the very means by which its own presuppositions are undermined. More recently, metamodernism has been championed by two Dutch cultural theorists, Tim Vermeulen and Robin van den Akker, who read Jameson into the term by dubbing metamodernism a "system of logic" and "structure of feeling" particularly suitable to the Internet Age and our collective exhaustion with irony.[19]

Metamodernity also posits an aesthetic response to subcultural communities produced by felicity—or infelicity—rather than design. For Moyo Okediji, metamodernism can be located in contemporary aesthetics by charting the literary art of African Americans who have at least once made a pilgrimage to Africa. The work of such artists, Okediji contends, performs simultaneously a sense of deviation from, and an assimilation into, the white culture of contemporary America—therefore, a juxtaposition of modernity and postmodernity.[20] Given the criticism of creative writing's academic and nonacademic institutions that they remain too white and upper class, it may seem odd to draw a parallel between Okediji's analysis and the present one, but the fact remains that to participate in a literary subcommunity generated by individuated admissions decisions is a bewildering affair for any student. Whereas in the early years of the Writers' Workshop admissions decisions were made in substantial part on the basis of referrals from those who had previously studied or taught in Iowa City—suggesting that the Workshop was implicitly perpetuating its own discrete subculture—today the conventional wisdom is that admissions decisions are made almost entirely on the basis of applicants' portfolios. Indeed, Benjamin Hedin, writing for *Poets & Writers*, has called such brief samples of student work "the only real determinant" in MFA program admissions.[21] Unlike other graduate programs, creative writing programs do not conduct interviews, nor do more than a handful of programs require applicants to submit supplementary essays. While the result of such a narrowly drawn selection process is at times a rather narrow aesthetic spectrum among each new class of matriculants, what the process does not do is consider other aspects of an artist's experience or temperament. The result is that the terminal-degree creative writing student is forever torn between a sense of common purpose, common toil, and the necessity of in-program cultural assimilation, on the one hand, and a sense of feeling ill suited to one's peers, on the other. One cannot imagine this juxtaposition of poles—alienation and belonging; rebellion and assimilation; antipathy and empathy—shows up nowhere in the poetry that results. In not dissimilar ways, the cadre of black artists spoken of by Okediji and the cadres of often white, upper-class students in graduate creative writing programs find themselves subjected to processes that at once pull them into and out of their own bodies; under such conditions, the "retention of the human figure" is ever a subject of literary preoccupation.[22]

In his 2000 study *The Subject of Art in Process*, Stanley Horner extends the metamodern model to include a "new" vision of arts education. Yet this vision reflects workshop pedagogy as practiced at both Harvard in the nineteenth century and myriad graduate creative writing programs in the third and current stages of the Program Era. According to Horner, the

> territorial specialists of Modernism are more and more being joined by border-crossing multi-practitioners of metamodernism. Whereas discipline-based art education endorsed the Modernist preoccupation with discrete domains of knowledge and a top-down hierarchy that focused more on the "subject matter" than on the "subject agent" . . . [I] propose an intra/interactive, interdisciplinary option . . . grounded in the practice of . . . individual subjects engaged as members in a community of voices . . . and, in particular, self-teachers in a community of voices that share both disciplinary and interdisciplinary knowledge.[23]

In Horner's metamodern critique of contemporary art education we can see the application of these terms to graduate creative writing programs in an increasingly interdisciplinary environment. And Horner is explicit about the application of these theories to the literary arts. As he writes, "[A] metamodern practitioner in letters and/or the arts is grounded in [criticism], and it is in being solidly grounded that they are able to make forays, skirmishes, into terrains above and below, where they can come into contact with others who are grounded in very different understandings about what constitutes a center of 'truth'" (III-C-2). While workshopping Harvard undergraduates in the late nineteenth century could hardly be called routinized practitioners of art, and while workshopping Iowans in the 1940s and 1950s could hardly be said to have grounded themselves in criticism, the contemporary graduate creative writing program in poetry is sufficiently affixed to its peer departments that what we see emerging is a generation of creative writing students grounded in the literary arts, the cynical and ironic postmodern temperament, and rudimentary poststructuralist literary criticism. While this juxtaposition of the creative and critical modes is less discernible in studio-oriented programs influenced by the Iowa model, the latter iteration of creative writing pedagogy has been in decline in this century and is now present in only a handful of graduate creative writing programs.

Though perhaps more esoteric than his emphasis on juxtapositive skill sets, Horner's linkage of what he terms "transitional time/space" to "the current metamodern period" is telling, as is the title of the treatise in which these terms appear: "The Subject of Art in Process." If conventional nonhistoricist (particularly neo-Marxist) literary studies scholarship emphasizes literary product over literary process, and if the emphasis on poetics in America's nonacademic avant-garde bohemia often favors the *isolato* model of neo-Romantic "genius" over communal writing processes, the creative writing workshop of today is very much a "transitional time/space" in which poets engage their own and others' writing as both procedural and always-already unfinished. Per Horner, "[T]ransitional discourse implies . . . a shift from text to speech, from singular styles to multiple struggles" (II-C-4). In the superlative creative writing workshop individual students' texts are not fetishized as sites of transference but exploited as occasions for speech on the multiple and overlapping struggles of all contemporary artists.

Popular criticism of the graduate creative writing workshop opines about its purported tendency to standardize the aesthetics of participants. A more historically oriented view would question first whether the workshop as it is now conducted remains true to the ambitions of its originators and second whether—despite any deviations from such origins—the diversity of contemporary creative writing curricula (if not always the operations of individual workshops) may, in the near future, do more than is currently anticipated to bring students' aesthetics and poetics into the Internet Age. In answering the first question, we may certainly see a streamlining of how creative writing workshops are led in today's academic-institutional writing spaces that belies the interdisciplinary idiosyncrasies of the nation's earliest workshops. This said, today's graduate creative writing programs, for all their broader curricular diversities, nevertheless comprise discrete literary subcultures in which normally oppositional principles—life and art; the critical and creative modes; compositional and performative spaces; communal and iconoclastic composition; administrative hierarchy and bohemian egalitarianism; intellectualism and anti-intellectualism—are juxtaposed. As students in graduate creative writing programs are given no formalized training in how to navigate these juxtapositions (in part because certain features of the workshop pedagogy widely prevail, in part because the discipline has only lately exhibited signs of such reflexivity), it is little surprise that creative writing students would perform such juxtapositions first and foremost in their literary art. The decades-long contestation between the modernist first principles of creative writing and the poststructuralism that sees the aesthetic instruction of the writing workshop as anathema to studied engagements with language qua language, fails to grapple with the juxtapositive qualities of contemporary workshop spaces.

It is for another day to offer in situ critiques of poetry written by those once subjected to the juxtapositive curricula of graduate creative writing programs. What we can say at present is that both sides of the pro- and anti-MFA debate wrongly presume that the Iowa Writers' Workshop has ever been and remains the archetypal creative writing program. In fact, this particular fallacy promulgates not one but two unfortunate straw men: first, the specious argument that graduate creative writing programs fetishize an anti-intellectual self-expression; second, the equally specious claim that such programs are not equipped to do anything else. What is more probable is that the Program Era—now in its fourth or fifth stage of development—is evolving into a forum for metamodernist pedagogies, literacies, and poetics that are responsive to this now-dominant Internet Age paradigm.[24]

NOTES

1. The material discussed here with respect to advanced composition studies in Cambridge in the last two decades of the nineteenth century is drawn in substantial part from D. G. Myers, *The Elephants Teach: Creative Writing since 1880* (Upper Saddle River, NJ: Prentice Hall, 1996).

2. Ralph Waldo Emerson, *Selected Writings of Ralph Waldo Emerson* (New York: Penguin, 1965), 230.

3. Rajeshwar Mittipalli and Claudio Gorlier, eds., *Modern American Literature* (New Delhi: Atlantic, 2007), 10.

4. This disparity is made more surprising by the fact that the historical linkage between Harvard's undergraduate students and the founders of the Writers' Workshop is well documented. Students of Hill, Wendell, Briggs, Gates, Gardiner, Copeland, and Baker at Harvard would go on to teach at universities such as the University of Nebraska and University of Chicago, and several of their students would in turn be associated with the founding of the Iowa Writers' Workshop.

5. Perhaps the most common historical misperception about the Program Era—particularly common, a review of the literature suggests, among graduates of the Writers' Workshop—is that the peculiarities of the Iowa model were adopted wholesale elsewhere shortly after they became entrenched in Iowa City.

6. Nick Lawrence and Alisa Messer, eds., "A History of Poetics at Buffalo: 1960–1990," *Chloroform: An Aesthetics of Critical Writing* (Buffalo: SUNY Press–Buffalo, 1997), 253.

7. This paragraph takes data from *The MFA Research Project*. See Seth Abramson, "MFA Program Foundation Dates," *The MFA Research Project* (blog), 17 Sept. 2011 (Madison: Wordpress, 2011), https://mfaresearchproject.wordpress.com/2011/09/17/mfa-program-foundation-dates/ (site unavailable).

8. This figure, as all the others here, has only lately been revealed by historical research. Previous estimates of the rate of program creation were largely speculative.

9. Natalie Kitroeff, "Four Charts That Explain Why America Has Too Many Law Schools," *Bloomberg Business*, 12 Dec. 2014, http://www.bloomberg.com/news/articles/2014-12-12/four-charts-that-explain-why-america-has-too-many-law-schools.

10. American Bar Association, "ABA-Approved Law Schools," American Bar Association, 2015, http://www.americanbar.org/groups/legal_education/resources/aba_approved_law_schools.html.

11. In creating *The MFA Research Project*, the nation's largest archive of creative writing–related hard data, between 2006 and 2015, I reviewed the curricula of every terminal-degree creative writing program in the world—except the two without websites—and interviewed more than a thousand prospective, current, and former MFA students about their in-program experiences. Many of the observations in this chapter are the by-product of these years of quantitative and qualitative research. Some, but not all, of the hard data here recorded were published in the annual "MFA issues" of *Poets & Writers* between 2008 and 2013.

12. Seth Abramson, "The Widening Gender Gap in Contemporary American

Poetry," *Huffington Post* (blog), 21 Apr. 2014, http://www.huffingtonpost.com/seth-abramson/the-widening-gender-gap-i_b_4213440.html.

13. See "Writing M.F.A.," Pratt, 2015, https://www.pratt.edu/academics/liberal-arts-and-sciences/graduate-writing/writing-mfa/.

14. Though a subjectively derived roster of such alumni would number in the scores, a representative sampling from just the last two decades might include Dan Beachy-Quick, Suzanne Buffam, Sandra Cisneros, Joshua Clover, T. Zachary Cotler, Ben Doller, Matthea Harvey, Cathy Park Hong, Katy Lederer, and D. A. Powell.

15. Bob Perelman, *The Marginalization of Poetry* (Princeton: Princeton UP, 1996), 13.

16. Mas'ud Zavarzadeh, "The Apocalyptic Fact and the Eclipse of Fiction in American Prose Narratives," *Journal of American Studies* 9.1 (Apr. 1975): 75.

17. Steve Almond, "The Problem of Entitlement: A Question of Respect," *Poets & Writers* (Sept./Oct. 2014): 29–32.

18. Justo L. González, "Meta-modern Aliens in Postmodern Jerusalem," *Hispanic/Latino Theology: Challenge and Promise*, ed. Ada María Isasi-Díaz and Fernando F. Segovia (Minneapolis: Fortress Press, 1996), 347–48.

19. See, generally, Timotheus Vermeulen and Robin van den Akker, "Notes on Metamodernism," *Journal of Aesthetics and Culture* 2 (2010): 1–14.

20. See, generally, Michael D. Harris and Moyo Okediji, *Transatlantic Dialogue: Contemporary Art in and out of Africa* (Seattle: U of Washington P, 2000).

21. Benjamin Hedin, "A Crapshoot You Can Bet On: The Psychology of Applying to MFA Programs," *Poets & Writers* (Sept./Oct. 2013): 88.

22. This phrase is used by Monni Adams in reviewing the work of Okediji. See Monni Adams, "Review: *Transatlantic Dialogue: Contemporary Art in and out of Africa*," *International Journal of African Historical Studies* 3.3 (2000): 725.

23. Stanley Horner, *The Subject of Art in Process: Undressing the Emperor's Nude Close* (Bloomington, IN: Trafford Press, 2000), i. For clarity, I have elided Horner's idiosyncratic capitalization practices, which are connected to his development of a terminological network in art education and do not substantively inflect the meaning of the terms used.

24. In just the past five years, the University of Notre Dame has founded the nation's second PhD program in poetics; the University of Washington Bothell has founded the nation's first MFA program in poetry and poetics; and numerous programs have opened their doors to foreground innovation and new media in both their pedagogy and curricula.

AFTERWORD

And Then What?

MARK MCGURL

Is the Program Era over, or has it only just begun?

As a lens through which to view recent literary history, at least, the essays in this collection leave no doubt that there was still a great deal to say about the unprecedented agency of university in its making. Here was so much ground for research that my book barely touched, or completely missed, or whose importance I may have underestimated: The Cold War. Black Mountain College. Marilynne Robinson. *Poetry*. In so convincingly illuminating the darkened regions of my original effort, these essays come "after" *The Program Era* only in the most superficial, chronological sense. They do more than continue to fill in a picture. As often as not they suggest alternative ways of framing the picture from the outset, even if they do keep faith with the idea that paying attention to the specificity of literary institutions yields innumerable analytical and interpretive insights. The examples here are so good, the case studies so convincing, one can only assume that there remain, even now, large stretches of territory to be explored in this dimension of the recent and contemporary literary field.

But what about the thing itself, the "era" of literary history characterized, in my account, by the rise of the creative writing program? With the help of the late D. G. Myers and a few others, my book traces its early stirrings in the late nineteenth century, its seedling growth in the first half of the twentieth century in the context of progressive education, its singular (and, as Seth Abramson reminds us, still unusual in many ways) manifestation in the form of the Iowa Writers' Workshop, and its slow and then sudden growth thereafter into the present. Whether implicitly or explicitly, and despite the apparently rude bureaucratic health of the enterprise, more than a few of the contributors to *After the Program Era* suggest that its days may be numbered, if it isn't already dead.

As cannily suggested by Donal Harris, the model here would again be Hugh Kenner's *The Pound Era* (1971). Kenner's wonderful tome supplied my book with the makings of a title, requiring but one crucial terminological switcheroo. But did it also portend the passing away of its object of study? If 1971 was still the Pound Era—still, that is, the era of literary modernism personified in the various projects of Pound—it was an era very much on the outs, a late, late Pound Era. Not only, as laid out in different ways by Greg Barnhisel and Eric Bennett, had the original interwar context of its radical cultural assertions drained away into the ideological necessities of Cold War propaganda and public relations, but even the latter were proving insufficiently compelling, at this point, to prop up the modernist project. Indeed, most accounts of the *post*modern place its advent sometime in the 1970s, but a few years after *The Pound Era*'s publication, with the final waning of twentieth-century revolutionary and decolonizing energies and lapse into low-profit, highly leveraged, but increasingly ideologically aggressive version of capitalism. After that, with no expectation of fundamental change from which literature might draw its own renovating energies and to which it might contribute its vision, the agenda could only be one of recycling, or envy of mass visual culture, or tighter and tighter involutions of form, the narrative navel gazing John Barth memorably dubbed the "literature of exhaustion." In this respect, Kenner's tome was tombstone.

Is the same thing true of *The Program Era*? Was it, unbeknown to itself, a kind of swan song? I find it intriguing that the answer to that question might validly be—simultaneously—absolutely yes and absolutely no. And I wonder if an equivocation this profound doesn't point to a real tension at the Program's core.

The book was researched and written in the first decade of the twenty-first century, in the long, awful reign of Bush II, but published in the immediate aftermath of global economic crisis, the Great Recession. Surely a disruption this profound, the largest since the time of the founding of the Workshop in Iowa, must matter to a set of institutions housed in universities that, in the era of mass higher education, find themselves on the front line of economic transformations of all kinds? Whether the general divestment of public funds from higher education we have seen in its aftermath was something quite new or simply an intensification of "neoliberal" logics in play at least since the Reagan administration, the idea would be that there has now been a fundamental bifurcation in the economic landscape of higher education for which a blanket term covering the period roughly from 1936 to the present is simply not adequate.

For Sean McCann, working toward a truly penetrating reading of one of the many strong writers of our time, Russell Banks, the essence of the Program Era had been in the strongly populist tint it took from the parallel rise of the era of mass higher education, when, juiced by the GI Bill and other forms of public assistance, the number of persons attending college of some kind quadrupled. If the Program Era was fundamentally about the institutional creation, as I put it, of an "aesthetic democracy" (a term I have had many subsequent occasions to regret using, given the ease with which it might be misunderstood as pointing to a real democracy, let alone a situation of general economic equality), then the alarming swerve back from the postwar Golden Age toward the historical capitalist norm of ever-rising inequality would need to be described as a *post*–Program Era. Granted, it's not as though writing programs are being shut down left and right—quite the opposite, in fact—but the original populist spirit of the enterprise has fled. For McCann, this reveals itself in the sudden incoherence of a novelistic project, Banks's, which made sense only while that spirit still hovered over it.

Donal Harris makes another version of the same argument, this time on the way to a fine reading of Chad Harbach's *The Art of Fielding* and other works of what Harris (retooling a term developed elsewhere) calls "peripheral realism." For him, a general sense of exhaustion with the institutionalized modernism of the Program Era in its triumphal phase yields a return to more traditional narrative forms. In a sense, this could be understood as exhaustion with John Barth's literature of exhaustion, exhaustion squared. David Foster Wallace (unlikely in some ways, given the fatal attraction to reflexivity in his writing) was one of its best exponents, and Jonathan Franzen another. An example like Harbach's—a big, fun, character-driven realist novel nurtured in the University of Virginia MFA program—can therefore be understood as a Program product, yes, but also one "held up to a dark mirror." Harris hypothesizes a *Program Era Volume 2* (God help me) that would begin with this eventuality, tracing the lines that link the reappearance of the realist novel at the highest levels of contemporary literary prestige to the "reorganization of the institutions that brought modernism indoors in the first place."

There's a lot to agree with in these accounts, especially if one keys the Program Era, in full flower, to the production of great literary works, to works that are not (as in McCann's account of late Russell Banks) at the mercy of their contextual contradictions but manage to successfully resolve them. From Flannery O'Connor toward the beginning, to Raymond Carver in the middle, to Wallace's *Infinite Jest* at the bitter end, the Program Era produces major works, even if in the first two of these cases, and for reasons detailed in my book, it does so mostly in the form of short stories. It produces major works and then—or so the argument would go—it does not. One offers *The Art of Fielding* to one's friends as a delightful read, the work of a richly talented storyteller of the old-new school, but it is not a work one expects to see appearing widely on the college syllabus anytime soon. (Not that there aren't a few enticing hooks there, including a middle-age/underage gay romance plot unthinkable in a popular novel until quite recently, and a knowing relation to classic American literature.)

As accounts of something good about the economics of higher education gone sour, however, they seem to me less convincing, and I might call critics like Barnhisel and Bennett to the stand as witnesses. For Barnhisel, the main weakness of *The Program Era* is in its loose usage of the term "modernist" and in how it downplays the centrality of "Cold War imperatives" to the whole enterprise. He paints a picture of insurgent interwar modernism captured by the institution and converted into another anodyne individualism meant to counter the repressions of the ideological enemy, the Soviets. I'm less interested in defending my book from these charges (although I think I could) than in drawing out one of their implications, that the "soul" of the program was never really in its populism or its headier dreams of aesthetic democracy. That populism was always at best a by-product of its real purpose: the defense of the American Way, that is, of capitalism.

In his own tremendously well-researched book on the Iowa Writers' Workshop, *Workshops of Empire*, Bennett makes a series of related arguments about creative writing and the Cold War, but here, with equal archival finesse, he is after something slightly different: a reading of O'Connor that explains her career as the expression of a turning point in American conceptions of canonicity right after World War II. For Bennett, this newly forward-looking, newly speculative understanding of greatness—one that made it possible for a young writer like O'Connor to be pervasively anthologized during her own short lifetime—is the belated reflection of a fundamental transformation in the economy as such, from measuring wealth in terms of real holdings to one oriented speculatively toward the future. One could certainly quarrel with this account on various grounds, forced as it is to generalize about vast stretches of economic and literary history, but again I want to focus on how it establishes the Program Era as always already fundamentally a creature of modern capitalism.

To the extent that, come the Reaganite 1980s, or the "neoliberal" world economic order that followed in its wake, some aspects of its essential capitalism were intensified, then the Program Era as we see it today is not on its last legs but living large, raking in mass quantities of tuition money for its host institutions, adding to a pile of higher educational debt that now grows toward the sky. Things may have lately gotten even worse, but the game had always been about the privatization of real and symbolic wealth. This makes sense of Abramson's strong assertion that the Program Era really doesn't arrive—there was no Program Era!—until the 1980s and 1990s, when, as he documents, the founding of writing programs really takes off in numerical terms, leaving behind a monument on the prairie, in the form of the Iowa Writers' Workshop, with not much relevance to the "metamodernist" phenomenon that interests him. (That said, as a monument to the *legitimacy* of the now-sprawling enterprise of the graduate creative writing program, of its ability to accrue cultural—and thus economic—capital to itself, Iowa has been utterly indispensable, no matter its peculiarities, and perhaps to some degree because of them.)

So from one perspective the Program Era is shutting down, turning out the lights, while from another perspective it is hoisting new neon signs aloft every day. It simply depends how, as an economic institution and entity, it is defined. Which leaves the question of how one should think about the Program Era, what sort of historical judgment we might begin to pass on it. In fact, that was already one of the concerns running throughout my book *The Program Era*, and if that book didn't exactly take a clear stance on the matter, the elusiveness may have been productive for the vigorous debates that have followed in its wake. Writ large, creative writing is a phenomenon complex enough to call forth ambivalence quite legitimately. Indeed, to not feel that ambivalence is, to me, a sign that one isn't looking closely enough. To either simply champion the enterprise, as its bureaucratic functionaries sometimes do, or (far more common) to summarily trash it on aesthetic and/or political grounds, seems to me a mistake. Yes, everything bad that is typically said about it has an element of truth.

To the extent that creative writing was a product of the Cold War, part of the PR apparatus of liberal capitalism, it did not escape those compromising bounds, but then that was true of every aspect of institutional life of the period, from little kids pledging allegiance to the flag to the contribution of basic scientific research to weapons technology. Similarly, my book hardly exempts the program from a set of self-compromising connections to the wider economy—whether that be the "information economy" or "experience economy" or "creative economy"—it inhabits. That is established right away as the platform on which the institution of creative writing is built. Still less does the book characterize creative writing (or indeed the university) as the *answer* to the problem of growing economic inequality that is such a striking feature of the neoliberal age. It is instead presented as, in theory, an *intrinsic* benefit. It is something good, like knowledge, like ice cream, that it would be good to share as widely as possible, which project, as Juliana Spahr and Stephanie Young make clear in their deeply informed contribution to this volume, has not yet happened to a satisfactory degree. Creative writing's problem-solving powers, such as they are, are confined to the domain of self-image construction on the part of institutions of higher education, on the one hand, and to the existential self-construction of students, on the other, only a precious few of whom can legitimately see an MFA degree as vocational training.

In asking us to pause briefly before proceeding to the highly emotionally satisfying act of sneering condemnation of creative writing, the point I was trying to make was a classically Jamesonian Marxist one: It might benefit us to seek the utopian element in even the most noxious ideological constructions, all of which encode a salvageable form of hope. And unlike, say, fascism, creative writing is far from a noxious construction. It is simply a complex and compromised one. But the aspirations at its core should be taken seriously. No one who dreams of a better world can forswear the value of creativity completely, no matter how compromised by New Economy cant that word has become. No one who has been involved in a satisfyingly collective endeavor can write off the program's desire to allow us to be creative together. Education should be responsive to our deepest desires for self-development and collective self-understanding.

Of course, all that is open to skepticism, debate, and demands for nuance.

What seems to me perfectly clear, after reading this collection, is that an adequate historical understanding of postwar literature, however one judges it, can be had only by paying close attention to the production and circulation of literature and literary practices in the culture of the school. Whether the Program Era as such is over or not, that scholarly project continues.

CONTRIBUTORS

SETH ABRAMSON is the author of five collections of poetry and an Assistant Professor of English at the University of New Hampshire. The Series Editor for *Best American Experimental Writing*, he writes a column on metamodernism and digital culture for both *Indiewire* and the *Huffington Post*.

GREG BARNHISEL is Associate Professor and Chair in the English Department at Duquesne University in Pittsburgh. He is the author of *James Laughlin, New Directions, and the Remaking of Ezra Pound* (U of Massachusetts P, 2005) and *Cold War Modernists: Art, Literature, and American Cultural Diplomacy* (Columbia UP, 2015) and coeditor of the journal *Book History*.

ERIC BENNETT is Assistant Professor of English at Providence College in Rhode Island. His scholarship on creative writing and the Cold War has appeared in *Modern Fiction Studies*, *New Writing*, and Blackwell-Wiley's *A Companion to Creative Writing*. His book on the topic, *Workshops of Empire: Stegner, Engle, and American Creative Writing during the Cold War*, was published by the University of Iowa Press in 2015.

MATTHEW BLACKWELL is a graduate student in English at the University of Iowa.

KELLY BUDRUWEIT is a graduate student in English at the University of Iowa.

MIKE CHASAR is the author of *Everyday Reading: Poetry and Popular Culture in Modern America* (Columbia UP, 2012) and coeditor of *Poetry after Cultural Studies* (U of Iowa P, 2011). He writes and maintains the blog *Poetry & Popular Culture* and is an Associate Professor of English at Willamette University.

SIMON DURING is currently an Australian Research Professor at the University of Queensland. He previously was a Professor of English at the University of Melbourne and then at Johns Hopkins University. His academic interests are broad, but he has worked most intensively on British literary history, cultural studies, literary theory, and postcolonialism. He is currently writing about the relation between God and literature in British literary history between 1688 and 1945. His books include *Foucault and Literature* (Routledge, 1993), *Patrick White* (Oxford UP, 1996), *Modern Enchantments: The Cultural Power of Secular Magic* (Harvard UP, 2002), *Exit Capitalism: Literary Culture, Theory and Postsecular Modernity* (Routledge, 2010), and *Against Democracy: Literary Experience in the Age of Emancipation* (Fordham UP, 2012).

LOREN GLASS is Professor of English with a joint appointment in the Center for the Book at the University of Iowa. His first book, *Authors Inc.: Literary Celebrity in the Modern United States*, was published by New York University Press in 2004. His history of Grove Press, *Counterculture Colophon: Grove Press, the "Evergreen Review," and the Incorporation of the Avant-Garde*, was published by Stanford University Press as part of its Post 45 Series in 2013. He has written extensively on the rise of creative writing programs in the United States.

DONAL HARRIS is Assistant Professor in the English Department at the University of Memphis. His work has appeared in *PMLA*, *Criticism*, and the *Los Angeles Review of Books*. He recently completed a monograph titled *On Company Time: Big Magazines and American Modernism*, which surveys the many ways that American mass-market magazines underwrote the production and popularization of literary modernism over the first half of the twentieth century.

MICHAEL HILL teaches about black literature and black popular culture, and his research publications focus on Ralph Ellison, Toni Morrison, and other post–World War II African American novelists. His book, *The Ethics of Swagger: Prizewinning African American Novels, 1977–1993*, was published by Ohio State University Press in 2013. Along with his wife, Lena, he is currently coediting *Invisible Hawkeyes: African Americans at the University of Iowa during the Long Civil Rights Era*, a collection about black students at the University of Iowa circa 1930–68.

BENJAMIN KIRBACH is a graduate student in English at the University of Iowa.

SEAN MCCANN is Professor of English and Chair of the English Department at Wesleyan University and author of *Gumshoe America: Hard-Boiled Crime Fiction and the Rise and Fall of New Deal Liberalism* (Duke UP, 2000) and *A Pinnacle of Feeling: American Literature and Presidential Government* (Princeton UP, 2008).

MARK MCGURL is Professor of English at Stanford University, where his scholarly work centers on the relation of literature to social, educational, and other institutions from the late nineteenth century to the present. He is Director of the Stanford Center for the Study of the Novel and also works with the Stanford Literary Lab. *The Program Era: Postwar Fiction and the Rise of Creative Writing* (Harvard UP, 2009) was the recipient of the Truman Capote Award for Literary Criticism in 2011.

MARIJA REIFF is a graduate student in English at the University of Iowa.

JULIANA SPAHR teaches at Mills College in an office right beside Stephanie Young's. Her most recent book is *That Winter the Wolf Came* (Commune Editions, 2015). She is in progress on a scholarly book about US literary production in English in the last half of the twentieth century, about the complicated relationship between literature and the political (both social movements of resistance and nation-state nationalism).

STEPHEN VOYCE is Associate Professor of English and a member of the Digital Scholarship & Publishing Studio (DSPS) at the University of Iowa. He is the author of *Poetic Community: Avant-Garde Activism and Cold War Culture* (U of Toronto P, 2013), editor of *A Book of Variations: Love—Zygal—Art Facts* (Coach House Books, 2013), and Director of the Fluxus Digital Collection. His work also appears in journals such as *Modernism/modernity*, *Criticism: A Quarterly Journal for Literature and the Arts*, *Postmodern Culture*, and *Open Letter*.

STEPHANIE YOUNG teaches at Mills College in an office right beside Juliana Spahr's. Her collections of poetry and cross-genre writing include *Ursula or University* (Krupskaya, 2013), *Picture Palace* (in girum imus nocte et comsumimur igni, 2008), and *Telling the Future Off* (Tougher Disguises, 2005). She edited the anthology *Bay Poetics* and is a founding editor of *Deep Oakland*. Recent projects include the Anti-Surveillance Feminist Poet Hair & Makeup Party, which works with performance and text to consider the relation of gender, visibility, surveillance culture, urban space, and policing.

INDEX

Note: An 'n,' 'f,' or 't' following a page number indicates an endnote, figure, or table, respectively

THE NEW AMERICAN CANON

Violet America: Regional Cosmopolitanism in U.S. Fiction since the Great Depression
by Jason Arthur

The Meanings of J. Robert Oppenheimer
by Lindsey Michael Banco

Workshops of Empire: Stegner, Engle, and American Creative Writing during the Cold War
by Eric Bennett

Places in the Making: A Cultural Geography of American Poetry
by Jim Cocola

The Legacy of David Foster Wallace
edited by Samuel Cohen and Lee Konstantinou

Postmodern/Postwar—and After: Rethinking American Literature
edited by Jason Gladstone, Andrew Hoberek, and Daniel Worden

After the Program Era: The Past, Present, and Future of Creative Writing in the University
edited by Loren Glass

American Unexceptionalism: The Everyman and the Suburban Novel after 9/11
by Kathy Knapp

Pynchon's California
edited by Scott McClintock and John Miller

Richard Ford and the Ends of Realism
by Ian McGuire

Reading Capitalist Realism
edited by Alison Shonkwiler and Leigh Claire La Berge